The Second Journey

Travelling in Literary Footsteps

The Second Journey
Travelling in Literary Footsteps

Second, revised edition

Maria Lindgren Leavenworth

Institutionen för språkstudier
901 87 Umeå
Umeå 2009

Umeå University
Department of Language Studies
SE – 901 87
http://www.sprak.umu.se
http://umu.diva-portal.org

Umeå Studies in Language and Literature 9
©Maria Lindgren Leavenworth
Cover illustration: Maria Lindgren Leavenworth
Cover layout: Gabriella Dekombis, Print & Media
Printed in Sweden by Print & Media, Umeå 2010
ISBN: 978-91-7264-927-9

Van—for travelling companionship and, to paraphrase the fabulous Dixie Chicks, for the absolutely incomparable way you keep the world at bay for me

Foreword

Ranked high on bestseller lists for 2009 is *The Lost City of Z*, a text in which the author, David Grann, carries out a physical journey in the footsteps of Perry Fawcett, a legendary British explorer who mysteriously vanished in the Amazon rainforests of Brazil in 1925, while searching for El Dorado. Grann's access to Fawcett's diaries and log books from previous journeys to the area, as well as the dispatches sent during the actual expedition, become initial maps to follow in his quest to ascertain the possible reasons for Fawcett's demise and bring an end to speculations about what possibly happened. *The Lost City of Z* illustrates that second journeys, in my definition contemporary travelogues which reiterate itineraries of previous travellers, still constitute an attractive, contemporary form of writing which renews the genre of travel writing by abandoning modes of expression which only chronicle the new and the novel and the traditional prerequisites of journeying to a 'new' destination. In contemporary criticism, however, the second journey form is still largely neglected. Instead, when contemporary travel writing is discussed, focus is on pronounced postmodern traits such as interrupted chronologies, self-reflexivity and experiments with the form of the journey itself. Although ten years have passed since the first publication of this dissertation, there is, consequently, still a need to discuss this form from a critical perspective and to situate second journeys within the genre of travel writing.

To revise a dissertation can in some ways be compared with making a second journey. You travel back in time (albeit not very far). To an extent you try to assess reasons for certain choices, for formulations and, in some instances, for conclusions drawn, and you try to recognise sights and sites that someone else (or so it seems) has signposted along the way. Also similar to a second journey, the revision does not present an entirely new picture of an old landscape. The revisions made here are of four kinds. Firstly, some additions have been made regarding primary sources. There are no added case studies; rather it is the discussions in chapter three that have been expanded in this regard. New online resources in particular have been added to the examples to show how second journeys are represented in another medium, and how they can be used by readers as convenient guidebooks. Secondly, revisions have been made to develop discussions about postmodern aspects and about discursive elements which structure both first and second journey. Thirdly, changes have been made concerning the use of secondary sources as discussions concerning influence (as opposed to intertextuality) have been removed from the text. Finally, the argumentation itself is more precise. This is especially noticeable in chapter five, the case study which has been most substantially rewritten in an attempt to more forcefully foreground the second journey. The structure of the text remains the same, with the exception of some subsections being removed.

The revision of the dissertation was made possible though the literal and figurative generosity of the Department of Language Studies. Any improvements in the text can be attributed to the very active, very critical and very constructive literary seminar at the department, led by Professor Heidi Hansson. The revised text itself has not been scrutinised by this group, but discussions concerning dissertation chapters and articles have during the last few years taught me worlds about argumentation, analysis and structure; about the writing process as such.

Table of Contents

INTRODUCTION. THE TRAVELOGUE AS MAP	11
CHAPTER ONE. WHERE HAVE WE BEEN, AND WHERE ARE WE GOING? TRAVEL, TOURISM, AND TRAVEL WRITING	21
DISCOURSES OF TRAVEL	21
DISCOURSES OF TOURISM	27
DISCOURSES OF TRAVEL WRITING	31
SECOND TRAVELLERS (AND TOURISTS)	35
CHAPTER TWO. AUTHENTICITY AND INTERTEXTUALITY: TO MAKE IT NEW AND TRUE	37
SPATIAL AND TEMPORAL AUTHENTICITY	38
HERITAGE, NOSTALGIA, AND BIOGRAPHY	41
FACT AND FICTION: AUTHENTICATING TRAVEL WRITING	46
INTERTEXTS	48
CHAPTER THREE. SECOND JOURNEYS	55
TRAVEL TEXTS, GUIDE BOOKS AND INTERTEXTUAL REFERENCES	56
RECOGNITIONS AND DISAPPOINTMENTS	60
IDENTITY: HOME AND HEROISM	67
WHERE ARE WE NOW?	72
CHAPTER FOUR. THE SCIENTIFIC JOURNEY: AFTER SCOTT TO THE SOUTH POLE	77
THE MALE, HEROIC EXPLORER	80
THE FIRST JOURNEY	86
THE SECOND JOURNEY	92
PREPARATIONS	92
CAPE EVANS	95
THE WALK SOUTH	98
THE RETURN	104
ANOTHER TALE TO TELL?	107

Chapter Five. Women Travellers: Following Kingsley in West Africa — 111
Gendered Discourses — 113
Departure: The Voyage Out — 123
Passage: Into Africa — 133
Homeward Bound: Negotiating the Return — 144

Chapter Six. The Biographical Journey: On Stevenson's Trail — 153
Biography and Authenticity — 157
Travels — 160
Travels with a Donkey in the Cevennes — 165
From the Clyde to California — 171
Tourism and Museums — 175
After the End — 184

Concluding Remarks —Where Do We Go From Here? — 187

Works Cited — 193

Index — 201

Introduction. The Travelogue as Map

In 1946 Evelyn Waugh announced that he did "not expect to see many travel books in the near future."[1] Although this worry can easily be allayed by a visit to any bookstore today, Waugh's pronouncement nevertheless points to a trend which can be found at the basis of this study. Post-war travelling, and by travelling Waugh, and others with him, meant adventurous pre-tourism journeying, was seen as coming to an end. As travellers 'became' tourists the possibilities of individual adventure and the attainment of what was seen as 'authentic' experiences were perceived as threatened.

More recent studies of travel literature take as a starting point the presumed exhaustion of the genre, even though they more often than not reach the conclusion that it is evolving and developing in new directions.[2] Theories concerning power structures that have long governed travel and travel writing are at the centre of contemporary criticism. The tensions between home and away, issues of representation, mediation and transculturation are discussed, as are questions connected to globalisation, colonialism and postcolonialism. In conjunction with this, in a time when voyages of exploration have become redundant, that is, when most places on the map have been filled in, and when mass tourism has made 'authentic' experiences impossible, the belatedness of the traveller and the different strategies he or she employs to balance the quest for 'authenticity' with the demands of the market continue to be discussed.

One strategy of renewing the genre, particularly visible in the last three decades, is seen in what I term second journeys. Although most journeys are undertaken in previous footsteps—texts and stories of various kinds informing even early travellers' forays—second journeys are

---

[1] "I rejoice," he continues, "that I went when the going was good" (9). Paul Fussell voiced a similar pessimism stating that the world left ruined by World War II was a place "in which the idea of literary traveling must seem quaint and a book about it a kind of elegy" (227).

[2] Patrick Holland and Graham Huggan, for example state that "the genre has proven remarkably immune to even the harshest criticisms, becoming one of the most popular and widely read forms of literature today" (vii).

carried out with the expressed aim of duplicating an earlier traveller's itinerary and as far as possible re-live past experiences. In second journeys, authors thus revisit destinations of earlier travellers and use previous travelogues as maps to follow. Second travellers are influenced by contemporary discourses; "[t]he distinctions made when we 'read' the world . . . which society has constructed and instilled in us through representations" (Mills, *Discourses of Difference* 10), visible in their texts in how they narrate place, people, notions of home and away, indeed the movement of the journey itself. Contemporary conventions connected to the genre of travel writing continue to dictate certain aspects of their texts, and since their works are so openly citationary, second journeys illustrate various forms of intertextuality, often of an exceedingly open nature. Close readings of second journeys therefore illuminate not only how an overt intertextuality becomes a valuable tool in a genre traditionally associated with originality. The second traveller's aim is to read contemporary conditions, places and people through the filter of the past, a process which also makes this filter discernible. That is, the reiteration of past itineraries and experiences and the close ties to a previous work entail a continued presence of discourses informing the first journey as well. Thus, close readings of second journeys reveal not only discourses connected to the form itself and to contemporary structures, but discursive elements shaping the first journeys.

Despite increased attention to travel literature in general and to women's travel and postcolonial perspectives in particular, the category of second journeys has been largely neglected by literary studies and culture critics. This neglect becomes curious when taking into account the variety within this subgenre and the large output of texts that can be defined as second journeys. In *Crossing Boundaries: Postmodern Travel Literature*, Alison Russell briefly comments on the group of "contemporary travel writers [who] choose the more difficult routes in an attempt to recapture the kinds of experiences that mass tourism has eliminated" (9). She mentions a few authors such as Sara Wheeler, Lesley Downer, Caroline Alexander and Stuart Steven, but although acknowledging that writers such as these "are attempting to revive travel writing by taking unconventional trips or by retracing the routes of others . . . employ[ing] the retracing trope to transform the mapped space into new territory"

(10), Russell's focus is on more expressly postmodernist forms of travel writing.3 Two short essays touch more directly on second journeys: Jacinta Matos' "Old Journeys Revisited: Aspects of Postwar English Travel Writing," and Heather Henderson's "The Travel Writer and the Text: My Giant Goes With Me Wherever I Go," published in the same 1992 collection. Matos rightly points out that the second journey (Matos does not use this term) is not unique to the last decades, but that contemporary writers "turn this duplication of former journeys into the raison d'être of their own trips." She identifies the second travellers as attempting to "deliberately shape their new journeys in terms of previous ones, retracing an already traveled route with the purpose of reliving another's experience" (219-20). Basing her arguments on Frederick Jameson's notions of historicism and simulacrum,4 Matos' focus is primarily on the journeys' relationships to history. Henderson, on the other hand, concentrates on how the landscape is first read and then written, and how the observer relates to the encountered scene by filtering his or her experiences "through the literary representation by which he [sic] first came to know it" (232), a filtering process which naturally can become problematic if too much has changed or if circumstances prevent the reiteration of certain acts. Henderson's identification of this filtering process and Matos' argument concerning first journeys "both as pretext and pre-text" (215) for the second journey are more thoroughly explored in my three case studies and in discussions in chapter three where the second journey form is analysed with examples taken from a number of contemporary travelogues.

The concept of 'authenticity' informs many of the discussions here and the term (just like the connected terms 'originality' and 'truth') has justly been problematised because of its inherent legitimating power, designating its opposite as fake. With this caveat in mind (and the single quotation marks now removed), second journeys illustrate a contemporary search for the authentic. The threat of mass tourism to

---

3 Her study concerns Thomas Pynchon's *V*, William Gaddi's *The Recongnitions*, Bruce Chatwin's *The Songlines*, Kenneth Lincoln's and Al Logan Slagle's *The Good Red Road*, William Least Heat Moon's *Prairy Earth* and William T. Vollmann's *The Atlas*.
4 Jameson defines historicism as "the random cannibalization of all the styles of the past," and simulacrum as "the identical copy for which no original has ever existed" (65-6).

destroy the possibilities of original, authentic experiences leads the second travellers to use, recycle and emphasise the first texts, which originate in a past in which authenticity is believed to be attainable. In a similar move not to interpret terms too literally, it should be pointed out that 'first' does not designate a narrative concerning a place never before visited or described. Who is to say, especially when considering the Western, white, male hegemony that has dominated travel writing, what constitutes a 'first' text, or if such a text even exists? Consequently, what defines 'second' is equally problematic. The usage here of the words 'first' and 'second' simply indicates the chronology between the two; the first text being the narrative that precedes the second journey: the textual map that the second traveller explicitly aims to follow.

The second journey can be likened to the pilgrimages and the Grand Tours as it is modelled on a previous text and as the traveller is lead to literally or figuratively marked sights/sites. In this sense it clearly has precedents within the traditions of travel and travel writing. Suggested emulations of earlier travels as indicated by the emergence of nineteenth century guidebooks, complemented by literary texts, also serve to illustrate the continuous development of the form. Problems of authenticity and originality have long been at the core of the travel genre in general but there are significant differences in strategies and aims visible in traditional travel narratives and their contemporary developments in the form of second journeys. The overtly expressed connection with an earlier work, the awareness of the tradition, the different forms of subversion, and the attempts to repeat experiences and situate them in new contexts, are all different strategies used to renew the genre of travel literature as well as to claim originality for the individual authors.

In the strictest sense of my definition, a second journey is based on a previous travelogue, that is, it is a text form which is concerned with two clearly delineated journeys. The case studies all illustrate variations on this form and, in the main, so do additional examples used in the analyses. When the definition is expanded somewhat, however, the wide spectrum of texts can be seen to include such diverse manifestations as Michael Palin's reduplication of Jules Verne's *Around the World in Eighty Days*, serialised for television in 1989, Bruce Chatwin's *The Songlines* (1987) fictionally retracing ancestral, aboriginal creation myths in Australia, and a website such as *Literary Traveler* where anyone with Internet access can publish articles on destinations approached through literary texts. The three case studies (all based on printed texts) illuminate differences in themes and structures rather than in media forms and focus attention on different discourses at work both in first and second journeys. The selection illustrates images of heroic and scientific exploration, the female, solitary journey and the second journey as a biographical project. The discourses at work are connected to gender, individual and group narrations, and biography. The texts considered further illustrate how the Antarctic, West Africa, areas in France, North America and the South Seas are discursively represented in both first and second journeys and the destinations' meaning are also seen as constructed in relation to the author's home: his or her point of departure and reference.

The first case study, in chapter four, concerns a second journey which is characterised by a scientific approach. Both the first and the second journey are projects involving several people and the second journey in particular is marked by a polyphony not found in the other case studies.[5] This kind of second journey is exemplified by Roger Mear's and Robert Swan's account of their expedition to the South Pole after Robert Falcon Scott: *In the Footsteps of Scott*, published in 1987. The predominantly male image of the hero, its traditional as well as its contemporary shape, is discussed and contrasted to the heroic images found in my other case studies. The first journey narrative, *Scott's Last Expedition: The Journals* (1913) also leads to a discussion about the truth-value of the diary form, connecting it with the more general arguments concerning authenticity. In this context the concept of the return is problematised since it is not accomplished in Scott's case. Succumbing to fatigue, starvation and cold, Scott and his men died within a short distance from their journey's goal. For the second travellers the question of authenticity then becomes problematic: how closely is it possible to emulate a journey that does not include a return?

---

[5] The scientific content of the journeys will not be evaluated here and it should further be noted that projects involving several people are not automatic to scientific journeys (even though it is a rule rather than an exception that scientific work is collaborative). Focus here lies on the second journey as a multi-membered project with clearly stated scientific aims.

The next form of second journey is characterised by a seemingly straightforward repetition of one first journey by one second traveller. Both travellers are more or less amateurs, a contrast to the professional and sponsored scientific projects. An interest in place is in the foreground, and the second journey traces one, clearly delineated, journey. This form, discussed in chapter five, is exemplified by Caroline Alexander's *One Dry Season: In the Footsteps of Mary Kingsley* (1989). Kingsley travelled through West Africa in 1896 and her journey is described in *Travels in West Africa: Congo Français, Corisco and Cameroons*, first published in 1897. When seen in the light of the expressly male tradition of Polar explorations and scientific journeys, Kingsley's and Alexander's narratives prove valuable to discussions about gendered discourses informing travel and travel writing.

The departure stage of the journey is discussed in some detail since it is problematised in Kingsley's narrative and since it indicates issues especially pertinent to women's travel texts. Not only does Kingsley depart from her Victorian identity, but the departure can be divided into more concrete stages, as she travels through the colonial settlements along the coast. Although Kingsley had anthropological and ethnographic interests, which resulted in extensive collections and in the volume *West African Studies* (1899), there seem to have been other and more important reasons for her journey. It should be emphasised that her journey was not a project in the same sense as many of her contemporaries' and she was not seen as a serious scholar until after her return and after the publication of her books. She also travels alone, which stands in marked contrast to many of her contemporaries. In this, she is emulated by Alexander whose journey raises questions about the (changed or static) status of contemporary women travellers and about the constructedness of both texts and the narrative persona depicted in them. In addition to these discussions, the diary form as it is used by Scott will be contrasted with how Kingsley employs it, emphasising discursive conventions and expectations connected to this narrative device.

The third form of second journey, discussed in chapter six, is characterised by its clearly stated biographical aims and is exemplified by Nicholas Rankin's *Dead Man's Chest: Travels after Robert Louis Stevenson*, published in 1987. It can be argued that all second journeys, in one way or another, result in this kind of first-hand biography, but Rankin comments on Stevenson's entire literary production: fictional works as well as travelogues. The second journey text also includes a vast number of references to sources other than Stevenson himself; letters from friends and relatives, interviews with and memoirs by the same. Rankin traces Stevenson's life journey from Edinburgh, via Europe and the United States, to the South Seas. Alexander, in contrast, concentrates on a specific travel text and a clearly specified time in Kingsley's life and Scott's three-month walk to the South Pole is at the centre of Swan's and Mear's second journey project. When discussing *Dead Man's Chest*, notions of biography-writing combine with discussions connected with museums and heritage trails used to illustrate a subject's life, as the second journey is presented as a more 'lively' way of representing Stevenson's life and works. Stevenson has been the subject of numerous more traditional biographies that extensively discuss his fiction and focus will therefore be on the parts of Rankin's work which concern Stevenson's travel texts, most notably *An Inland Voyage* (1878) and *In the South Seas* (1900), and the texts pertaining to his immigrant journey (*The Amateur Immigrant* and *Across the Plains*), published in 1985 in the volume *From the Clyde to California*. Rankin decides not to emulate Stevenson's journey narrated in *Travels with a Donkey in the Cevennes* (1879) and Richard Holmes' *Footsteps: Adventures of a Romantic Biographer* (1985), which focuses on this specific route, is used as an additional example of the biographical second journey.

Although limited in number, the case studies serve as examples of the diverse nature of the second journey. The focus on Western English-speaking authors can also be construed as a limitation, but the focus on discursive elements, which are often culturally determined, makes a clearly delineated scope necessary in order to deepen the analyses and show discursive points of contact between authors. Additional examples of the second journey are discussed to emphasise certain aspects and draw attention to wider discursive structures.

A consideration of the history of travel, tourism and travel writing is necessary to position the second journeys in relation to other forms of journeying and to various types of travel texts. Since the presumed exhaustion, both of original places to visit and of the travel genre itself, is intimately connected to the emergence and development of tourism, sociological discussions within this field are also of importance. This especially since second journeys combine several traits of tourism with more traditional characteristics from travelogues, thereby suggesting that the hierarchical divisions between travel and tourism cease to be of importance in the postmodern society. Chapter one thus presents a brief look at the history of travel and more detailed discussions concerning tourism. The history of travel writing is then discussed separately, to emphasise the concern with different discourses, travel and travel writing, as well as how these discourses come together.

In chapter two different strategies employed to renew travel writing will be considered, starting with a discussion about the problematic concept of authenticity. The return to earlier texts illustrates a desire to make connections with a past in which authenticity is perceived as possible to attain. In what ways does the present situation within travel writing and tourism stand in the way of authentic experiences? And how can the past be used as a repository for authenticity? Intertextuality as a device to make writing as well as experiences new will also be discussed. Travel writing is at its core a highly intertextual genre, and this is especially striking in the second journeys' recycling of the first texts. How does this paradoxically work to renew the genre?

In chapter three the second journey form is analysed in greater detail with emphasis on the key notions of intertextuality and authenticity. The examples in this chapter are not all second journeys in the strictest sense, rather, the aim is to illustrate the diversity of the form. Of particular interest here is how traditional divisions between categories such as travel and tourism, and travel texts and guidebooks are destabilised by the second journey form. Moments of recognition, but also of disappointment, are reported by all second travellers here. These subjective experiences and feelings are to a great extent consequences of the quest for authenticity, but the problematic notion of the heroic traveller who is often questioned in both first and second text can also be seen as a reason for both success and failure.

Close readings of second journeys, whether detailed as in the case studies or more sketchy as in the general discussions in chapter three, reveal different strategies in the employment of "the retracing trope" but the result in all cases is that the previously described space is transformed "into new territory" (Russell 10). Each second traveller has a different approach to issues concerning authenticity, and negotiates disappointments, perceived failures, and recognitions of the past in an individual way. The first text, the filter of the past, is also handled differently, and is used to different ends, by each analysed second traveller in this study. That is, although all second journeys are governed by discourses connected to authenticity and intertextuality, the close readings reveal individual ways of traversing an already mapped space and illustrate how new accounts of it are produced. As one postmodern development of the travelogue, the second journey further raises questions concerning the constructedness of both first and second text, and problematises representations of both self and Other.

Chapter One. Where Have We Been, and Where Are We Going? Travel, Tourism, and Travel Writing

The easier it becomes to travel the harder it is to be a traveler.
John Julius Norwich

The journey is a common and versatile textual motif. It is used as a concrete topic in a travelogue but authors also use it as a metaphor for worldviews or identity constructions, or as a narrative device in fiction. The metaphor of movement, whether it is geographical or symbolical, effectively illustrates the human propensity and need to define ourselves in relation to others and here in relation to there. On a concrete level, most of us share some experience of travel whether we are referring to the actual movement of individuals or entire peoples: migrants, exiles, nomads and tourists, or cultural encounters involving negotiations and expectations. These shared experiences make the journey metaphor both recognisable and relatable.

In this chapter, discursive structures connected to travel, tourism and travel writing are analysed to problematise seemingly straightforward metaphors and to situate second journeys in the textual and conceptual history preceding them. Mainly appearing from the 1980s and onwards, second journeys still share discursive traits with travel writing from earlier time periods and the second traveller often combine traits from two, traditionally separate, travelling personas: the traveller and the tourist.

Discourses of Travel

Metaphors of travel need to be critically investigated, related to history and to their position within that history, especially since in contemporary culture, literature and criticism there is an awareness of the problems of generalising the idea of the journey. Dislocations (voluntary or forced) need often be divorced from more romantic notions of travel and movement. To encompass all forms of human mobility and movement under the heading of travel is impossible, Inderpal Grewal argues, because "[s]uch a use erases or conflates those mobilities that are not part of [the] Eurocentric, imperialist formations . . . that reinscribe European hegemonic aesthetic forms" (2). Western thoughts and ideas as well as political, social, financial and cultural systems have prevailed during the colonial period and to a certain extent they still do. This means that a disregard for all movements that have not been voluntary (such as the slave-trade, human trafficking and war refugees, to mention only a few examples) would result in the maintenance of old hierarchies and value systems. Romanticised notions of exile and otherness and the more uncomfortable contemporary dislocations resulting in "new concerns over borders, boundaries, identities and locations" (Kaplan 2) illustrate that several discourses are at work and these are further accompanied by issues connected to the gender, class, sexuality and ethnicity of both the journeying subject and the people he or she encounters and describes. Travel and travel literature are political in the sense that they cannot be divided from prevailing ideologies and even works written against the (most often) patriarchal discourses of travel must be read in relation to dominant modes. Travel does not only mean a movement in space; it may also entail a removal out of the class (and sometimes gender) context, and may move the traveller up or down the social scale, illustrating that the traveller may be situated within several and sometimes conflicting discourses.

The distinction between home and away, between the unknown and the familiar, is presented as a profoundly unsettling experience in many early texts in which the journey is a test rather than a leisurely activity. The possible changes the traveller underwent, subverting notions of stability and identification, were seen as threatening not only to the journeying subject but to society. In texts depicting these kinds of journeys, the traveller often portrays him- or herself as unusually heroic to emphasise the courage and stamina required to withstand the physical ordeals and the psychological disorientation in the unfamiliar environment. Distinctions between self and Other[1] are not absolute,

---

[1] Concerning the definition of 'the Other' and processes of 'Othering' I am using Sara Mills' discussion which focuses on discursive elements. She argues that: "In periods of imperialism, 'Othering' is one of the ways in which the conquering nation organises thoughts and actions towards the colonised nation, but

however, not even in colonial travels with their seemingly fixed power hierarchies. Steve Clark argues that "travel is *not* the simple inscription of an established meaning over a neutralised, identityless other" but rather that "the process of transition, and its associated liminal rites [can be] theorised as modes of 'unsettlement' rather than transcendence or occupation" (39, original italics). Contemporary travel writing is influenced by postcolonial discourses which further problematise descriptions of the encountered culture and the traveller's position and movement within it. Trinh T. Minh.ha argues that the "critical relation" to the colonial projects has led writers "to see in travelling a socio-historical process of dispossession that leads the contemporary traveller to a real identity crisis" (22). which, in turn, results in a heightened awareness of the traveller's inability to accurately represent foreign people, places and experiences. The sites of representation become doubly problematic; that is, the site which the writer intends to present to the readers as well as the site he or she occupies as an individual (Duncan 39-56). Both first and second travellers can thus be seen to struggle with discourses of "unsettlement" and problems of representation. The filter that the first text constitutes can, in combination with postcolonial discourses, further make the second traveller aware of prejudiced views expressed in the first texts; views which will then need to be addressed in some way in the contemporary text.

Ambivalence concerning representation can to varying degrees be seen in both past and contemporary travel and a temporal distancing of what and who is encountered similarly connects journeying from different time periods. The romanticised notion of the Other and of the past Golden Age stems from a long tradition of descriptive narratives of the unknown. The Western "propensity to temporalize the Other" (Duncan 46) is naturally not unproblematic. By distancing what is foreign not only in space but in time, the Other becomes perceived as backward, as childish;

---

each colonial context develops a specific range of colonialist discourses dependent on the type and length of colonial relation" (*Discourses of Difference* 88). In a footnote, Mills continues: "It is important that this form of Othering is not simply seen as an inbuilt psychological mechanism, but a strategy for dealing with nations in conflict" (*Discourses of Difference* note 15, 206). In descriptions of the Other in contexts which is not marked by any conflict between nations, representation of people marked as the Other from the outset (through other texts and political moves) make the discursive descriptions the norm regardless of the context.

ideas which helped legitimise colonisation. The image of the Other has been discursively constructed to represent her or him as existing in an earlier phase of human development which meant that he or she had to be governed and educated for his or her own good by the 'adult' or 'civilised' Western traveller. In postcolonial travel, discursive shifts have caused the Other to be represented in less static ways, but temporal distancing between cultures affects the travel industry to this day. James Duncan contends that "[o]ther cultures are often portrayed as occupying remote places that are rare or unique and therefore desirable, places where one can escape the social and psychological pressures of modernity and retreat into a 'simpler', more 'natural' place and time" (46). Discourses which temporally distance the Other thus prove to be remarkably tenous. The authenticity sought by second travellers through their return to earlier texts is connected, in part, to this approach to and view of encountered peoples, places and customs. The added postcolonial concerns produce tensions in the second journey narratives, illustrative of the resistance to discursive practices in representing both the travelling subject and the encountered culture.

Places of escape; cultures that appear (however illusorily) to offer alternative ways of life, are propagated in both texts and travel advertisements promising escapism on several levels all aiming to get the traveller away from mundane, everyday life. These places and cultures are quickly disappearing in a world of mass-travel, of charter tourism and of Westernisation of the destinations.[2] In *Tristes Tropiques*, Claude Levi-Strauss designated travels as "magic caskets full of dreamlike promises" but concluded that they "will never again yield up their treasures untarnished" as the Western world has impacted both destinations and journeys as such and has "doom[ed] us to acquire only contaminated memories" (37-8). Levi-Strauss' romantic view of journeying in the past raises questions about how travel has been regarded, but also about how it is considered today. What treasures have ever been untarnished and according to whom? Why is the illusion that they have existed so important? Second journeys resist these common ideas as the

---

[2] The term Westernisation should be taken to indicate not only that the majority of contemporary travellers and tourists are from the Western world, but also that this imbalance has shaped the destinations as such.

"memories," there in textual form, are not seen as "contaminated" but rather as the impetus for the journeys.

There is no question that the Westernisation Levi-Strauss laments has had effects on discourses surrounding destinations, on how to narrate people and customs, indeed on travelling as such, and added to this are effects of a more prosaic nature. Qualities, earlier associated with the adventurous or involuntary aspect of the journey, either as prerequisites for travelling at all or rewarding additions to the personality upon the return, are now threatened as the traveller, safely delivered at the destination, can have American hamburgers or Swedish meatballs (depending on inclination and taste) for dinner, and rest assured that a Coca-Cola is a Coca-Cola even if it is purchased in Borneo.[3] That is, there is a contemporary ambivalence towards travel when many want to travel but no one wants to be a tourist.

Levi-Strauss' pronouncement is somewhat misleading, however, as it suggests that it is the twentieth century which exclusively deals with the "contaminated memories" when, in fact, the idea of an elsewhere as a place of exoticism and authenticity has existed for longer than that. Indeed, it is difficult to exactly pinpoint when the discourse of belatedness first comes into existence as few journeys do not trace some form of footsteps. Medieval pilgrimages might be the most obvious example of travelling in both actual and textual footsteps as pilgrims journeyed in groups, were led by a guide and stopped at designated places along the way, still, the repetitive and citationary nature of this form of travelling is seldom discussed with emphasis on any expressed sense of belatedness.[4] Chris Bongie argues that the final decades of the nineteenth century may be a starting point as the exotic at this time becomes a sign "of a constitutional absence at the heart of what had been projected as a possible alternative to modernity." Writers of this period then "register the exotic as a space of absence, a dream already given over to the past" (Bongie 22). Similarly, Ali Behdad uses the nineteenth century as a point of departure for authors "under[taking] an exoticist project marked by an

---

[3] Here I am paraphrasing Jacinta Matos (218).

[4] Pilgrimages were in this sense early manifestations of second journeys. Not only did the pilgrims repeat a spatial movement, they did so with an earlier text at hand, alerting them to what to observe and how to respond.

anxiety of coming after what had come before." Behdad's work focuses on orientalism in this time period and notes the influence on the Western world and its impact on what it deems as exotic. Colonial discourses had by this time "transformed the exotic referent into the familiar sign of Western hegemony," Behdad argues, causing in the orientalist traveller "either a sense of disorientation and loss or an obsessive urge to discover an 'authentic' Other" (13).

The late nineteenth and early twentieth century writers who constitute the first travellers in the case studies do not overtly express a sense of belatedness but as well-informed readers on the geographical areas they traverse, they still display a resistance to the idea that their destinations have already been textually mapped. Although Mary Kingsley makes several references to Count de Brazza and Dr Robert Nassau, for example, Caroline Alexander (the second traveller) voices suspicions that Kingsley tried to keep these references to a minimum and argues that evidence in other texts suggests that the nineteenth century traveller purposely omitted several stories in her attempt to present herself as more isolated than she was in the colonial areas of West Africa. Robert Louis Stevenson's view of and search for the exotic is most clearly manifested in his travelogue *In the South Seas*. Compared to his earlier journeys in North America and Europe; textually more 'covered' spaces, it is the relatively 'unexplored' Pacific Islands that appeal to him the most. Robert Falcon Scott is the only first traveller whose text I analyse who does cross a region, Antarctica, which is not extensively mapped, either textually or physically. In his case, belatedness takes a different and more literal shape as the race to win the South Pole is won by Roald Amundsen.

The second journeys considered are part of a contemporary exoticist project, the "recovery of the past and of all that a triumphant modernity has effaced" (Bongie 15). As such they illustrate the continuation of discourses of exoticism rooted in the late nineteenth century, and the consequence of imperialism's aim to conform the Other and the elsewhere to Western standards. This view of an elsewhere is an elitist one which excludes all those who are not part of, or not fully part of, the community of the privileged (and sometimes blasé) jet-traveller. Bongie states, in response to Lévi-Strauss' pessimism about the monoculture of the world, that Lévi-Strauss demonstrates a lack of focus on the *process* (4). That is, new horizons, new experiences, new boundaries, are in the process of disappearing, at least in theory, while in the reality of most people, the elsewhere still exists.

DISCOURSES OF TOURISM

Second travellers are acutely aware that others have been at the destination before them (this is a given simply by the fact that they are tracing someone else's journey), but they also wrestle with discourses of tourism, both within and outside their texts. Most second travellers find themselves immersed in tourist groups at one or another occasion, either because they literally take part in events organised for tourists, interact with tourists, or are labelled tourists themselves by other observers both from within the encountered culture and from the outside. The desire to differentiate between travellers and tourists can be seen in the second journey form, through a resistance to this labelling and by emphases on experiences off the beaten track, but since authenticity is associated with the past and since the first text in several ways functions as a destination with sights/sites to respond to, second journeys also represent a conflation of two, previously separate discourses: travel and tourism.

Traditionally, the line between travellers and tourists has been emphatically drawn and may account for some of the hesitation with which tourism has been incorporated into academic studies (sociology excepted). Jonathan Culler observes that the tourist has "few defenders, constitutes an embarrassment, and [. . .] it seems, is the lowest of the low" (153). The hierarchical division between traveller and tourist is, in Culler's view, paradoxically inherent in tourism itself. He claims that "[t]he desire to distinguish between tourists and real travellers is a part of tourism—integral to it rather than outside it or beyond it" (156). The desire to differentiate oneself from the loathed tourists finds one expression in what is perceived as adventure, promoted by contemporary tourist ads in which experiences out of the ordinary are promised and in which the word tourist is never mentioned. Discourses connected to the journey as either a trial or a pleasure are at work here but contemporary stress on the former is complicated by the diminished possibilities of experiencing real adventure. Just as it is now considered "touristy" to only climb Mount Everest (one would have to hang-glide from its summit or perhaps climb in darkness if one wants to distinguish oneself), modes of travel undergo transformations so that what was once considered unusually adventurous is now an everyday occurrence. The traditional sense of adventure, or the possibility thereof, has gradually disappeared and been replaced by unnecessary risks. Eric Leed argues that the attempt on the traveller's part to distinguish him/herself from the tourist "is merely evidence of the fact that travel is no longer a means of achieving distinction. It is a way of achieving and realizing a norm, the common identity we all share—the identity of the stranger" (*The Mind of the Traveler* 287). Contemporary travelling thus echoes the fragmented reality of the everyday world in which boundaries are blurred and where movement and strangeness are rules rather than exceptions, making exceptional experiences even harder to attain.

In the absence of clearly defined adventure, psychological effects on the traveller can supply a sense of experiencing something new and different, an experience which can be perceived as "a disturbing yet potentially empowering practice of difference" (Minh-ha 23). The disturbance in Minh-ha's discussion is connected to the shifting perspectives of the travelling subject. She argues that "[t]o travel can consist in operating a profoundly unsettling inversion of one's identity: I become me via an other. Depending on who is looking, the exotic is the other, or it is me" (23). To travel entails more than leaving a place, it also means that you may gradually leave behind what has defined you; the identities you have assumed in your more familiar environment. The traditionally stable and secure position of the traveller as observer may be subverted as the encountered Other gazes back. These qualities of a more inward journey which question and overturn means of identification as well as power structures may still supply the sense of adventure, to travellers and tourists alike.

A strategy used to emphasise the difference between travellers and tourists is seen in the search for experiences found off the beaten track, away from scheduled trips. Dean MacCannell's analyses of the division of sites into "back" and "front" regions suggest that there is always a desire on the part of the tourist to visit the back regions where the (sometimes staged) performance of the front region is prepared. It is through access to the back region that the tourist can become traveller again. The same imagery can be used when describing the traveller's desire to reach what he or she believes to be the authentic, a process which "is marked off in stages in the passage from front to back" (McCannell 105). Transitions between front and back regions can be represented through knowledge gained by communication and interaction with the inhabitants of the back region, but also through choosing old-fashioned means of transportation (in some cases no longer used by the native population) or planning living arrangements which are thought to represent an authentic experience (again, regardless of how the encountered people may live). In this sense, back regions are not only manifested in actual places and people, but in an idea of the past. Temporally, first journeys are comparable to back regions where authenticity is thought to be located. The past itself, indeed, becomes the back region. The present reality, the re-visit to the places encountered in the first text, consequently becomes the front region. The trick for the second traveller is then to (re)produce a version of the authentic and a closeness to the back region. The use of the first journey as a filter and its descriptions as markers of sights/sites are ways of accomplishing this.

The attempts to completely enter the world of the Other, to seek out and remain in the back regions, to imitate and/or disguise oneself as part of the encountered culture have become increasingly common ways of avoiding being labelled a tourist. The attempt to assume an identity of the Other while still remaining uninfluenced by the foreign environment becomes especially problematic when the aim is to faithfully and objectively report experiences in the written form. The double identity of the traveller "at the same time *representator* and *representative*, reporter and legislator" (Porter 14-15, original italics) also means that the writer can never fully separate him/herself from the narrative. By representing an Other, by assuming a (any) perspective, the writer also discloses him- or herself.

The use of a previous text as both inspiration and guidance is not limited to second journeys tracing a previous travelogue, but is also seen in what is termed literary tourism, persisting in contemporary culture when read experiences become ways to attract tourists to a certain places or site. Ian Ousby compares secular literary tourism to medieval pilgrimages and argues that the quest for a higher motive can be found in the tourists' "belief that the experience will in some way educate or uplift them" (8). Literary pilgrimages and heritage trails take tourists to the birthplaces and tombs of writers, or to the house or countryside in which a specific text was written. Entire towns such as Stratford-upon-Avon and Lyme Regis[5] are marked by the works of authors. In contemporary culture, visual and written fictions are used in tourist advertisements to attract visitors to certain areas, sometimes with spectacular results. Ystad, on Sweden's southern coast, is an example of a town whose number of visitors has increased markedly as it is the setting of BBCs Wallander series, starring Kenneth Branagh. The series is based on Henning Mankell's novels, and tourists may be familiar with either the written texts or the visual but travel to Ystad to personally walk in the fictive detective footsteps and learn more about both police work and forensics. The educational and uplifting aspects are touted as additional rewards for the tourist and the physical presence in Ystad as an opportunity to gain a sense of authenticity.

However tenuous the distinction between travellers and tourists is, the different strategies employed to uphold it illustrate the discursive power of both categories. Caren Kaplan's discussions concerning modernity in connection with the tourist trope are useful as a last example of the destabilisation of boundaries and a convergence of discourses. Kaplan points out that tourism has been used by theorists who by privileging "tourism seek to account for the anomie of modern, urban life through recourse to a powerful metaphor of travel." This is beneficial, Kaplan argues, for the destabilisation of the "elitist formations of some forms of cultural modernisms and demands a more historically specific, economically grounded theory of cultural production" (57). The tourist thus provides a vantage point from which to study modernism and Kaplan establishes one of the central links between the modernist exile and the postmodern tourist or vacationer:

> [T]he expatriate modernist writer and the vacationer may share the same desire for new experiences or places in order to "see" or "feel" differently.

---

[5] When Tennyson visited Lyme Regis he was less willing to discuss the historical importance of the place, i.e. the Duke of Monmouth's landing on the pier in 1685, than Jane Austen's *Persuasion*. "'Don't talk to me of the Duke of Monmouth', the Poet Laureate told his host. [. . .] 'Show me the spot where Louisa Musgrove 'fell down and was taken up lifeless'." Cited in Ousby 21.

> They may share a need to escape for longer or shorter periods from a routine or a mode of life that may be less than inspiring. They may both look to whatever trace of the past or of the alternatives to the modern they may be directed to find. (59)

The very rejection of the tourist in favour of the 'real' traveller is not only a celebration of the modernist elitist displacement, but signals the modernist hierarchical set of values rather than the de-differentiated postmodernist view. Kaplan remarks that "[t]he more the point of view of the tourist is rejected by the modernist, the more it reasserts itself as a structuring gaze" (79). Several traits from tourism, similar to the ones Kaplan observes, are combined in the second travellers' attempts to capture the past or, at least, see in the present condition differences that illuminate the time elapsed between the two journeys.

Discourses of Travel Writing

During the latter part of the eighteenth century, travel literature becomes increasingly discussed as a genre and writers turn to the journey as a motif, either in the form of travel journals or as a fictional device. The increased popularity of travel books drew additional attention to the belatedness of the traveller and Karen Lawrence notes that "[e]ven voyages of discovery betray anxiety that someone else's marker has preceded the explorer both geographically and textually" (24). Even journeys charting 'new' territory can thus be perceived as infringements upon areas that someone else has claimed, albeit only theoretically. The need for the travel writer to contribute something new and specifically his or her own to the accumulated works in the tradition is added to the perceived impossibility of undertaking a truly original journey. One consequence of the need to make it new is that subjectivity and self-discovery enter travel writing by the end of the century, giving rise to alternative discourses of self and Other. As Casey Blanton notes, there is a shift in focus from descriptions "to accounts of the effects of people and places on the narrator" (15). Although issues concerning the self and the world continue to be crucial there is an imperial tone in much writing continuing into the next century—a condescending, albeit at times benevolent, view of people and places encountered.

The nineteenth-century European Continental Tour and the beginning of tourism brought particular issues of awareness and originality to regard in connection with travel writing. The Tour was surrounded by guiding texts, in that sense making it a predecessor to the second journey and to literary tourism. "Traveling and reading" James Buzard notes,

> were seen to complement each other, constituting a cyclic ritual in which readers both shaped their expectations and relived their past travels through texts. It had long been true that preparatory readings—not only of travel books but of histories, poems, plays, novels—could help to establish future travellers' expectations; that travel could test those expectations; and that further reading could strengthen remembered expectations and experiences, recharging the reader's sense of having accomplished something meaningful by travelling. (160-61)

The awareness of the literary tradition helps the traveller to make sense of the experiences and as textual representations designate sights/sites as important, the visits to these automatically become meaningful. The journey in this sense becomes educational and not just a time of leisure. Travel texts, guidebooks, poetry and fiction surround the travelling subject as preparational material and are on the actual journey used to distinguish travellers from tourists. Buzard gives as examples Lord Byron's texts which not only worked as guidebooks but also as markers of the authentic as they both had a "capacity to revivify the well-known tourist haunts" and worked to "distinguish . . . genuine from spurious ('touristic') cultural experience" (120). The Byronic emulation thus worked as a means to authorise the traveller and distinguish him or her from tourists, even though this gesture is performed within tourism. The reading of Byron was furthermore complemented by more traditional guidebooks such as Murray's or Baedeker's. The two distinct but connected works filled different functions during the journey: the guidebook proper gave practical information, while Byron instructed the tourist in how to feel.

If the traveller intended to publish an account of these experiences, the literary-historical awareness presented a problem. The new text had to situate itself within the boundaries of the earlier tradition or somehow claim new territory within the field. While some sights/sites along the route were more or less required in a description, the cyclic ritual with texts surrounding the inception, the journey itself, and its aftermath, became what Buzard aptly refers to a "prison of prior texts" (170), a prison the travel writer at times desperately wishes to escape. James Duncan and

Derek Gregory observe that "the citationary structure . . . threatened the very integrity and 'authenticity' of the experience itself" (7), an observation which highlights the added pressure to contribute something new and original while still moving surrounded by texts to which references should be made to illustrate the traveller's own erudition. This is a tall order indeed, and tracing the development of the travel genre it is noticeable that many contemporary works have left the citationary structure altogether and instead present the experiences of the journey as highly individual. In second journey narratives, however, the cyclical structure persists and the citationary elements are used to other ends. Second travellers' embracing of earlier texts as pretexts and pre-texts (Matos 215) rather than prisons is an open process, inviting the reader to take part in the repetitive form. Repetition, that is, supplies a sense of authenticity.

The highly individual travelogue is one development in contemporary travel writing, and it is complemented with a mix of genres and forms as well as alternative strategies for representing both self and other. Fernando Galván notes the "marked increase in texts that break with the classical dichotomies 'fiction'/'reality' and 'literature'/'non-literature'" (78) which signals the postmodern tendency to disintegrate binaries. Other changes revolving around the writing process, and more specifically around the texts' subjects, are observed by Blanton who argues that they come "at the nexus of the narrator's sense of him or herself as creator of a text and of the involvement with the other (as persons, places, and moral and aesthetic universes) about whom the text is written" (xi-xii). The biographical element which is always part of a travelogue is thus characterised by an increased self-reflexivity, and the travel text's constructedness is emphasised in contrast to travel writing in previous centuries in which experiences are often presented as being the travel writer's unedited notes from the journey. The contemporary stress on the creation of the text also means an increased emphasis on descriptions as textual representations, coloured by the travel writer's own prejudices, expectations and (mis)conceptions.

The foregrounding of unstable subject positions and the blurring of epistemological and ontological boundaries which characterise postmodern writing in general might seem well suited to be embraced by travel writers.

> Travelers tend to present themselves, after all, as unusually flexible people, who are more open than most to alienating experience, and who seek out places that defy quotidian expectation and preformed assessment (Holland and Huggan 157).

However, the majority of contemporary travel books resist postmodern influences perhaps, as Patrick Holland and Graham Huggan conclude, because "the potentially transgressive, destabilizing character of travel seeks a compensatory stability in both its subject and its destination" (158). These stabilities are not enforced in all contemporary travel narratives, however, and there are several authors who experiment with the form in postmodern ways. Among these can be mentioned Italo Calvino, Umberto Eco, Bruce Chatwin and Pico Iyer; names which repeatedly return in works on postmodern travel writing, such as Holland and Huggans *Tourists with Typewriters*, James Duncan and Derek Gregory's *Writes of Passage* and Alison Russell's *Crossing Boundaries*.[6]

Second travellers are not discussed in any of these works, although Russell briefly mentions Sara Wheeler's *Terra Incognita*, Alexander's *The Way to Xanadu*, Lesley Downer's *On the Narrow Road* and Stuart Steven's *Night Train to Turkistan* as examples of texts which experiment with the genre. The resistance to incorporating second journeys into discussions about postmodern travel writing likely comes from the fact that they fall back on a more traditional format, modelled as they are on earlier texts.

However, close readings of second journeys reveal several postmodern concerns. The blurring of temporal boundaries and the readiness to report failures, misgivings, fears, disappointments and vulnerabilities draw attention to the fact that second travellers are aware of the constructions of their narratives and to their own subject positions. The travelling subject's place in the narrative is highlighted by the continuous retracing

---

[6] The lack of female travel writers among the examples is striking and in Russell's Coda "Whither the Women?" it is suggested that the feminist concerns about ahistorical and dehistoricised aspects of postmodernism make analyses of female travel narratives difficult to align with the project of mapping out postmodern developments (189).

of an earlier journey which in most cases presents a more stable and unified travelling persona. The critical and postmodern edge in second journeys stems from these continuous comparisons and from implications about what resulting questions contemporary travel writing can pose regarding exploitation and representation in a globalised and over-travelled world.

Second Travellers (and Tourists)

Travel writing is not the only literary field which is currently seen as suffering from a sense of exhaustion or belatedness, neither is it the only cultural field. What is clear, however is that there is indeed a contemporary longing for times past, for an age in which travelling was still adventurous, in which there was still some sense of blank spaces on the map, still a desire and a need to explore the *terra incognita*, no matter how illusory these notions may be. It is perhaps not surprising that all second journeys considered here are from the late twentieth and early twenty-first centuries as contemporary travel writers employ different strategies when travelling through and describing the world, and while some of these texts strive to find new starting points, others, "constitute a reappropriation of older routes" (Matos 216). The need for new strategies is pressing in a time of mass tourism and of Westernisation, both of which can threaten potential adventures and a perceived originality.

The presumed exhaustion of the travel genre exists alongside other literary, historic and individual fields which all experience the same "end of things-as-we-know-them" symptoms (Matos 215). Travel writing today is diverse and, despite the often expressed worries concerning the genre's demise in an over-travelled world, very much alive. The second journey is one contemporary expression which grows out of texts, concepts and discourses of previous centuries. In her article "Old Journeys Revisited" Jacinta Matos defines a group of texts that corresponds to my category of second journeys. "There exists," she states,

> a significant body of writing whose main purpose is to revisit places and retrace journeys made in the past and written about by others. They are, therefore, journeys that deal not only with the present reality of the traveler but also with a past encoded in narrative form. Thus a double focus is created: a journey made by somebody in the past is duplicated by a

> contemporary traveler, and a prior text is articulated with a present narrative. The old journey serves, that is, both as pretext and pre-text. (215)

The second journeys, as I identify these texts, attempt to establish links to the past by re-creating spatial movements. Although the process of rewriting is not specific to contemporary writers, the second travellers' openly stated dependence on the first text, inviting the reader into the citationary structure of the narrative, illustrates a development within travel writing which clearly places second journeys within the postmodern field. Not only does the second journey supply a new mode of travelling in an over-travelled world, but it also establishes links to the past and an opportunity to juxtapose and to compare, as closely as possible, the past and the present. The comparisons and juxtapositions make room for a postmodern use of intertextual references, and they also entail a higher degree of self-reflexivity. Where the first travellers write in accordance with their travelling personas (the heroic explorer, the eccentric creature/the scientist, the adventurer/writer of fiction), the second travellers continuously question their project and themselves, as travellers and writers.

Chapter Two. Authenticity and Intertextuality: To Make it New and True

> *In short, isn't the authenticity of an original a matter wholly distinct from the authenticity of a copy? No it isn't, not now. The culture of the copy muddies the waters of authenticity. We who can never exactly repeat the past are left to revive and hear ourselves out through devices that descend from music boxes and player pianos. Are we little else but futile reenactments, or is reenactment the little enough that we can be truly about?*
> Hillel Schwartz, *The Culture of the Copy*

As a text form, the travelogue is highly intertextual. The usage of other texts (fictional or factual) as inspirational or as sources of information can feature into the inception of a journey, its preparation, its realisation and its aftermath. Intertextual references in the resulting works are also common, be they to previous travel texts, works of fiction, geographical or cultural descriptions, or guidebooks. This chapter traces how textual influences and intertextual references have bearing on travel and travel writing in general and on second journeys in particular. These discussions are paired with a seemingly paradoxical juxtaposition. How, in a discourse where the authentic and original is so central, do the authors place themselves in relation to previous descriptions?

But first, a repetition and elaboration of the caveat from the introduction. There are many questionable ways in which authenticity has been used and which exclude many cultural expressions from discussions simply by situating them in opposition to what is deemed authentic. I want to emphasise here that my use of the word in no way aims to place any intrinsic value on the experiences sought or recounted, nor that exclusions should be suggested when I use the term. The travellers themselves may signal an experience out of the ordinary, but my use of the word does not legitimate their findings or make these out to be more valuable than other observations. When I use authenticity and the search for it, I see it as a concept crucial to travel in general, and to contemporary second journeys in particular. Authenticity may be staged, forged, fake, seen to be fake, or almost real, but the quest for it underlies most journeys. The problem is that what is perceived as authentic by the predominantly Western traveller is often a fantasy, situated in places and times perceived to be removed from everyday life and constructed from the Western (predominantly male, white, hegemonic) point of view. These reservations aside, the notion of authenticity informs many discourses within which both first and second travellers move.

Spatial and Temporal Authenticity

Travellers' and tourists' views of the past and of the unknown can be construed as sites in which true experiences are perceived as possible to attain. The modern world sees artefacts, souvenirs, and other markers of place and time transferred into the domestic sphere and an all-prevailing search for authenticity may be discerned as the reason. Dean MacCannell argues that:

> Authentic experiences are believed to be available only to those moderns who try to break the bonds of their everyday existence and begin to "live". [. . .] But everyday life is composed of souvenirs of life elsewhere. In this way, modernity and the modern consciousness infiltrate everyday existence and, at the same time, subordinate it to life elsewhere. (159-60)

Surrounded by souvenirs, modernity's citizens are told to always aspire for somewhere and something else, and the search for this illusive authenticity has become a contemporary discursive structure. The link between authenticity and place, however, follows from developments during the nineteenth century when, James Buzard notes, "the authentic 'cultures' of *place*—the *genius loci*—was represented as lurking in secret precincts 'off the beaten track' where it could be discovered only by the sensitive 'traveller', not the vulgar tourist" (6, original italics). The discourse of the authentic, placing it away from common routes, links this nineteenth century development to contemporary culture, but added in the past discourse is the more clearly pronounced division traveller/tourist.

On a journey, then, authenticity on the one hand resides in experiences or sights that are believed to exist off the beaten track, away from other tourists. On the other hand, as Jonathan Culler argues, we find "the authenticity a sight derives from its markers, so that tourists want to encounter and recognize the original which has been marked as a sight"

(161). An original can be marked in several ways and reproductions (small replicas of monuments, souvenirs, postcards and other markers of place commemorating the journey) are all connected to the notion of authenticity. Culler continues:

> The existence of reproductions is what makes something an original, authentic, the real thing—the original of which the souvenirs, postcards, statues etc. are reproductions—and by surrounding ourselves with reproductions we represent to ourselves . . . the possibility of authentic experiences in other times and in other places. (160)

The links between this line of reasoning and McCannell's conclusions illustrate that discursive structures informing the notion of the authentic posit the idea of an elsewhere removed both spatially and temporally from the contemporary subject. The created reproduction becomes the authentic through an imitational process that previously would have rendered it inauthentic. The second journey becomes a manifold reproduction. It is a sign of the longing for times past in which the fantasy of unmediated experiences flourishes, and it is connected to this past by its very existence in literary form: the book becomes, if you will, a souvenir. The journey in search of the original, unmediated experience connects with the first notion of authenticity (it ostensibly takes the traveller off the beaten track) and distinguishes (at least apparently) the traveller from the tourist. If we consider the marker as literary, that is, the first text as marker, we also find the other kind of authenticity: the authenticity the sight has derived from its marker (the first text). In this context, then, the second traveller becomes similar to the tourist wishing to encounter the original, marked as a sight.

When journeying in the footsteps of an earlier traveller with the previous text immediately at hand, the first journey furthermore takes precedence over contemporary reality. The "past sight dominates [the] present site" as Heather Henderson has it (231), a situation which further questions the possibility of authenticating experiences. The expectations the second traveller has are inextricably linked to the marker rather than the actual site, or, at any rate, to the relation between the two. The conscious foregrounding of the earlier journey designates it as the original and its descriptions become the markers against which the present reality will be measured. The authenticity sought through eyewitness experiences becomes increasingly problematic in postmodern travel writing as notions of subjectivity are problematised and the political, economic and cultural discourses underlying any claims to absolute truth are revealed.

The act of imitation is paradoxically essential to contemporary notions of authenticity,[1] and it is particularly important to the second journeys' repeated emulations of the first journey. The paradox has led culture critics, James Clifford among others, to ask the pertinent question: "[d]oes inauthenticity now function, in certain circles at least, as a new kind of authenticity?" (178). Regina Bendix touches on the same idea, suggesting that we are in fact concerned with different discourses converging in the twentieth century (and continuing into the twenty-first): "By submitting to the same process of representation and commodification those things that were proclaimed to be opposites, the genuine and the spurious are converging, their identities separable only by their narratives" (3-4). As is demonstrated by the second journeys' open processes of rewriting and emulating, they at least partly answer Clifford's question in the affirmative and illustrate the convergence of previously separate discourses.

Contemporary tourism has reacted somewhat differently to the search for authenticity. We have seen that there is a desire to seek out the 'back' regions of the destinations, but when too many tourists visit these, the quest for what is perceived as authentic results in the destination becoming marked by this desire or even constructed out of this need and so losing its pretensions to authenticity. 'Alternative' tourism, seeking uncharted territories off the touristic beaten track, moves against mass-tourism, but is effective only as long as the destination remains visited only by a select few. More often than not, however, mass tourism invades the area, driving the alternative tourists to abandon it in search of new and unspoilt destinations. Even if travellers and tourists do not intend transformations of this kind, they still take part in the economic, social, ecological and cultural discourses that lead to that effect. Discussing the

---

[1] Regina Bendix has noted that "[f]or all of our senses and all of our experiential cravings, we have created a market of identifiable authenticities. Recent decades has seen an interest, if not delight, in imitation as well" (3). She goes on to say that "[p]rocesses of authentication bring about material representations by elevating the authenticated into the category of the noteworthy. In the last decades of the twentieth century this process has accelerated exponentially, and so much has been declared authentic that the scarcity value is evaporating: once tomato sauce carries the label 'authentic,' the designation loses its special significance" (7).

public concern about these issues, Eric Cohen asks: "should tourists, even alternative ones . . . be contained within set confines even if this might preclude their having 'authentic experiences'?" (14). The question highlights the fact that nature and cultures are felt to be in need of protection from tourists and that tourists should be directed towards specific destinations, such as heritage sites and marked attractions. To focus on the contrived sites, to deflect tourists from certain destinations may, Cohen warns, foreshadow the end of tourism as we know it. "The crucial distinctive feature of tourism is that it involves travel," he states, and the destinations provide experiences that are not available in the home environment. This "distinctiveness of the destination," Cohen continues, can "be termed 'placeness'" (23). The development of contrived sites, the blurring of boundaries between real and manufactured experiences and the reduced prominence that postmodernism endows such distinctions with make way for the possibility of enjoying at home what one previously had to travel to experience. Experiences are thus de-placed and this may, in its extreme, threaten tourism as such.[2]

Heritage, Nostalgia, and Biography

A contemporary phenomenon, connected to the past and the authenticity perceived to reside in the past, is the increased interest in heritage which re-evaluates, invests with value, and presents the past to the traveller or to the audience. Barbara Kirshenblatt-Gimblett observes the positive effects of heritage projects as they "ensure that places and practices in danger of disappearing because they are no longer occupied or functioning or valued will survive" (150). However, there is an inherent legitimising problem in the notion of heritage as someone, somewhere necessarily has the power to decide what sites should be included in a heritage project and as Clifford points out, "[h]eritage replaces history, contributing to a hegemonic articulation of national and class interests" (216). Second travellers assume this privileged position determining not only what places and practices should be represented in their own texts but who are deemed interesting enough to travel in the footsteps of. Seen as a part of

---

[2] The death of tourism may be taking the issue too far and Cohen remarks that the shortcomings of the contrived sites will surface at some point bringing back the longing for spatially removed adventure, remoteness and genuine placeness. What will remain, he suggests, is space tourism (25).

the heritage industry, the second journey narratives ensure the survival of the first travellers in contemporary travel literature, by continuous references to and foregrounding of the first texts.

Heritage sites, historic sites and literary trails are all features of postmodern culture in which distinctions between separate fields and between the modernist binary opposites (such as the distinction between past and present, between past reality and contemporary experience) have, to an extent, collapsed. Chris Rojek explores the heritage site and several other modern forms of leisure, drawing upon the postmodern notion of de-differentiation "a condition in which former social, economic and political distinctions cease to obtain" (5). There are no longer any clear divisions between binary opposites, he states: "the divisions which gave stability to the Modernist order of things seem to be untenable—they do not correspond with people's actual experience of things" (5). The postmodern blurred boundaries between past and present, and between previously distinct spheres such as work and leisure, then find one expression in the heritage site, created to recapture the past and manifestly illustrate bygone eras. One of the examples Rojek mentions is the Plymouth Plantation in New England, complete with its own calendar. Instead of letting the past reside in the past, as it were, this is a creation of the past in the present; an attempt to deconstruct the temporal boundaries. This deconstruction is visible also on literary trails which traverse landscapes connected to a certain writer and aim to have the past come 'alive' along the route. These trails present not only the literary settings and characters, but also introduce biographical information about the author much in the same manner as the second journey narrative. Authenticity, in this sense, becomes connected to the past even though the literary landscapes are created (or represented) and manufactured.

A similar set of issues is connected to museums. Translating and/or framing a subject, culture, or area is also a form of staged authenticity, this time working within the public space of the museum setting and the power to include and exclude is pronounced here as well.[3] The second

---

[3] The complicated structures governing these notions are discussed at length by Clifford who argues that "[t]he spaces of collection, recollection, and display marked by the term 'museum' are multiplex and transculturated." The reasons for collecting and displaying are multifarious, "for purposes of prestige, political mobilization, commemoration, tourism, or education," as Clifford further argues (216).

journeys explored in the case studies all illustrate the second traveller's attempt to frame and translate the subject: the first traveller. In addition, the second travellers (most notably Nicholas Rankin, Robert Swan and Roger Mear), comment on official frames and translations in the forms of museums, preserved (or represented) homes and other places and objects with tangible ties to the first travellers.

When drawing a parallel between literary landscapes, heritage trails, the more traditional museums, and the second journey, it is clear that many of the perceived failures of the second traveller can be found in the difference between preservation and representation. That is, rather than being preserved in his or her original state, the first traveller is represented through objects, constructed places, writings, photographs, letters and other peoples' recollections, and it is this representation and constructedness that will sometimes disappoint the second traveller, regardless of the impossibility of encountering a 'preserved' first traveller.

Biography writing is connected to the heritage industry and to museums in that a biography too aims to frame and present its subject while simultaneously preserving the interest in him or her. It may also strive to evoke appreciation or understanding for the time-period to which the subject belongs. All second journeys analysed in the case studies are in some ways biographical projects; the aim is to shed light not only on a past movement, but a past traveller. The second journey narrative is in these cases often presented as a more dynamic, or, at least, alternative portrait of the first traveller than any conveyed through museums. This is especially clear in *Dead Man's Chest* where Rankin continuously criticises Stevenson museums and Stevenson collections, while giving prominence to his own work—the second journey as a biography—as presenting a more vivid image of his subject. In the case of Mary Kingsley, the notion of biography is problematised by gendered nineteenth century discourses which posit female, personal narratives as inferior and untrustworthy. Caroline Alexander wrestles with Kingsley's strategies employed in self-representation a century later and *One Dry Season* becomes, in fact, a biography of other travellers as well, most notably Trader Horn. Swan and Mear set out to rescue Robert Falcon Scott from past and contemporary detractors, proving that it was bad luck, not bad judgement, which resulted in the death of five men. The aim is to evoke an appreciation for the heroic project as such and the textual representation of Scott and Antarctica in Swan and Mear's book ensures a continued interest in the man and a sustained respect for the geographical area.

The blurring of boundaries between past and present is not confined to travel narratives. As Rojek argues, blurred boundaries of this kind are multifarious and easily detected in contemporary media. He states that:

> branches of the mass media keep the past constantly 'alive' in the present. Nostalgia industries continuously recycle products which signify simultaneity between the past and the present. [. . .] Increasingly, popular culture is dominated by images of recurrence rather than originality. (4)

In connection with second journeys we can note the instances in which the first text is used as a replacement for the second text. These instances are signs of the repetitive feature of contemporary culture—the past text is, to a certain degree, recycled, the nostalgia for past experiences takes over the present reality. We see it in Alexander's use of the previous travellers' descriptions of waterfalls she cannot reach, we find it in Rankin's reliance on Stevenson's texts when he decides not to emulate certain trips, only to mention a couple of examples. The use of whole paragraphs from the first texts then illustrates the second travellers' desire to uphold the sense of simultaneity between the past from the first text and their own experience. In the second journeys, this recycling is less a sign of commonality than what makes the second journey a distinct and inventive category.

Furthermore, the second journey can be said to belong to the "nostalgia industry" as the information given in the narratives centres on the past traveller, on the past experience. The blurring of boundaries between past and present takes place in the instances in which the first narrative completely takes over and/or where comparisons between experiences, between past and present, cause the second traveller to establish a connection with the first that falls outside traditional experiences. Richard Holmes' journey through the Cèvennes after Robert Louis Stevenson contains a telling illustration of the blurred boundaries. Holmes is coming into the town of Lagogne, hitherto satisfied with his journey and the closeness to Stevenson he has experienced, a closeness which is so powerfully felt he likens it to "a hallucination" (26). Holmes reaches a bridge Stevenson has written about, ceremoniously takes his hat off "as if to meet a friend, and pace[s] up and down, waiting for some sort of sign" (26). In a sudden switch, Holmes then begins to suspect that something is amiss. He looks around for a tangible reason for this feeling and notices the town's old bridge.

> It was about fifty yards downstream, and it was broken, crumbling, and covered with ivy. So Stevenson had crossed *there*, not on this modern bridge. There was no way of following him, no way of meeting him. His bridge was down. It was beyond my reach over time, and this was the true sad sign. (26, original italics)

The seemingly naïve and vain wish to meet Stevenson is made all the more poignant since Holmes is clearly aware of his role as biographer, and the temporal distance this role entails. He subsequently acknowledges that the past is "unattainable," saying that "[y]ou could not cross such bridges any more, just as one could not cross literally into the past" (27). In instances like these, the realities of the first and the second traveller become intermingled and developments or dilapidation of the former's surroundings make any real meeting impossible. A result of the impossibility to meet is often that the second traveller to a certain extent disappears from the text and is instead found in comments voicing disappointment, in omissions, and in the communicated feeling of letting the earlier traveller down by failing to relive experiences, or even by realising that too much has changed.

In these instances nostalgia is coupled with a sense of failure and disappointment, feelings which are highly individual and are not to be seen as signalling the failure of the journey as such. The subjective, emotive phrases pertaining to failure and disappointment are further problematised by the awareness, on the second traveller's part, of the difficulties inherent in the project as such—to trace footsteps made many decades ago. The paradoxical fact that failure in this sense stems from a known impossibility is one of the intriguingly problematic aspects of the second journey.

In this context it is also worth stressing that second journeys can be seen as translations and as such they are never unproblematic.[4]

---

[4] Many critics have considered travel narratives a form of translation. "Just as textual translation cannot capture all of the symbolic connotations of language or the alliterative sound of words, the translation of one place into the cultural idiom of another loses some of the symbolic loading of the place for its inhabitants and replaces it with other symbolic values. This means that translation entails both losses and

Describing his own work with cross-cultural translations, Clifford contends that "the moment of failure is inevitable. An awareness of what escapes the 'finished' version will always trouble the moment of success" (183). The word failure, although dramatic, is appropriate he argues,

> because the consciousness of being cut down to size, refuted by a constitutive "outside," is painful. It cannot be cured by revisions or by adding another perspective. If confronted consciously, failure provokes critical awareness of one's position in specific relations of power and thus, potentially, reopens the hermeneutic process. (183)

The repeated use of words like failure and disappointment in second journey narratives can thus be seen to illustrate the process of travelling, the process of writing, and the process of translating the encounter. When the second traveller is questioned, by the reader, by the previous text(s), by the awareness of power structures and the genre's tradition, the revelation of the failure and the ensuing disappointment open the text up, giving it additional postmodern features.

FACT AND FICTION: AUTHENTICATING TRAVEL WRITING

Another aspect of authenticity is connected to the travel report, the writing process as such, and to the long tradition within travel writing to balance descriptions of the unknown (always threatening to be unbelievable) with truth claims. When the educational journey superseded the pilgrimage, the humanist idea that the whole world was of interest led to the emergence of a new genre: "the multipurpose travel report" (Stagl 50). Its aim was to supply rhetorical information about "*memorabilia, insignia, curiosa, visu ac scitu digna* (things memorable, striking, curious, worth seeing and knowing)" (Stagl 50, original italics). The contents of the report were chronologically ordered, often in the form of a diary, and constituted a corpus of experiences which the traveller upon the return could pick and choose from. He or she was then at the mercy of the readers who chose whether or not to believe the story. Even when the

---

gains, and as descriptions move from one place to another so they circulate in what we have called 'a space in-between'. This space of translation is not a neutral surface and it is never innocent: it is shot through with relations of power and of desire" (Duncan and Gregory 4-5).

interest in the surrounding world was so widespread, the problem of 'truth' was pressing.

These issues continue to be of interest during the development of the travel genre. In earlier compilations of travel texts, the editing meant that old and new travel reports were presented side by side. The editor was seldom the actual traveller. The retold, printed story became distanced from the traveller and the actual experience. It became easy to invent stories, to interject with descriptions, in fact, to tell stories of travels that had never taken place. The methodology of travel, the *ars apodemica* arose partly because of this problem and grew from the humanistic instructive and descriptive writing aiming to increase travel in the interest of education. In an attempt to regularise travel and to deal with both empirical and non-empirical knowledge, the *ars apodemica* consists of a vast number of things to bear in mind when travelling. A systematic definition of travel was needed as well as a consideration of the arguments for and against travel. Medical, religious and practical advice is given, including advice on how to use instruments useful on the journey, such as maps, travel guides, etc. It is also specified what is to be observed. The travellers should note things of interest but also bring home interesting objects, make sketches of sights and natural specimens (Stagl 47-94). Empirical evidence, careful notes and a systematised way of regarding and reporting experiences were thus seen as ways of circumventing possible exaggerations and 'lies' about the encountered world.

The tensions between fact and fiction and problems associated with assigning truth to a text persist, however, in contemporary travel writing. In the introduction to *Travel Fact and Travel Fiction* Zweder von Martels states that:

> In our age, the gap between observation and scholarly discovery on the one hand and fiction and literary tradition on the other seems greater than ever before. Both observation and discovery are connected with originality and reality, with truth and sparkling results; fiction and literary tradition rather with fancy, with imagination and the world of books and the mind. But any sharp division between these terms is artificial and becomes untenable as soon as we look closely at the examples where authors rely on their observation. (xiv)

The blurred boundaries and the postmodern disintegration of dichotomies follow from the realisation of the artificiality of binaries and few travel books today contain only "observation" and "truth" or only "imagination" or "fancy." The perceived discrepancy between fact and fiction may also, in part, arise from the inclusion of other texts into the narrative at hand which may be perceived as lessening the authenticity and originality of the traveller's project. In second journeys this is especially clear in the use of quotations, sometimes inclusions of entire paragraphs when failures to reach specific destinations or re-live specific experiences occur, and when the second travellers are unable to trace the first footsteps to the extent that they wish. In these instances "reality" is pushed into the background in favour of descriptions from the first text.

These kinds of inclusions, however, are also found in the first narratives. As a telling example von Martels uses the encountered peoples and places from Columbus' descriptions of the so-called New World. He continues: "To the modern reader it can come as a surprise to realise that explorers often expressed themselves in words that reflect their reading of literature instead of what they actually saw" (xiii). Intertextuality, in this sense, is an important feature of travel literature in general and of second journeys in particular. The second travellers have decided to embrace the idea of belatedness, departing from traditional norms of travel writing, and have thereby quite deliberately opened themselves up to comparisons.

Intertexts

The process of rewriting as a mode of textual transformation naturally involves rereading. The return to the first texts primarily concerns the writer of a second text, but it also involves his or her readers. In many postmodern travel narratives, references to other works within the genre are oblique—links are hidden and quotations are left unexplained etc., but in the second journeys there is a clear tendency towards the opposite; the authors openly state their connection to earlier works, not only through titles and itineraries, but also through lengthy quotations, footnotes and explicit references. The "prison of prior texts" Buzard discusses in connection with preparatory readings (170) is as a consequence a raison d'être rather than an encumbrance. Matei Calinescu argues that the idea of the world as a text has become so worked into our view of existence that rewriting is inevitable. Focusing on the blurring of boundaries "between language and reality, fiction and fact, thought and action" he concludes that writers are "not only justified to rewrite earlier texts, they do not only feel an urge to do so, but being caught in an infinite textual maze, they have no choice but to rewrite" (Calinescu 245).

The time elapsed between first and second journey is of importance here and a parallel can be drawn to Walter Jackson Bates' work on Neo-classical poetry in which the return to earlier texts constituted a great deal of its appeal. Neo-classical poetry did not compete with the writings immediately preceding it, but instead gained authority through its affiliation with a still earlier period. This authority is "pleasing," Bate argues,

> when you can invoke it from a distant (and therefore "purer") source; pleasing because it is not an authority looming over you but, as something ancestral rather than parental, is remote enough to be more manageable in the quest for your own identity—more open to what the heart wants to select or the imagination to remold. (22)

The century, or in some cases centuries, between the first and the second journey makes the first texts authorities in a similar manner. Rather than situating their texts in close temporal proximity with the first, second travellers remarkably often choose to emulate journeys carried out further back in time. The discourses structuring the first texts do not necessarily conflict with those governing the second and rebellion against a 'parental' source is not necessary. The temporal remoteness makes it possible for second travellers, just as for Neo-classical poets, to pick and choose; to make the first text manageable. The second travellers can affiliate both with an earlier writer and an earlier text and by doing so create a sense of authority in their own narratives.

The authority of an earlier text, the rewriting of it, and the repetition of a movement made in the past might suggest that we should be concerned with influence rather than intertextuality, however, the growing insistence on the autonomy of the text and on texts as non-hierarchical social products reveal the limitation of theories of influence. Jay Clayton emphasises the static nature of the concept of influence, arguing that it

> is unidirectional, flowing from an earlier to a later author, whereas intertextuality establishes a flexible relation among texts. The itinerary of the reader, which is shaped by individual interests and experiences,

> determines the "direction" of the relation, and that direction can change over time as the reader develops new interests and accumulates further experience. (50)

The diminished authority of the author and the emergence of reader response theory also lead away from influence as the second traveller to all intents and purposes also is a reader. That is, he or she is a reader and also, at times, an interpreter of the first text, who is placing him/herself and his/her text between the first text and the new reader. While this is not unique to second journeys, the conscious foregrounding of the earlier text in the later narrative needs to be emphasised. Readers of the second journey are invited to read the texts side by side: the intertext becomes both a pretext for and a pre-text to the second journey. At the same time, the reader of the second journey does not necessarily have to be familiar with the original narrative. To a greater extent than in many other forms of intertextuality, the first journey is ever present. It is continuously quoted from and referred to. Knowledge of the first text, however, brings a deeper understanding to the reading of the second text.

New discoveries and knowledge will play a part in any interpretation of the first journey narrative. Things that the first travellers conceal, for actual reasons or because of discursive constraints, may be revealed by the second traveller and make it possible to read the first texts in a new light. Simultaneously, the second travellers are aware of the history of travel narratives; they bring to their own reading other sources of inspiration from both outside and inside the travel genre. Instead of a steady line of descent through the history of travel writing, maintaining canons and reinforcing modernist distinctions between high and low art, between past reality and contemporary experience, intertextuality stresses the mosaic quality of the narrative: parallel, overlapping, complementing or conflicting strands of inspiration or discussion.

Discourses surrounding both first and second journey illuminate what Linda Hutcheon has defined as an especially prominent feature of postmodern parody: "repetition with a difference" (*A Theory of Parody* 32). The form and characteristics of the travel genre, traditionally associated with notions of originality, are employed by the second travellers only to emphasise the fact that their journey is not an original, that it is, in fact, the opposite: a clearly formulated attempt to follow in the footsteps of an earlier traveller. By departing from traditional norms of travel writing, norms that demand originality, exploration of the 'unknown' and descriptions new to the reader, the second journeys set themselves apart. They acknowledge the impossibility of originality in the traditional sense by clearly stating that they are concerned with *re*-visits and *re*-creations, thus turning the very idea of exhaustion into the pretext for their journeys. They repeat, but with a difference.

Hutcheon's notion of trans-contextualisation (*A Theory of Parody* 32), that is, the situating of an earlier text in a new social, historical and/or cultural context via the parodying text, is also useful when considering intertextual elements in second journeys. Even if quotations from the first journey narrative are literal, they take on new meanings due to the trans-contextualisation—our, and the second travellers' knowledge, situation, and/or new perspective transform (slightly or profoundly) the quotations. Examples include Scott's comments, thought to be heroic by his contemporaries, now with the knowledge of the outcome of the expedition, glaringly naive. The trans-contextualisation of quotations from Kingsley reveals that parts of her narrative were probably exaggerated or even fictional, and descriptions in her narrative informed by colonial discourses can also be seen in a new light through the same process.

The second travellers' narratives display an awareness of limitations to travel literature. The limitations are perceived as set by the fact that there are no places left to travel to, but also by the genre's development, and the second journey's place within it, as well as by the second travellers' relations to previous works. In this, they are exceedingly postmodern. Hutcheon remarks that

> the postmodernist ironic rethinking of history . . . critically confronts the past with the present, and vice versa. In a direct reaction against the tendency of our times to value only the new and the novel, it returns us to a re-thought past to see what, if anything, is of value in that past experience. (*A Poetics of Postmodernism* 39)

She goes on to say that "[p]ostmodern intertextuality is a formal manifestation of both a desire to close the gap between past and present of the reader and a desire to rewrite the past in a new context" (*A Poetics of Postmodernism* 118). Within travel writing, the new and the novel can be seen to be attached to experiences. It is by experiencing something exclusive that authenticity can be gained. At the same time, and paradoxically, authenticity is predominantly seen to reside in the past. This past, when repeated, then brings new value to the present. The gap between past and present is, to a certain degree, reduced by the contemporary emulation of a past movement and the trans-contextualisations of the past experiences as well as the comparisons with the contemporary present rewrite the first texts.

In contemporary theoretical discussions about intertextuality, emphasis is mainly on fiction and other contemporary art forms, and the focus remains on self-reflexive, obscured and/or hidden references to other works of art (not necessarily belonging to the fiction genre). In contemporary literature, and especially in the non-fiction works with which we are concerned here, the links to earlier works are more and more open. David Cowart notes that

> such attachments have become increasingly common in recent years, doubtless as part of the postmodernist tendency towards self-consciousness and self-reflexivity–the tendency to let the machinery show. A study of these "symbiotic" attachments, especially as they involve formal or thematic revision, will reveal something about how contemporary writers engage in a kind of "epistemic dialogue" with the past, meanwhile forcing readers into a recognition of the historical or diachronic differences between the voice of one literary age and that of another. (1)

Symbiosis in Cowart's discussion is not construed as something negative. Rather than signalling a one-sided parasitic relationship, the symbiotic text exposes "the myth of originality" (3) by sustaining interest in the original and inspire new readings of the same. In second journeys, the overtly expressed connection with the earlier text, working on several levels from subtitles, maps of the earlier journeys, quotations and biographical material concerning the first traveller, puts the first text side by side with the second, inviting or carrying out comparisons. In this way a dialogue with the past is created which clearly illustrates how discursive structures have been reshaped or remained the same, indeed how epistemological and ontological concerns have shifted and changed (and in some cases remained the same). By departing from traditional norms of travel writing, norms that demand originality, exploration of the unknown and descriptions new to the reader, the second journeys set themselves apart.

By openly embracing the idea of a precursor the second traveller deviates from earlier notions of belatedness, turning the first journey(s) into the very motivation for the second journey. By retracing a previously journeyed route, the second traveller thus aims to experience what the first traveller experienced and heighten the authenticity of the second journey. The intertextual element in second journeys is one means of achieving the desired connection with the past. Heather Henderson remarks that "[t]he pleasure of imagining scenes from the past on the spot where they took place is often greater than the pleasure of witnessing scenes of today" (232). The filter, or grid, that the first journey constitutes can be perceived as an encumbrance when the first journey limits or controls the experiences of the second traveller, resulting in the present having to be ignored in favour of the past the second traveller has come to see. It can also be seen as a liberation when textual elements define and justify the second journey text.

CHAPTER THREE. SECOND JOURNEYS

> *In the recesses of his imagination everyone, I believe, must carry a secret map given him in childhood with the sites of treasure trove marked upon it where the rest of the world sees only a town's name, and to travel is to try and reach these sites, pickaxe in hand, hoping against hope for the ring of its blade on the buried casket.*
> Philip Glazebrook, *Journey to Kars*

"Was I too late?" The question is asked by Gavin Young in his 1991 book *In Search of Conrad* and stems from his worry that "[t]hese day, places change very quickly" (2). Young finds Joseph Conrad's novels on his grandmother's shelves, by his father's deathbed, and brings them along on his own journeys as a war correspondent. He "translates" people he meets on his journeys with the help of characters from the texts until the latter "became as real as actual Singaporeans or Thais passing me in the street" (2). Looking for Conrad through a series of journeys in his fictional (and sometimes actual) footsteps becomes a project for Young, but the initial question remains as a shadow hanging over his narrative as places have been too altered to support or make possible recognitions of the kind he seeks. It is also a question which illustrates the discourse of belatedness which informs contemporary travel and travel writing. Second journeys are, however, in part an expression of the belief that it is not too late to experience what the travellers of past times experienced—it is merely a question of finding the correct map to follow.

The texts analysed in this chapter introduce some of the features found in second journeys which will be explored more thoroughly in the case studies. Caroline Alexander's *The Way to Xanadu* (1993) raises questions about the multitude of previous texts that precede any single narrative. Bruce Chatwin's "A Lament for Afghanistan" (1980) illustrates how nostalgia can actually come to be the essence of the second journey and Philip Glazebrook's *Journey to Kars* (1984) shows how expectations are both negotiated and met. Frank Delaney's *A Walk to the Western Isles* (1993) suggests that a second journey can be used to familiarise yourself with new texts and authors, and Sara Wheeler's *Terra Incognita* (1996) illustrates an attempt to pay respect to first travellers, simply by trying to see what they saw. Texts from the two volumes of *Literary Trips* (2000, 2001) and from the website *Literary Traveler* are examples of how second journeys are used also as forms of guidebooks.

This chapter illuminates the wide range of second journeys through analyses of specific issues; it situates them within the textual history preceding them and traces how intertextual elements and the notion of authenticity affect the texts. The chapter further maps out some perceived disappointments, but also the successful recognitions experienced by the second traveller, and problematises aspects connected to both the first and the second traveller's identity in relation to home and to heroism.

Travel Texts, Guide Books and Intertextual References

The travel book is a (somewhat) chronological description of one or several journeys whereas the guidebook is a rather more referential text, which includes information about hotels, currencies, visas, languages, etc. While the travel text is presented in a single, authoritative, present voice, the guidebook most often contains information from different sources, and expresses this information in a less personal, less unified, but still authoritative voice. These differences have led to a seemingly natural division between the two forms, but the citationary nature of travel writing also entails similarities. Ali Behdad investigates the change from travel texts to guidebooks occurring in the nineteenth century with the rise of tourism and although he designates the guidebook as a new discourse within the travel genre, he argues that it builds upon and, in many senses, repeats the travelogue's form. Further, "the guide quotes the statements of previous travelers, incorporates them as part of its informational apparatus, and then acknowledges them as truthful representations" (Behdad 38). That is, information gleaned from travel texts often appear in guidebooks, whereas the opposite is less common. This characteristic feature of the guidebook is clearly seen in the second journey as previous voices are incorporated and represented as truthful,; however, as a contemporary, postmodern form, second journey narratives also question the single, authoritative voice and make room for more self-reflexive comments which echo both concerns regarding the position of the travelling subject and the constructedness of the text.

The traditional guiding text, be it a reference work containing practical information instructing the traveller what to see (such as a Murray or Baedeker volume), a work of fiction (such as Lord Byron's texts) instructing the traveller how to feel, or a religious text (indicating ways in which the site/sight should be approached and appreciated), would most often be a concrete artefact, brought along and consulted on the trip. First journeys work in both these capacities as the second traveller is led to sights/sites and has expectations on experiences which stem from the first traveller's descriptions. The companion on the journey does not, however, have to exist in a concrete form. In second journeys, it is not only the first text which influences perceptions and descriptions but often, memories of other read or real experiences are incorporated. The quotation in the title of Heather Henderson's article "My Giant Goes with Me Wherever I Go" is taken from R. W. Emerson's essay "Self-Reliance" (1841), and Henderson contends that "[t]he giant that accompanies every travel writer is constructed in part by the books he or she has read" (230). These texts, and what they depict, can take precedence over the people and places actually encountered. Expectations raised by the previous narrative(s) make way for potential disappointments and sought-after recognitions, and the effects of the literary inspirations can be sustained throughout the journey. Henderson argues that

> the value of a scene, landscape, or monument lies not so much in its own intrinsic qualities as in the pleasure of seeing for ourselves what someone else has seen and described before us. The observer's relationship to the scene is indirect, filtered through the literary representation by which he [sic] first came to know it. (231-32)

Recognition of a place encountered in writing thus supersedes the importance of the present site and in second journeys the most important filter is, naturally, the first journey which illustrates an opportunity to capture previous experiences, perceived as authentic. Earlier texts become markers which the second traveller wishes to encounter.[1]

---

[1] I intend the word 'marker' to be interpreted according to Dean MacCannell's use of the word. See the discussion in chapter two and MacCannell, *The Tourist* (110).

The past preserved in writing and the awareness of earlier travellers pose problems for second travellers because the "mediated" desire (Henderson 238) of the journey inspired by other texts may restrict or limit the second traveller's experiences. Henderson's discussions concerning a first journey by Alexander Kinglake (*Eothen, or Traces of Travel Brought Home from the East*, 1844) and a second journey made by Philip Glazebrook (*Journey to Kars: A Modern Traveller in the Ottoman Lands*, 1984),[2] illustrate that the belatedness of the traveller is a notion with some history as Kinglake wrestles with the same problems Glazebrook later will. There are differences, however, in how first and second travellers in these cases negotiate previous texts. Kinglake experiences anxiety when unable to fully appreciate sights that have been described in the literature he has read, although he is aware of the fact that earlier writers may have employed exaggeration. His "awareness of the ways in which the landscape is already 'written' imposes on him an obligation to think, feel, and see in a particular way" (Henderson 238). Although restrictive in the sense that Kinglake feels obliged to react in certain ways, his references to previous works which filter the scenes he encounters also signal a desired mediation of the landscape. The ability to recognise sights from literature has long been seen as a sign of education and a certain status. Instead of being overcome by earlier narratives and descriptions that seem much more vivid, Kinglake, writing in the middle of the nineteenth century, attempts to make earlier travellers part of his own narrative rather than displaying himself as a follower. By recognising and thereby mastering the previous texts inscribing the landscape, Kinglake controls the world he encounters.

The awareness of the prior travel text(s) as well as knowledge of the area surface in all the first travel texts discussed in the case studies but there is a difference in how first and second travellers use the intertextual references. The tendency to master previous narratives, to subsume them and obliquely work them into one's own text, as is the case with Kinglake, stands in contrast to Glazebrook's openly stated connections with earlier works, with his emulations signalled by clearly marked quotations and

---

[2] Glazebrook's second journey belongs to the group of second journeys that centres on an area rather than on a specific writer and/or text and Kinglake is one of several writers that Glazebrook quotes.

explicit references. Simultaneously, rather than a marker of education and status, the references in the second journey narrative can be seen as signalling a sometimes unwanted influence as the second traveller is aware of the notion of the exhaustion of the genre and the position of the future reader. The awareness of earlier texts becomes, in this context, highly problematic. To enter the literary tradition that he or she is so influenced by means an awareness of the fact that "[t]he travel writer inevitably interposes his [sic] own text between the sight and the reader, just as previous writers interposed their texts between him [sic] and the sight" (Henderson 241). The second traveller, that is, may realise that he or she reproduces the same pattern as the first traveller, inserting his or her own text as an additional layer or filter to be negotiated by the presumptive reader. In doing so, and expressing an awareness of this repeated pattern, second travellers draw attention to the constructions of their own texts and often emphasise their individual reaction to an experience, rather than making pronouncements of a more general nature.

As the case of Kinglake shows, the narratives preceding the first journeys are numerous and sometimes difficult to discern. Concerning the second journeys analysed in the case studies, it is clear that Robert Falcon Scott read extensively what little was known about the region he set out to explore and also got continuous information about the progress of his competitors from daily dispatches. Mary Kingsley had undoubtedly read much on West Africa before she departed; she mentions Robert Hamill Nassau and Count de Brazza as sources of inspiration. Robert Louis Stevenson did not investigate the areas he was travelling to in the same scientific manner as Kingsley and Scott, and the diversity of his destinations also meant that he had varied access to information about them. The information he *did* have in some cases mis-prepared him for his travels, and the influences in many ways made him regard both travelling and locations in an excessively romanticised way.

Henderson points out another consequence of this awareness of other texts. She states that:

> Travel literature is so highly intertextual that at times texts are actually substituted for experience itself, and the attempt to control crucial

> passages, whether in the Bosphorus or in Victorian prose, represents an essential strategy in the campaign to make a place one's own. (246)

Intertextuality is here presented as a common feature of the travel genre, but it is visible to an even greater extent in the second journey narratives. At times the second traveller simply surrenders and quotes the first description in full, rather than attempting a narration of his or her own, perhaps disappointing, experience. At other times, the second traveller abstains from visiting a certain place, but, instead, comments on the earlier text. These instances illustrate the control exercised over the first text rather than over the experience. However, the interposing of textual elements can in other instances be seen as a defence mechanism: a strategy designed, by the insertion of textual layers, to distance the writer from what he or she is reporting.

RECOGNITIONS AND DISAPPOINTMENTS

The relationship to the first text differs between (and within) second journey narratives and the motive for travelling in someone else's footsteps also varies although the desire for a connection with an authentic past is ever present. This past is represented as tangible only when the second traveller physically enters the scene, and the very landscape is often presented as holding the key to an increased understanding of previous travellers and their motives. When Glazebrook first sees the Danube he says that:

> This was the view I had come for, and these were the travellers I had hoped to *glimpse* as they pushed off on their adventures. I meant to *meet* them again and again . . . and to understand, if possible—by seeing some of the scenes they travelled through—something of what was in their minds; why they came, what they wanted of the East, who they thought in their hearts they really were. [. . .] I had thought about these strange individuals, and their motives for Eastern travel . . . now I wanted to see whether the ideas and theories I have evolved seemed watertight . . . when tested against experience of lands they had travelled through. [. . .] I have been there . . . in the company of *ghosts*, the *shades* of real travellers, whose voices I have tried to overhear, and whose thoughts I have tried to understand. (Glazebrook 8-9, emphases added).

By recreating the movement in space, by attempting to see, hear, smell and feel what previous travellers have experienced, Glazebrook's aim is to understand them. He cannot do so only by reading their works: it is by the attempt to recreate the physical sensations that he can approach the sentiments and emotions earlier travellers have wished to communicate. By moving where they moved, by reading their words in the surroundings in which they supposedly originated, he hopes to understand them and their motives for travel. Glazebrook clearly realises the distance between first and second journey although he metaphorically speaks of the chance to meet or glimpse earlier travellers, and the temporal distance is signalled by his use of terms like ghosts and shades, that is, a presence that is no longer a presence.

The biographical element inherent in second journeys entails an emphasis on making connections with the writing subject of the first text which is sometimes illustrated by a certain distance and at other times by a more intrusive, voyeuristic pleasure. Sara Wheeler repeatedly voices a desire to "pay homage" to the Antarctic travellers she has encountered in reading (148). When visiting Scott's hut at Cape Evans she expresses closeness to the early explorers. "I saw them everywhere," she writes (55). By travelling through the area the first travellers crossed, by recognising landmarks described by them she notes: "I hadn't realized how close we had become, these dead explorers and I" (150). By situating herself in the environment she has read about, Wheeler approaches an understanding and experiences a connection with the past, even though this is a past of male travelling that she as a woman would not have gained access to in the early twentieth century.

Frank Delaney formulates his project, a journey to the Western islands of Scotland in the footsteps of Samuel Johnson and James Boswell, as follows:

> 'Discovering' them by following in their footsteps grew more and more appealing. On the Hebridean journey, the pair became Life itself and Life's recorder, and pursuing them thus could I not unveil them gradually and very fully? [. . .] Therefore, I could judge the two men from how they responded to what they viewed. Spending so much time in their company would implant them so clearly in my mind that any further reading would, for the rest of my life, be done against a background of 'first-hand' personal knowledge. I would absorb them almost without knowing—acquaintance by osmosis, and my tongue not too far from my cheek. (4-5)

Delaney travels to familiarise himself with Johnson and Boswell rather than to "meet" old acquaintances like Wheeler and Glazebrook. Like the latter two, however, Delaney stresses his own presence in the landscape and his reiteration of the physical movement through it as crucial to an increased and very personal understanding. Any future information concerning Johnson and Boswell will, Delaney suggests, be measured against what he, though his intimate connection with them, deems logical or likely. "There is only one method of discovery better than reading a book on a subject," he says, "and that is by writing one" (Delaney 4). *A Walk to the Western Isles*, the textual result of this discovery process, illustrates Delaney's growing appreciation for the first travellers, their texts, and the landscape—both past and present—he is travelling through.

Preconceived notions about what the journey should yield and how these make way for moments of recognition and pleasure are crucial to the notion of authenticity, but the expectations can also cause disappointment. Glazebrook supplies a good example. "Here was an arrangement of nature and art which satisfied my imagination," he says of the theatre of Dionyssos in Athens, and when he sees a man sitting there he remarks that "[h]e might have been Warburton's Turk, in the way he harmonized to my mind with the scene in which I found him" (29). Later, walking around in the garden of the Agora, he finds "another scene which exactly suited what I wanted from Athens" (30). These scenes correspond well to Glazebrook's expectations raised by his read experiences. He sees Eliot Warburton's Turk, and the Greece depicted in travelogues, rather than contemporary people and places. Where the time elapsed has altered the landscape, feelings of disappointment supplant the feelings of successful recognition. Glazebrook formulates a theory about the source of his disappointments:

> The truth is that few individuals have ever travelled, in modern times, to see what other countries are like nowadays; in general people travel in search of traces of past eras, and they have in consequence almost always been disappointed by what exists when they get there. [. . .] The disappointments are brought about by the mis-preparation of your mind for what really exists; yet it's the mis-preparation—the treasure trove buried in your mind under certain place-names in early days—which draws you on to travel in the first place. (151-52)

Glazebrook here makes the personal observation (albeit lending it a more general air) that the preparatory readings, resulting in a "mis-preparation" are, indeed, what constitute an attraction for the traveller. The contemporary destinations, indeed the authentic destinations, are not what the traveller desires to see; it is the past as it predominantly has been presented in literature that supplies the authentic experience, serving as the initial inspiration for the journey and constituting the goal for the traveller. Feelings of disappointment thus stem from a more or less known (and more or less clearly expressed) impossibility, but do not always lessen the experiences had. Rather, disappointments can, at times, in themselves be markers of authenticity.

An instance during Delaney's journey serves as an example of when a disappointment (caused by physical impossibility) is turned into a moment of epiphany. Due to bad weather, Delaney is unable to visit the island of Coll. At first he terms this non-event a "significant failure" but then proceeds to quote extensively from Johnson's and Boswell's narratives. "Curiously," he says,

> my failure to land on Coll brought me closer to them than I had so far come, as if the geography, economy and society they recounted became the colour and brush-strokes by which we see the artist through the painting. [. . .] By not seeing Coll, but with the habit of standing in their footsteps now formed, added to the way they stimulate the imagination. (Delaney 231-35)

The Coll of Johnson's and Boswell's narratives remains untouched and unmediated in Delaney's mind. At the same time, he paradoxically comes closer to them by focusing solely on their words. In a similar vein, Caroline Alexander quotes Kingsley's chapters on the overland trip to the Remboué, a leg of the journey which Alexander herself is unable to duplicate. "I have generally tried to avoid plundering Kingsley's *Travels*," she says, but contends that these particular descriptions are "too brilliant and too devastatingly funny to pass over in silence" (*One Dry Season* 219). Not only are they too funny to pass over—Alexander has no choice but to quote them since seasonal circumstances prevent her from following the same route. The past of Kingsley's narrative thus takes precedence over the present as no comparison can be made. Nicholas Rankin, on the other hand, chooses not to emulate Stevenson's journey across the Cévennes. The availability of the trip, and the many authors who have already traced Stevenson's route make it uninteresting to him. Rankin does not take recourse to Stevenson's own words in lieu of a trip of his own, instead he briefly outlines how reiterations of the itinerary (complete with donkeys for hire "at exorbitant rates") are now marked for tourists and he concludes "you could go yourself one summer" (Rankin 115-16).

In Bruce Chatwin's "A Lament for Afghanistan" which traces Robert Byron's 1933-34 journey, chronicled in *The Road to Oxiana*, nostalgia for the past combines with predictions for the future to form an image of a time and an experience which will be lost forever. The first travelogue has worked as a powerful influence on the second traveller who has "raised it to the status of 'sacred text'" (286) and learned all he can about Byron through letters, texts and interviews. To follow in his footsteps becomes a logical step in this familiarisation process. The journey itself is carried out in 1962 and Afghanistan is a relatively easy destination to access and travel through. Chatwin's text, however, is written in 1980 and the 1979 Soviet invasion of Afghanistan is a shadow hanging over it. Byron foresaw many of the developments in the Middle East, and Chatwin mimics him in this as well, ending his short piece as follows:

> We will not stand on the Buddha's head at Bamiyan, upright in his niche like a whale in dry-dock. [. . .] And we shall lose the tastes—the hot, coarse, bitter bread; the green tea flavoured with cardamoms; the grapes we cooled in the snow-melt; and the nuts and dried mulberries we munched for altitude sickness. Nor shall we get back the smell of the beanfields, the sweet, resinous smell of deodar wood burning, or the whiff of a snow leopard at 14, 000 feet. (Chatwin 293)

The "we" in this quotation pertains to both Chatwin and Byron, and, one might argue, other travellers, past and future. Throughout the text there are comparisons not only between the landscapes and people encountered but between the travellers' similar reactions to these. From the perspective of 1980, Chatwin thinks back on his experiences, wondering what has happened to the people he met on his journey, and being convinced of tragic outcomes in many cases. The loss of sensations, smells and textures in the quotation are thus to be read more symbolically as the loss of a country's future.[3]

British traveller Tim Severin has written a number of travelogues which can be characterised as scientific second journeys, many of them

---

[3] Post 1980 events make Chatwin's lamentations even more prophetic, as the two Buddha statues were destroyed by the Taliban in 2001.

carried out with the aim of 'proving' that ancient legends were, in fact, accounts of previous travellers (although not necessarily only of the individuals lending their names to the legends). Among Severin's books of this type can be mentioned *The Brendan Voyage* (1977; tracing the route of the sixth century eponymous monk on his trip from Ireland to North America), *The Sindbad Voyage* (1982; which sets out to explore the possible truths behind the tales of the *Arabian Nights*), and *The Jason Voyage* (1985; reiterating the journeys of the Argonauts). In addition, Severin has travelled in the footsteps of, among others, Marco Polo and Ghengis Khan, and attempted to establish, through journeys, the real-life background of Herman Melville's *Moby Dick* and Daniel Defoe's *Robinson Crusoe*.[4]

In several of these texts, the pronounced focus is on achieving a sense of authenticity by constructing a vessel as similar to the original as possible, a process which necessitates significant background research into sometimes quite unorthodox texts and painstaking work in finding and assembling the right materials. This kind of authenticity is crucial to achieve the aim of proving that the ancient voyages were indeed carried out and that many of the tales related through them were, in fact, descriptions of real events. In *The Sindbad Voyage*, Severin writes that his earlier journey in the wake of Brendan "had demonstrated that the technique of building a replica of an early vessel was a useful research tool" (15) which signals that it is not only the finished product but the very process which is valuable and pedagogical. He continues to say that the experiences of sailing the boat had gains of a more subtle nature as they gave "a taste of what life aboard an open skin boat must have been like for the early sailors" (15). Knowledge can thus be gained not only pertaining to the first journey, but to early seafaring travels in general. The success of Severin's own second journeys is then used to gauge the probable (or possible) success of the first. Although success is absent from Scott's return journey, aspects connected both to authentic means of transportation and to the issue of finding evidence in favour of a claim,

---

[4] See Severin, *Tracking Marco Polo* (1986), *In Search of Ghengis Khan* (1991), *In Search of Moby Dick* (1999) and *Seeking Robinson Crusoe* (2002).

link these types of journeys to Robert Swan and Roger Mear's second journey, more extensively analysed in chapter four.

In *The Way to Xanadu*, Alexander carries out a journey to places found in fiction, in this case Samuel Coleridge's poem "Kubla Khan," and, although not a second journey in the strictest sense (as it does not trace a previous travelogue), it highlights the propensity for disappointment and for the perception of the journey (or aspects of it) as a failure. After lengthy preparations and research Alexander travels to Nei Menggu, Inner Mongolia to Shangdu where Khubilai Khan once had a summer residence referred to by Coleridge in the poem. The city is in ruins, but still impresses Alexander with its melancholy air. It does not, however, live up to her expectations as she seeks the poetic quality behind the stanzas. In doing so, she goes back to Coleridge's "Notebook" in search of his inspiration. As is demonstrated by Coleridge's biographer John Livingston Lowes "the poem's most dominant imagery can be attributed to a small nucleus of books of travel and discovery" (Alexander 49). Although it is "not possible to travel to the Xanadu of 'Kubla Kahn', one might" Alexander contends, "traverse its landscape" (49). Alexander's crossing of the landscape depicted in the poem is then literal as well as literary.

As it turns out, Alexander's second journey comes to encompass four additional journeys. The first one goes to the southern parts of North America as Coleridge was influenced by a book by William Bartram.[5] In the north of Florida, Alexander finds what she believes served as literary inspiration for Coleridge's "mighty fountain," his "incense-bearing trees," and "spots of greenery" (Coleridge 56). Alexander then travels to Kashmir in search of the "caves of ice" (Coleridge 57), and finds them in the company of pilgrims journeying along a traditional route that takes them to the foot of the Himalayas and to the Amarnath Cave. Kashmir becomes the logical destination as Coleridge frequently mentions Reverend Thomas Maurice, Major James Rennell and François Bernier, all of whom have written on that region. Alexander's penultimate journey takes her to Ethiopia. As many of his contemporaries, Coleridge was fascinated by Abyssinia, but Alexander maintains that the most lasting impression was

---

[5] Cumbersomely entitled *Travels through North & South Carolina, Georgia, East and West Florida, the Cherokee Country, the Extensive Territories of the Muscogulges, or Creek Confederacy, and the Country of the Chactaws.*

made by James Bruce's *Travels to Discover the Source of the Nile* (1790). Her own journey becomes a disappointment to her in some respects and leaves her with one final destination. "My travels had awarded me with glimpses—albeit scattered—of the landscape of Xanadu. Now," Alexander says, "nothing remained for me but to turn to the place where it had been conjured up and to the poet who had dreamed it" (*The Way to Xanadu* 170). She travels to Exmoor, and to the place where Coleridge awoke from the repose induced by opium to write the poem.

The journeys in different geographical directions and the return to Exmoor do not result in the "heightened poetic vision" with which Alexander has hoped she would eventually see "Kubla Khan." She concludes that the image the poem conjures up remains "reminiscent of nowhere" she has gone (184-85). *The Way to Xanadu* is a later work of Alexander's and in it she reaches the conclusion that is in many ways foregrounded in *One Dry Season*, that there are "difficulties inherent in attempting to revive the symphony and song of an experience" (167). There is always a pre-knowledge on the second traveller's part: an organisation of the things he or she expects to see, made through and by the first text. To rely so heavily on the markers that the previous texts (be they travelogues or poems) constitute is therefore to invite more than the usual problems into the translation, understanding or even appreciation of the surroundings.

IDENTITY: HOME AND HEROISM

Most travel writing reflects the image of the traveller's home in various ways. The writing from home and from a perceived centre can supply the traveller with a formally stable identity, even though this identity is at times subverted in texts. The home, and the identity the traveller has in the home environment, can further be used in comparison with and in contrast to people, places and customs encountered on the journey. In early travel literature, and especially in texts from the colonial period, the home and the traveller's initial identity are often presented as models in comparison with which the encountered person, place or custom is inferior, uncivilised or savage. However, the identities connected to home can be problematic in various ways, and variations on this problematic aspect are present in all the first texts in the case studies. Scott's heroic persona is dependent on the audience at home to which he makes repeated textual returns, especially towards the end of his journal. His national identity is further made important, because he is out to win the Pole, indeed Antarctica, for Britain. Kingsley's identity is based in the conservative British Victorian society and even though she gradually distances herself from it, it is against Britain that many of her experiences are measured. Stevenson, finally, imaginatively returns to his native Scotland, both in his fiction, his journals and his correspondence. It is even possible to argue that the spatial difference makes it easier for him to see his home country but as his travels last for most of his life, the images of home fluctuate and fill different, sometimes conflicting, functions. In their travelogues, however, neither Kingsley, Scott nor Stevenson return home in the sense that an actual return is recorded or hinted at in their narratives. It is through comparative discourses that homes and identities connected to these are revealed.

Identities connected to home are questioned in the postmodern condition in which the centre itself is fragmented and scattered but textual returns are not uncommon in second journey narratives. Comments pertaining to what has transpired after the return to the home environment and during the writing of the travelogue are indicative of the self-reflexivity characteristic of contemporary travel writing and draw attention to the text's constructedness. But while identities and subject positions connected to home are worked into second journey narratives, the nationality of the traveller seems less important. Patrick Holland and Graham Huggan argue that several reasons can be discerned for the lack of a homogeneous place in today's society:

> the metropolis itself is clearly a multiethnic entity, a place where different, often contradictory, realities mix and mingle. And for another, the older anthropological conception of a distinctive (separate) culture has been largely replaced by a longer view that sees all cultural forms, interacting in a transnational context, as strands in a global, hybridized pattern of dis- and relocation. (8).

Whereas the first travellers whose texts I analyse are revealed to be determinedly British or Scottish though comparative discourses, the second travellers remain almost nation-less. The alignment with a national identity in the first journeys and a nation-less identity in the second journeys raise questions about who or what constitutes the Other and it brings to attention issues about representation both of self and of other(s).

Gendered discourses as seen in the first journey indicate another set of identity constructions which problematise the second traveller's ability to relate to the traveller he or she is tracing. Alexander's difficulties in reviving an earlier experience are connected to the genre-conventions of travel writing, specifically to the romantic element requiring a hero, but also to the gender this trope presupposes. "The modern traveller" she states,

> will inevitably find himself walking self-consciously in the footsteps of an earlier, more illustrious predecessor, compared to whose adventures his own may seem prosaic and dull. Yet . . . I do not believe that making journeys to regions remote from one's ordinary life will cease to allure and fascinate. I do believe, however, that it will become increasingly difficult for the traveller to cut the dashing figure of the old romantic epics; or . . . to pretend to himself that he has done so. (Alexander, *The Way to Xanadu* 170)

I have left Alexander's exclusive use of the male pronoun unchallenged to indicate that the heroic character, both where the first and second traveller is concerned, is often influenced by its traditional maleness. Although this is more pronounced in the first journeys made in previous centuries, Alexander's statement above concerns the modern traveller and the sole use of him/his indicates that the problems persist.[6]

The gendered aspects of travel are visible in modes of travel, modes of expression and in how the second journey emulations are complicated by these notions. Traditionally, that is, the traveller has been a man, and a man travelling for a long time had to strive to be heroic.[7] The significant differences between Kingsley's and Scott's texts, and the ways with which the second travellers handle the traditional heroic role reveal differences in male and female travel narratives. Kingsley identifies sporadically with the heroic persona, but her text also illustrates a resistance to it. The oscillating between textual selves causes Alexander some problems, and

---

[6] Alexander herself does not comment further on gender as posing a problem for duplicating a heroic travel narrative.

[7] By this I do not mean that all men unproblematically assume the role of hero.

rather than stressing Kingsley's heroism in terms of outward exploits, she finds it in the first traveller's lonely quest for knowledge and independence. In contrast, the heroic traveller is naturalised in Swan and Mear's narrative, *In the Footsteps of Scott*. Scott was very much a product of the heroic age and the explorational journey met all standards required of the heroic journey. In the second journey, Scott's walk to the South Pole is seen in comparison to the achievements of Ernest Shackleton and those of Roald Amundsen, thus introducing a competitive element into the heroic journey. Although Scott failed to beat Amundsen to the Pole and although subsequent studies present Scott in a more nuanced light, Swan and Mear's project remains an attempt to reintroduce Scott as a hero.

Nicholas Rankin has an even more romantic view of Stevenson's heroic persona and sees different forms of heroism informing aspects of his life.

> You could take the writer from the man and still be left holding the full-blown cloak of romantic myth that flourished in the twenty years between his death and the First World War. It was the story of an artist from Walter Scott's 'old romantic toun', born into a family of engineers who built lighthouses which shone in the wild dark. Born bourgeois and turned bohemian, he quarrelled with his father's faith and ignored the dress-codes of his caste. Brilliant and ill, he wrote romances, ghost stories, adventures like *Treasure Island* and *Kidnapped*. He had roughed it to California to marry for love, and later sailed off into the tropical Pacific. In faraway Samoa he made his home among barebreasted women with flowers in their hair and muscular warriors who carried axes for cutting off heads. He became Tusitala, the 'Writer of Tales', and when he died, aged forty-four, they buried him like a chief on the top of a mountain. (7)

This romanticised view of the heroic traveller is partly influenced by Stevenson's adventure fiction, partly by Stevenson's own romanticised notions about travel and about himself as an adventuring hero. However, the image presented here of a lifelong affinity with the heroic persona through lineage, family profession, and resistance to parental and cultural norms is largely Rankin's construction and its placement in the first chapter is significant. *Dead Man's Chest* is biographical in a more pronounced sense than *In the Footsteps of Scott* and *One Dry Season* and painting this initial picture both naturalises Rankin's choice of subject and indentifies a theme which will run though his subject's whole life.

A heroic travelling persona seems harder to both create and maintain in contemporary, postmodern second journeys and feelings of disorientation, anxiety and loneliness are often juxtaposed with the first traveller's representations of heroism and courage. That these are representations and not necessarily truthful renderings of an actual situation is discussed by Glazebrook in connection with an incident when Warburton (one of Glazebrook's first travellers) comes across a band of smugglers on a deserted beach. Instead of fleeing, Warburton attacks them. Glazebrook sarcastically remarks that Warburton's tone is "all that Sir Gawaine's should be when challenged at the Beach Perilous by the Knight of the Literary Device" (100). The danger is presented as real and the situation perfectly suited (perhaps too much so) to the arm-chair traveller at home. Glazebrook has greater difficulties with the heroic figure than his nineteenth-century counterparts, instead he reports how the loneliness in a hotel room or the sensations of not understanding the language far remove him from what is traditionally considered heroic.

Despite the readiness with which Glazebrook reports his doubts and fears, he cannot completely let go of the discursive stress on a heroic figure in his own travel narrative and concludes that two characters are needed to create a balance. "One was the narrator," Glazebrook explains, "the Traveller who was to be the protagonist of my novel; the other was his alter ego, the invented companion whom he would make into the Hero of his travels" (169). The implication here is that all heroic characters are to a certain extent fabrications and that this too is a convention of the genre. Ironically, the idea of the fabricated alter ego is termed by Glazebrook as "the device" he will use for the bridging of "[t]he gap between literal truth and dramatic truth" (169) and in this sense a "Knight" comes to his aid as well.

The supposed heroism of travellers is closely connected to issues of exoticism. With the rise of modernism and the increased emphasis on the belatedness of the journeying subject what exists, in lieu of the traditional hero, is, in Chris Bongie's words, a "phantasmic afterimage." He continues: "The individual is, from the beginning, a posthumous figure of and in crisis, an afterimage in search of what is itself no more than an afterimage" (10). Behdad has similarly observed that with the rise of tourism and with the emergence of guidebooks, the travel text comes to paint "a prosaic picture without the poetic horizon of the earlier travelogues, and a vague narrative that lacks the heroic adventures of a romantic traveler" (36). Although I do not see the images as automatically "prosaic" and dull because of tourism, I do see in the second journeys clear problems stemming from the fact that the contemporary travellers hesitate to assume the heroic role while travelling in the company of texts that present their authors as more traditionally heroic journeying subjects.

WHERE ARE WE NOW?

The texts hitherto discussed have been traditional travelogues with few hints or tips for other travellers or tourists wishing to retrace the same route. Two other collections of texts illustrate a clearer convergence of the traditional travel text and the modern guidebook. The two volumes of *Literary Trips* have the subtitle *Following in the Footsteps of Fame*, and contain essays tracing a specific text (such as Tennessee Williams' *A Streetcar Named Desire* in the essay "Streetcar Named New Orleans"), a specific place (as in the essay "The Beats: Visions of San Francisco), or focusing on specific writers such as Shakespeare and Tolstoy. The essays, organised according to geographical destination, are accompanied by a more informational section entitled "The Writer's Trail" in which hotels, restaurants and air fares are listed along with suggestions for further reading. In her acknowledgements, series editor Victoria Brooks in guide book fashion points out that the rates given in the information sections range from: "Extremely expensive—more than $300" to: "Inexpensive—under $100". Although the essays focus on geographical locations (New Orleans is more important than Blanche DuBois and Stanley Kowalski, the streets of San Francisco are described in more detail than Jack Kerouac and Allen Ginsberg), most texts in the volume have fictional texts rather than travelogues as their points of origin. There are a few, however, which can be termed second journeys as they trace a previous travelogue and all essays featured in the books are suggested as a model for other travellers, and the first texts heralded as inspiration.

The website *Literary Traveler* offers a relatively democratic venue for the publication of short texts which, similar to the *Literary Trips* volumes, read a contemporary place through the filter of a previous text. Added to straightforward allusions to the first text are suggestions of how to approach a site, what to keep in mind, and even what to bring for a picnic. Author Jennifer Eisenlau contends that Robert Graves' *I, Claudius* is "Rome's Ultimate Guidebook" and argues that scenes from it "will come alive in a reader's imagination, as they eat a mozzarella and tomato panini on the grounds where Claudius himself limped along." Again, the physical presence in a landscape brings a greater sense of authenticity and a closeness to the first (in this case fictional) text.

Many of the essays both on the website and in *Literary Trips* evidence the same sense of belatedness as Gavin Young, who I quoted at the beginning of this chapter, voices. Monique Filsnoel notes in her online essay "Karen Blixen's Kenyan Paradise" that changes are inevitable and that the suburb she sees makes it "hard to imagine this home in the middle of a wilderness in which Karen's favorite dog Dawn was taken by a leopard." Jennifer Huget states that "being at Hartford, Connecticut's Mark Twain House puts me as close as I am likely to get at the turn of *this century*" (*Literary Trips* Vol 1, 176, original italics) and Marda Burton looking for a connection with William Faulkner in Mississippi states a similar concern about time: "I feel that the shiny asphalt ribbon might ne taking me off to another planet, or another time" (*Literary Trips* Vol 2, 147).

In all three texts, however, the authors' contention is that a connection with the past can be reached, albeit fleetingly, and all of these moments of recognition take place in houses in which the first authors and travellers have stayed or lived and which are promoted as tourist destinations. Filsnoel notes that the clocks in Karen Blixen's preserved house "have stopped to mark the passage of time" which gives the illusion of an arrested state. Although artefacts connected to Blixen's life are mixed with replicas, the literal and figurative timelessness gives Filsnoel ample opportunities to "imagine" various aspects of the first traveller's life. Huget states that the reason for her early morning start is to avoid "the din of rush-hour traffic" which would make difficult or impossible her aim "to transport [her]self to a different era" (176). In Twain's house she then experiences a "transcendent moment" as past and present merge; in the quiet billiards room she has a sense of Twain walking next to her (179-80). Significantly, this moment occurs at the very end of the house tour, when Huget is left by both tour guides and fellow tourists to ruminate on the original author's existence at the site. Burton, finally, has some reservations concerning the development of tourist activities in "Faulkner Country." She starts her essay by drawing attention to the deep greenery of the area, setting nature and simplicity in contrast to human-made structures and contemporary changes and foregrounding Faulkner's interest in these qualities. While no connection with Faulkner, similar to how authors' are "found" in Filsnoel's and Huget's texts, is established in Burton's essay, she makes a connection on a more subtle level as Faulkner's home Rowan Oak "offers the serenity of simplicity" in comparison with other, more contrived sites and as she encounters two deer while leaving the premises, which "turn and silently disappear into the deep green woods" (155). That is, although the house itself and its carefully framed collections put her in the right frame of mind, it is unchanged nature which supplies the desired connection with the first author.

More clear-cut second journeys (tracing previous travelogues) also suggest the awareness of the time passed. In the online essay "*Songs of Blue and Gold*: Lawrence Durrell's Island of Corfu," Deborah Lawrenson searches for the first traveller on the Greek island. She expresses a desire to see Durrell's "unforgettable word-pictures" as relayed through his travelogue but wonders about the "chance of finding [them] seventy years later" Although she voices a suspicion that knowledge about the traveller through the retracing of his steps might, in the end, be "illusory," Lawrenson's physical presence on Corfu and various details in the surroundings do bring a sense of "continuity" between her experiences and what Durrell noted in *Prospero's Cell*.[8]

The essay section of the website is accompanied by sections providing information about literary tours focusing on geographical areas (such as the Montreal Literary Tour), a fictional figure (such as the King Arthur England Tour) or on an author (such as the Flannery O'Connor Tour). Following links on the page gives the reader access to information concerning times, fees and accommodation, along with advice on preparatory readings. These very brief examples illustrate that forms of

---

[8] Lawrenson's time on Corfu leads to thoughts about other aspects of Durrell's life and other journeys he undertook and results in "a fictional version of" him; Julian Adie in Lawrenson's novel *Songs of Blue and Gold*, published in 2008.

second journeys have been appropriated in a more clear-cut tourist discourse.

All examples further illustrate the initial awareness on the part of the second traveller of the difficulties inherent in attempting to capture the past, and of the realisation that changes and developments necessarily prevent an immediate contact. Simultaneously, however, there is a suggestion that literature can take you there and that previous texts can constitute the map necessary for the desired experience. The fictional works which constitute the first texts in these examples can be compared to the use of Byron or Shelley in the instructions to the eighteenth- and nineteenth-century traveller on the Grand Tour; the sentiments found in fiction and poetry can instruct the traveller on how to respond in the appropriate setting. In this sense, fiction and poetry work as emotional maps. Travelogues, when employed as first texts, also contain a certain amount of 'emotional instruction' which the second traveller negotiates with during the course of the journey. The reiteration of the actual routes, however, means that first journeys also function as more straightforward road maps, textually outlining paths which may or may not be paved, signposted or overgrown.

CHAPTER FOUR. THE SCIENTIFIC JOURNEY: AFTER SCOTT TO THE SOUTH POLE

And does history repeat itself, the first time as tragedy, the second time as farce?
Julian Barnes, *A History of the World in 10 1/2 Chapters*

On November 12, 1912, after wintering at Cape Evans, a rescue party of eleven men found the tent belonging to the expedition that had walked to the South Pole earlier that year. The hope of finding Robert Falcon Scott and the rest of his party alive was lost; the main goal was instead to obtain records confirming or denying the expedition's success. The objective of being the first at the Pole was a known impossibility however, as Roald Amundsen had reached it a month before Scott and his men. The discovery of the tent brought about powerful emotions in the rescue party, and they were hesitant about looking inside.

When they finally did, they found only three men of the original five: Henry Bowers, Edward Wilson and Scott himself. Edgar Evans had died a month before the final camp was made and had been buried. Lawrence Oates had, badly frostbitten and unable to continue, walked out of the tent into a blizzard a few weeks later, never to return. Bowers and Wilson had apparently died in their sleep with faces calm and peaceful, while Scott had died later, half sitting up, with his left arm across Wilson and his sleeping bag open "as if he had meant to let the cold in and life out" (Thomson 292). Scott's last notebook, farewell letters and an official message to the public were found and brought back along with some personal items, but the bodies were left in the tent and a cairn of ice was built on top of it, crowned with a cross made out of two skis. The men had perished from a combination of starvation and exposure. The unusually bad weather had prevented them from reaching the next depot only eleven miles away. On their sledge were found rock samples collected on the journey, which they never contemplated leaving behind, but brought with them in the name of science.

This is a well-known story. It stirred the public imagination at the time the news was brought back and when Scott's edited notes, *Scott's Last Expedition: the Journals*,[1] were published in 1913 any reader could form his or her own opinion about the events which shaped the tragedy. Fifty-five years later Robert Swan's attention is caught by the cover of a book at the library. His ensuing interest results in a 1985 expedition and in a book *In the Footsteps of Scott*,[2] co-authored with Roger Mear and published in 1987: the second journey with which this chapter is concerned.

In calling this form of the second journey scientific, I do not propose to ascertain the validity of any scientific findings. The definition is rather a consequence of the fact that the first journey is part of the exploration tradition and the fact that Scott stresses the scientific aspects of his undertaking. The second journey, following in Scott's footsteps, also takes its place within this tradition and aims to retain some scientific aspects.[3] Swan and Mear's second journey includes charts, maps, tables, schematics and other visual comparisons between first and second journey in the form of photographs.[4] A description of the painstaking work to raise the funds for the project is included as part of the narrative. A form of dialogue between Swan and Mear occurs as statements made by the former in the introduction and the epilogue are commented on by the latter in the main text and it illustrates the sometimes conflicting aims the two travellers have. There is an additional polyphonic quality to the text as there are sections in which other project members get an opportunity to insert excerpts from their own diaries. This feature stresses the fact that this is a multi-membered project and as such markedly different from the other forms I will discuss.

---

[1] Subsequent page-references to this primary source will be preceded by the letter *J*.

[2] Subsequent page-references to this primary source will be preceded by the letter *F*.

[3] One of the studies carried out aims to chart the expedition-members' "basal metabolic rate and its response to strenuous physical exercise under highly controlled conditions." As such, the expedition "in keeping with the spirit and goals of ... Antarctic endeavours ... was in the process of conducting a very valuable and significant study" (*F* 238).

[4] The photographs are used to compare Antarctica and Scott's party in 1911 to the area and the expedition in 1985. The other two second journeys analysed in this study include no photographic comparisons between past and present. Nicholas Rankin includes one frontispiece photograph of Robert Louis Stevenson and Caroline Alexander a frontispiece map of Gabon which outlines her own and Mary Kingsley's journeys.

Another difference pertains to the intertextual feature as, compared to the other second journeys analysed in this study, Swan and Mear's references to the first text are few. Although the 1985 expedition's progress is measured against Scott's, we find few direct quotations despite the claim that they read his diary "each night [which prevents them] from becoming complacent" (*F* 190). Dates, meteorological conditions and distances covered, that is, concrete comparisons using similarities and differences in the landscape and meteorological conditions seem more important than the first text itself. In this way, the climate and the potentially hostile landscape become markers of an intertextuality centring on experiences rather than readings and quotations from the written text.

The Scott-text is continuously there, however, if we by text infer the awe-inspiring tale of an expedition without a return and a mystery surrounding the tragedy. Swan and Mear, together with the three other members of the main expedition, John Tolson, Michael Stroud and Gareth Wood, travel to Antarctica along the same route as Scott. They record meteorological conditions, take part in physiological and psychological surveys but, more importantly, their aim is to find out why Scott's expedition failed. Swan, Mear and Wood will also walk the same stretch across the ice as Scott did, with roughly the equivalent supplies, with the aim of reaching the South Pole. This second journey's approach aims to 'prove' how and illustrate why the first journey was carried out, and why it failed.

Among other examples of this form can be mentioned Tim Severin's series of books tracing legends like Jason and Sindbad, and second journey narratives like *The Viking Voyage*, where the construction of a vessel as similar to the first one as possible becomes more important than itineraries, communication of similar feelings, indeed the first texts themselves.[5] As Matos has observed when discussing Severin's texts, he does more than emulate the geographical dimension of the journey. His aim is rather "to recreate as far as possible the immediate context of these journeys—that is, he seeks a greater authenticity" (Matos 223). This

---

[5] See Tim Severin, *The Sindbad Voyage*, *The Jason Voyage: The Quest for the Golden Fleece* and Judi Lomax, *The Viking Voyage: With Gaia to Vinland*. See further the discussions about aspects of Tim Severin's work in chapter three.

recreation is the intention also of Swan and Mear, but as they cannot duplicate either meteorological conditions or the social climate in Britain at the time of Scott's journey, their heroism and the authenticity of their project become closely bound up with somewhat unnecessary risks and with the isolation of Antarctica.

A discussion about why the legend of Scott was and is so vivid and at the same time so contradictory is necessary to understand aspects of the second journey concerning nationalism, science and the particular brand of heroism which to a great extent influence second travellers. The history of the exploration of the Earth was in one of its last and most controversial stages at the beginning of the twentieth century and national pride and jealously guarded areas characterise Antarctica to this day which problematises the second journey.[6] The scientific project in itself, as well as the specifics of the geographical area, also highlight the development of heroism and the geography that seems to produce this heroism. What, in Scott's time period, made the heroic figure so accepted and popular, and why did he achieve an almost legendary status? In what ways is heroism important to the second travellers? The unproblematic attitude both first and second travellers have towards heroism will be contrasted to the attitude of the other travellers in this study. The heroic persona presents difficulties both for Mary Kingsley and Caroline Alexander. Robert Louis Stevenson remains a hero to Nicholas Rankin and this is in part influenced by his fictional writings, but there are significant differences between Rankin's view of heroism and the one emphasised in Swan's and Mear's text.

THE MALE, HEROIC EXPLORER

Past travelling and travel writing, although by no means unproblematic, was seen as automatically heroic, and this is especially visible in texts concerning exploration and discovery. Patrick Brantlinger argues that "[t]he great explorers' writings are nonfictional quest romances in which the hero-authors struggle through enchanted, bedeviled lands towards an ostensible goal" (cited in Henderson 245). Since the "hero-authors"

---

[6] I do not intend to discuss the scientific and political developments in Antarctica in any detail. Mear and Swan's book offers insights into the contemporary situation and Sara Wheeler's *Terra Incognita* illustrates the historical developments in the area.

describe places that are new to the audience, there are no or few previous works against which their texts are measured, and they are relatively free to present the unknown lands they traverse as fraught with dangers and a traditional sense of adventure. By the early twentieth century, few unexplored territories remained, but Antarctica and the illusive Pole were still there to claim. Francis Spufford argues that the Antarctic area in itself—uninhabited, icy and dangerous—affected both the explorers and the public imagination. He remarks that the travellers' "presence is as astonishing as their astonishing surroundings, something to be wondered at. And one asks, of course, everyone asks, *why*? Why did they do these insane things?" (Spufford 1, original italics). An answer is not provided, Spufford continues, because "explorers are notoriously bad at saying *why*. [. . .] It may be that no answer is really expected, that the question does all it is intended to do by registering astonishment, and signalling the difference between sensible us and mad them" (2, original italics). The implied and/or inherent danger in the unexplored areas, the absence of motives required for the audience to arrive at an understanding and the physical distance between the explorers and their home environment thus served as a means to create almost mythical characters.

The popular press also articulated an emphasis on explorers as extraordinary men, for men most of them were, as it helped create the legends of exploration. Beau Riffenbaugh stresses the very time period as one of the determining factors as to why this legend-making occurred. He draws on theories by Joseph Campbell, John Ruskin and John MacKenzie[7] when discussing the pattern of the heroic journey and finds that the case of Scott aptly illustrates the makings of a true legend. Here we find, he notes,

> the young naval officer plucked from obscurity by Sir Clements R. Markham (the call to adventure); the farthest south of the *Discovery* expedition (the threshold); the years of planning a new expedition, the trek to the South Pole, and the discovery of Amundsen's priority (the trials); his

---

[7] See Joseph Campbell, *The Hero with a Thousand Faces* (1949), John MacKenzie, ed. *Popular Imperialism and the Military 1850-1950* (1992), and John Ruskin, *The Crown of the Wild Olive; Three Lectures on Work, Traffic and War* (1866). Although the latter two seem to have stronger ties to military life and war situations, Riffenbaugh argues that their criteria perfectly fit those of exploration, especially concerning the relationships between men and the sharp division in both capacity and temper between the men in distant lands and the women waiting patiently at home.

> relationship with Edward Wilson (the close-knit brotherhood); the desperate march to One Ton Depot (the magic journey); the death of the entire polar party (martyrdom); the return of his letters and notebooks to Britain and its public (the return, conveying the boon of national inspiration: "Had we lived, I should have had a tale to tell of the hardihood, endurance, and courage of my companions which would have stirred the heart of every Englishman") . . . and the role played by his widow in the creation of the icons of his myth. (Riffenbaugh 7)[8]

Scott's figurative return can be problematised to a greater extent than Riffenbaugh seems willing to do, but the outline illustrates that several separate events and developments worked together in the creation of Scott, the legend. The mythical and timeless quality of the story makes it possible for each age to choose how to interpret the legend and what elements to emphasise, be it natural science, post-war heroism or contemporary eco-tourism.

The fact that Scott died on the return journey was in many ways crucial to the way he came to be portrayed as a legend. Elspeth Huxley observes that to cut it as a national hero a man "must be brave; he must be bold; and it is a great advantage, if not a necessity, that he should die in the attempt to reach his goal" (10). In connection with death as a prerequisite for lasting fame, David Thomson has also noted the case of Oates. When Oates walked out into the blizzard that would kill him, uttering his famous last words: "I am just going outside and may be some time" (J 430), Thomson observes that "time has made Oates very tidy [and that] he may have guessed that the graceful exit would fix him securely in history" (282). Whether or not this is true is anyone's guess. Oates was severely ill at the time and lasting fame may have been less important to him than to increase his companions' chances of survival, but seen in the light of the heroic tradition and remembering Scott's partiality to it, it may very well be a possibility. The dead hero is also important, Riffenbaugh contends, "since it is through his death for the cause that his heroic status can be most easily created, interpreted, and manipulated" (6). The function of the new and unexplored landscapes Brantlinger's "hero-author" struggles through and the dead hero intersect here since both offer possibilities for manipulation and make the readers'

---

[8] The quotation from Scott is found in the message to the public, found with his dead body (J 442).

further interrogations difficult and/or impossible. Following Scott's death, the mediators, principally Clements Markham and Kathleen Scott, were free to manipulate and develop the heroic myth without having to situate it further within the realities of the expedition. The second travellers also work as mediators, manipulating the legend, emphasising certain aspects of heroism that can be applied to themselves and their journey.

In a comment, made especially pertinent because of Swan and Mear's subsequent journey, Thomson notes that "Scott's journeys were ostensibly geographical, but their deepest appeal has always been to armchair and sick-bed explorers, to the imagination of people going about ordinary, domesticated lives" (2). He then proceeds to equal Antarctica with the moon in the escapist tradition, that is, hardly an inspiration for second journeys. Although considerably more accessible to contemporary travellers, the area remains one of the geographically most remote places on earth, its vast distances difficult to cross on foot, its ever-changing qualities challenges to any traveller. Although strategic bases are set up and small towns built along the coastlines, Antarctica is still the target of much debate. These geographical and political discourses consequently influence the concept of heroism, in both first and second journey.

The relationship between the Britain of Scott's time and Antarctica is complex and entails both geographical distance and a peculiar familiarity. During the time gap between Captain George Nares[9] and the exploits of Scott and Ernest Shackleton, the area was in a sense being kept 'alive' in the minds of the public. This is partly due to the novels of the time in which writers occasionally used the dangers of the icy wilderness to test the fictional hero.[10] But there was also a continuous tradition to regard Antarctica as essentially British. A "sense of proprietorship over Antarctica partly rested on the curious conviction that the continent was *not foreign*," Spufford claims and delineates Scott's journey as conducted through "a corridor of Britishness" as stops along the way were made in South Africa, Australia and New Zealand (250, original italics). This extension of Britain resulted in "the sense that even [in Antarctica] the

---

[9] Nares went South with the steamer HMS *Challenger* in 1874, but did not land on the Antarctic continent.

[10] Spufford mentions writers G. A. Henty and Jules Verne among those who have made use of the Antarctic setting (272-73).

expedition existed within the envelope of a familiar order" and that the space in which the expeditionaries found themselves was "natural . . . rather than foreign" (Spufford 251). This natural space then provided a stage on which the hero could test his strength, be it physical or moral, and emerge victorious. Although Scott failed physically, his last letters and the message to the public were thought to display an extraordinary moral victory, completely in line with the purpose and spirit of the heroic explorer.

The unchallenged male pronoun in these discussions indicates that Antarctic exploration, indeed the entire geographical area, is saturated with *male*, heroic figures and, equally male, heroic imagery, that is, created and sustained by a male discourse. It was argued that the unusually harsh conditions made it impossible for women even to survive there.[11] Despite their exclusion from both the geographical area and the discourse, women were able to identify with the male heroes as "endurance, perseverance and resignation," qualities traditionally associated with women, became associated with men in the Antarctic setting (Spufford 103). This "means that Arctic heroism, strangely, was relevant heroism, with the natural environment of the poles compelling men to wait, suffer, and be patient, in the same way as the human environment compelled women" (Spufford 103).

The theoretical affinities between women and explorers may have helped increase the popularity of the endeavours, but the fact remains that women were closed off from the area. Recent years have seen several women travellers on the continent and female staff members are included in the scientific expeditions, but a certain resistance to women's inclusion in Antarctic projects seems to remain. Sara Wheeler observes, while preparing for her journey in the 1990s, that "[i]t was male territory all right—it was like a gentleman's club, an extension of boarding school and the army" (xviii). The fact that women now *do* travel to, and work in, Antarctica has had consequences for the heroic discourse as the presence

---

[11] Sara Wheeler writes that "[m]en had always wanted to keep Antarctica for themselves, and since the Norwegian Caroline Mikkelsen became the first woman to set foot on the continent on February 20, 1935, the cause had advanced with the speed of a vegetable garden" (220-1).

of women on the continent is perceived as making it difficult for men to present themselves as heroes at all.[12]

The 1985 party is not exclusively male, women staff members are mentioned at the preparation stage, and work on board the ship. The core expedition wintering at Cape Evans is exclusively male, however, and few female voices are represented in the polyphonic sections of the text. The male tradition of heroism is thus retained to some extent in the second journey narrative and in the introduction Swan does not hold back on the drama inherent in the project. "Mine was a bold dream," he states, "conceived in a time when it was fashionable to decry the exploits and achievements of bold men and women. I was going to retrace Scott's footsteps to the South Pole" (*F* x). The second journey is thus, already at the outset, depicted as something unusually heroic, necessarily so, perhaps, to justify the undertaking at all. Even Swan's formulation of the fact that the journey in Scott's footsteps has not been undertaken before: "no one had ever *dared to venture* upon Scott's journey again," underlines the heroism of the project (*F* xii, emphases added). Swan claims to be alerted to the project almost by accident at the library, as the book *Scott's Men* catches his attention. He describes the cover photograph of the starved and exhausted men and "the haunted expression in their eyes" (*F* xi). He also watches Charles Frend's 1948 film *Scott of the Antarctic*. "I identified closely with its portrayal of the simple bravery of men against the elements," Swan writes. "Scott symbolised qualities of courage, determination and single-mindedness that struck a chord in me" (*F* xii). The identification with Scott and other members of the 1911 party is a recurring element in the second journey text, especially where Swan is concerned, and he later describes his experiences with words like reunion and homecoming.

The mythical quality of Scott's expedition seems to be the most powerful incentive for the second journey: "the legend as much as their achievement" the inspiration (*F* xi). The legend has thus survived despite Scott's failure to become the first person to reach the South Pole. This failure is peculiarly transmuted into success, Scott's actions emerging as

---

[12] In a magazine article, published as late as 1966, Antarctica is referred to as "the womanless white continent of peace" and a U. S. commander proceeds to say that "I think the presence of women would wreck the illusion of the frontiersman—the illusion of being a hero" (cited in Wheeler 221).

noble rather than misguided. Furthermore, Scott and his men walked across the ice and through the snow where Amundsen used dogs and sleds, and Swan sees the unaided walk as glorifying Scott's project. "For him [Amundsen] the journey went like clockwork and there is not much more to say about it" (*F* xii). Scott's unsuccessful journey, on the other hand, presents a greater challenge and much, Swan suggests, remains to say about *it*.

Scott has many defenders, but he has also been severely accused of placing himself and his men in so many dangers. Swan attributes the failure of Scott's expedition less to bad judgement than to bad luck. By retracing the journey he aims to prove that it can indeed be carried out, setting "the record straight on the gallant man's behalf" (*F* xiii), that is, defend Scott from his detractors. In addition, Swan expresses a desire "to uphold the tradition of Polar exploration and draw attention to the pressing need for conservation in the last great wilderness on earth. It was a tall order" (*F* xiii).

THE FIRST JOURNEY

The original journey is described in Scott's notebooks: those found with his body, as well as those that were left at the base before the walk south. Had Scott returned to complete his narrative the *Journals* would possibly have looked different, with descriptions of lengthy preparations in Britain[13] and diplomacy ensuring the mentioning of sponsors in the first chapter. As they stand, however, the text begins with the last few days in New Zealand before leaving for the voyage south.[14] In most respects, the entries conform to the common standard of the scientific journal, mixing records of meterological conditions, descriptions of the treatment of dogs and horses with slightly more personal comments about expedition members and worries about weather- and other conditions. It is the last part of the *Journals*, especially the last pages in which the party is awaiting death, that sets it apart and, although Scott instructed a friend to

---

[13] For an idea of how much planning went into the *Terra Nova* expedition, see Thomson 130-64.
[14] There are also twelve quarto volumes of scientific work assembled by his staff and published after the homecoming.

censor parts of the notes in one of his farewell letters, they may still strike the reader as painfully honest.

The published journals in diary form connect with the idea of mediators, instrumental in organising and manipulating the textual remains of the expedition. The use of the diary form is not uncommon to scientific texts; in fact, an accurate daily recording is seen to heighten the authority and authenticity of the narrative. However, the gender of the diary-writer may influence how the text is perceived, and to what extent it is judged to be of general interest. Mary Kingsley, for example, views the diary form as a 'lesser' form of writing, influenced by the notion that women's personal narratives were untrustworthy. Different receptions and views of the diary form thus serve as additional reminders of the male tradition, markedly different from the female not only in travelling, but also in travel writing.

The tale of the quest for the South Pole centres on Scott and Amundsen, but would be incomplete without a number of minor characters. This is certainly in the nature of the scientific and exploration journeys in which significant numbers of staff members, each specialising in different areas, were included in the expeditions. Although this case study centres on the second journey in the footsteps of Scott it is necessary to comment on Amundsen as well, partly because he was instrumental in Scott's failure, partly because exploration in this time period was so closely connected to nationalism. Polar exploration in particular became, as Eric Leed puts it, "a trophy of manly and national competitions" (*Shores of Discovery* 229). Apart from the works the travellers wrote themselves, several books portray them and chronicle their journeys. Many of these choose sides, preferring one to the other, stressing either Scott's bad judgement or what was perceived as Amundsen's foul play.[15]

The race did not start out as such, however, and Scott's attainment of the South Pole had not entered into the discussion other than as a minor project in the entire scientific endeavour. This all changed when Ernest Shackleton came farthest south in 1909. This had as one result that the walk south changed its character. Farthest south was no longer an issue,

---

[15] Among these can be mentioned Roland Huntford's *Scott and Amundsen* (1979) and *Kappløbet* (1974) by the Norwegian Kåre Holt, the former championing Amundsen, and the latter Scott.

what remained was instead only to get to the very Pole and be the first one there. Shackleton thus inadvertently turned the scientific journey that Scott planned at the time into a race. The scientific pretext remained, however, and this must also be seen in relation to the romanticised image of the explorer. To have the attainment of the Pole as a sole purpose would not sit comfortably with the image of the serious explorer solving the problems of the unknown and supplying scientific answers to age-old problems.

The scientific work carried out by the *Discovery* expedition (Scott's first expedition, 1901-4) had been questioned by the British scientific Societies. This undoubtedly caused Scott to resolve even harder to make the *Terra Nova* expedition successful in this respect. The idea of a race appealed to the public, however, and to win this race became a question of national pride. As if Shackleton's perceived intrusion was not enough, an added threat entered in the shape of Amundsen. The Norwegian had originally planned an expedition to the Arctic, but different circumstances made him unofficially change his plans. On 10 November 1910, on Madeira, Amundsen's brother Leo sent one of history's most famous cables, which would reach Scott in Melbourne: "Am going south. Amundsen" (Thomson 171). This unexpected turn of events forced Scott to further emphasise the scientific nature of his journey. While this earned him respect in several circles, the pronounced interest in science simultaneously worked against Scott and made it possible for Amundsen to openly state that the South Pole was his main and only objective. He felt that he did not infringe on Scott's territory since the British expedition travelled under the scientific flag.

Amundsen reached the South Pole on 15 December 1911. Scott arrived on 17 January 1912 and died on 29 March, although he confused the dates during his last days. The news of Amundsen's victory reached the world. Newspaper reports were confused, however, and for a short while Scott enjoyed the fame of having been the first to reach the Pole before all such rumours were extinguished by his widow, Kathleen. The reports in British newspapers were harsh on Amundsen, never letting an opportunity go by without reminding the public that he had gone behind Scott's back. Even later, when Amundsen came to London to give a lecture, the introductory speaker, the president of the Royal Geographical Society, Lord Curzon, made overt references to Scott while criticising the way Amundsen had 'won' the race.[16] He even went as far as to end the evening with the following: "I almost wish . . . that in our tribute of admiration we could include those wonderful, good-tempered, fascinating dogs, the true friends of man, without whom Captain Amundsen would never have got to the Pole" (cited in Thomson 288-89).

Several different causes for Scott's failure have been proposed. He had to balance the desire to get to the Pole with the more general scientific research that was to be carried out by the expedition and which supplied its raison d'être in the eyes of the scientific societies that had provided the money. This double focus was one that never entered the mind of Amundsen who, in this sense, was more single-minded and perhaps therefore also more successful. Lord Curzon's references to dogs, however, echo a central part of the debate concerning Scott's failure. Scott brought both dogs and horses to Antarctica, but they were not as hardy as Amundsen's animals and the latter's successful use of dog-pulled sleds was a contributing reason for his attainment of the Pole. Scott expressed a negative attitude to this form of assisted feat already in *The Voyage of the Discovery* (1905):

> In my mind no journey ever made with dogs can approach the height of that fine conception which is realized when a party of men go forth to face hardships, dangers and difficulties with their own unaided efforts, and by days and weeks of hard physical labour succeeded in solving some problems of the great unknown. Surely in this case the conquest is more nobly and splendidly won. (343)

Scott was not opposed to the use of dogs, nor was he particularly sentimental concerning their sacrifice in the name of exploration; he weighed pros and cons, and used his own experiences of using dogs to form an opinion on the matter (Murray 304-05). The repeatedly voiced idea of self-sufficiency, however, here and in the *Journals* is formed within a discourse in which man, noble and heroic is solitary set against

---

[16] Lord Curzon said "and even while we are honouring Amundsen this evening, I am convinced that his thoughts, no less that ours, are turning to our brave countryman, Captain Scott, still shrouded in the glimmering half-light of the Antarctic, whose footsteps reached the same Pole, doubtless only a few weeks later that Amundsen, and who with unostentatious persistence, and in the true spirit of scientific devotion, is gathering in, during an absence of three years, a harvest of scientific spoil, which when he returns will be found to render his expedition the most notable of modern times" (cited in Thomson 288).

nature. Goals attained and feats accomplished through the unaided efforts carry another, and higher, significance. As Thomson points out, however, there is a continuous and "fatal British romanticizing of the unassisted effort of the explorer" (68) and it is sustained in the second journey narrative as Swan echoes Scott's sentiments and, too, sees the unaided walk as a more heroic and worthwhile feat, regardless of its fatal outcome (*F* xii).

Scott's journals were brought home, edited (with some passages deleted), and published. They became widely read and the harrowing last entries have become classics in the literature of exploration. Aware of the fact that they will not make it, Scott's thoughts are on the death awaiting them "We shall stick it out to the end, but we are getting weaker, of course, and the end cannot be far. It seems a pity, but I do not think I can write more" (*J* 432). The message to the public ends as follows:

> Had we lived, I should have had a tale to tell of the hardihood, endurance, and courage of my companions which would have stirred the heart of every Englishman. These rough notes and our dead bodies must tell the tale, but surely, surely, a great rich country like ours will see that those who are dependent on us are properly provided for. (*J* 442)

This is what Riffenbaugh refers to as "the boon" (7) to the nation; the inspiration to accomplish great things was badly needed in the years before World War I, and could, in theory, be found in the exploits of Scott. Scott's thoughts were centred around those who remained at home which may seem strange considering his own predicament, but which agrees with his way of looking at himself and his men as examples to follow. Scott's last words also illustrate that the heroic journey, with the objective to win an area for the home country, and to fix the traveller's persona in the conquered area (or the area about to be conquered), must assume "an observing public without whom there can be no fame" (Leed, *The Mind of the Traveler* 27). That is, the home, the people and places left behind as well as the intended readers are crucial to the formulations of, and by, the heroic traveller.

The style of writing found in the message to the public is also, despite impending death, romantic. Thomson observes that "the message has the freedom that comes with release and abandon. [. . .] [A]nd the prose—written *in extremis*—is fit to end an epic" (293-94, original italics).

That is, even stylistically, as the myth comes to its almost predestined conclusion, the language and the sentiments strive for the romantic, glossing over the failure leading to it. There are obvious differences between the last pages, written "[w]ith the authority of death" (Spufford 333) and the rest of the journals. Earlier, Scott is sparing with personal comments about the men and about his own emotions. When he does talk about his companions, and especially when he criticises them, the descriptions are vague as if he is aware of future readers. It must also be stressed again that the journals to a certain extent were censored and manipulated. As Thomson points out, the change from constrained to free is visible from the entry when it is clear that Amundsen had reached the Pole before them, and onwards:

> Scott emerged as a writer only when failure was unmistakable and tragedy crowding in with the cold. In the last stages of the second expedition no one looked over Scott's draft; but by then he had no need of editing. He was free as soon as he saw Amundsen's black flag in the distance ahead. (83)

Here again, we return to the romanticised image of the gentleman struggling against the elements and against his own fate. Although the time was soon to pass when this kind of rhetoric was truly appreciated, the context in which the message was written still made it powerful. "And many still respond to the message," Thomson contends,

> whether mountain-climbers, round-the-world sailors or those eccentrics striving to perform some daft feat undone by others but likely to find a place in the *Guinness Book of Records*. To go where no one else has gone may look absurdly precarious, vain and wasteful; but the impulse behind it is still capable of producing a 'tale to tell'. (294)

Scott's particular brand of male heroism thus continues to appeal to contemporary travellers and the Antarctic remains a well suited place in which to test oneself against the elements. In this sense, to a greater extent perhaps than other geographical areas, Antarctica still offers the traveller an opportunity 'to go where no one else has gone.' Although this is a contradiction in terms where the second travellers are concerned—they do after all travel with Scott's *Journals* as a guiding text—their emphasis on originality comes to depend upon the specificities of the area that make it possible for them to regard themselves as travelling through an unknown continent.

The tension between the different nations staking claims in Antarctica is also connected to the problematic concept of originality. Here it takes on a different form, closer to its traditional meaning. There are no indigenous peoples in Antarctica, no formal government, and in Scott's time the continent was a blank space on the map in a very literal sense. The race towards the Pole was thus an attempt of a very concrete kind to charter new territory. As the spirit of the time would have it, we have also seen that such feats were seen as national accomplishments to a greater extent than now. Scott's identity as an Englishman, at the time so important to the 'nationalness' of the project, has other implications for the second travellers. Their national identity is important only in the clashes with another country's authorities; by and large they see themselves as part of a project belonging to individuals, and in this sense they remain almost nation-less.

THE SECOND JOURNEY

PREPARATIONS

Since Scott's journey, Antarctica has been divided between nations but some areas remain unclaimed. The necessity to winter at one of the bases depends on the meteorological and geographical conditions which are hazardous. Combined, these features still provide ample opportunities for a tale to tell, possibilities that are carefully underlined in the second journey text. Still, Mear is initially hesitant to proclaim the heroism of the project. "Those who seek adventure can no longer set out under the banner of science and close communion with the great forces of nature is no longer possible from within the restrictive protection of the modern Antarctic base," he argues. Then he formulates the driving force behind the second journey: "So it was that we looked back for our inspiration" (*F* 20).

The introductory chapters are dedicated to the preparations for the second journey. The contacts made with future sponsors are painstakingly described, as are all the setbacks that the expedition faces. The preparations take up much time and are described in detail, in this sense emphasising all the forms of departure. Appendices are added, meticulously noting temperatures and meteorological conditions to be contrasted and compared with the findings of the 1911 scientists, and elaborate lists of all items brought are added, corresponding to the lists included in the works by Scott and his men. The detailed descriptions of initial problems, fundraising, listings of names of people that contribute, of businesses that helped by sponsoring, strengthen one aspect of the authenticity and place the second narrative within the tradition of scientific writing.

The fact that Scott and his men died on the return journey challenges the second journey's intended emulations since the objective is not to copy it to such an extent. The second travellers are aware of the fact that the emulation can (or should) never succeed fully in this respect. Mear mentions "the artificiality of a one-way journey" (*F* 9), and stresses that the return will make the second journey's reiteration of the first trip problematic. Swan, however, does not seem to mind the idea of dying in the footsteps of Scott when the plans are initially made. In this sense, he harkens back to the glorified notion of sacrifice.[17] Swan's excessively romantic view of the journey and of sacrifice approaches an extreme kind of authenticity and the quest for it seems to take precedence. "Robert's obsession grew," Mear notes,

> [h]e would let nothing and no one prevent the fulfilment of his dream. His one idea was to march to the South Pole. It seemed that he had no ambition or thought beyond it. His life appeared to end with its conquest, and I began to wonder whether he was looking for a heroic death. Success was so important that he no longer contemplated failure, while I spent each day trying to imagine every hazard we might encounter walking the 900 miles to the Pole. Out there one mistake, one wrong decision could cost us our lives and I no longer believed that Robert in his fervour would not be driven solely by ambition, the same ambition that had killed Scott. (*F* 32-33)

Two attitudes to the project surface here; Swans "obsession" and "dream" and Mear's attempts to foresee and plan for potentially dangerous developments. Other key terms in the passage: "conquest," "ambition" and

---

[17] When discussing which three will undertake the walk, Mear says to Swan: "Your whole being was directed to one point and there was nothing after it. Everything weighed on getting to the Pole, nothing was more important. I was the first to feel relief when suddenly you had ambitions beyond it, for that meant you also wanted to come back. That was a big change" (*F* 123).

"success," are also connected predominantly to Swan's attitude to the project, but also place the second journey within the heroic discourse. They also suggest a persistent competitive element, despite the fact that this element, so crucial to the first journey, is lacking in the second. Although emphasis will stay on what dangers remain, a balancing act ensues between Swan's obsession and what realistically can be done. A brochure, catering to sponsors and contributors, finally characterises the endeavour as: "[a]n Expedition whose intention is to retrace Captain Robert Scott's footsteps to the South Pole and to restore the feelings of adventure, isolation and commitment that have been lost through the employment of the paraphernalia of modern times" (F 21).

The second travellers copy the original in that they will travel by boat to Antarctica, and winter at Cape Evans. They will then walk to the Pole in the spring. From there they will be flown out in a private Cessna, independent of the American base at the Pole. "I wanted to demonstrate beyond conjecture that the journey could be made without outside assistance" (*F* 202), Mear writes. Any help from the outside would, it is felt, diminish the authenticity of the project since Scott was independent of assistance, but the tensions between the nations staking claims in Antarctica are also weighed in in their discussions. The second travellers will bring no radios "for with them we would never come close to the commitment Scott had found," as Mear argues (*F* 78,) and only supplies large enough to carry them through.[18] One mistake may very well cost them their lives, and in this sense, they use danger to emphasise the authenticity of the project.

The perilous mathematics of the journey are also to be found in the very distance covered. With each day that passes, they will be closer to the point where they will be prevented from returning and this will also give rise to a mounting tension within the group. The first part of the second journey text clearly illustrates the mixed feelings Mear, in particular, harbours for the project. While the aim is certainly not to die in Scott's

---

[18] Mear quotes Charles Lindbergh when discussing the dangerous mathematics of the journey. "Safety at the start of my flight means holding down the weight for take-off. Safety during flight requires plenty of emergency equipment. Safety at the end of my flight demands an ample reserve of fuel. It's impossible to increase safety at one point without detracting from it at another" (*F* 42).

footsteps, the dangers are stressed as they provide points of contact between first and second journey.

CAPE EVANS

When arriving at Scot's hut on the beach at Cape Evans the impression is almost ghostly; the area is deserted and devoid of human footprints. Swan comments on this arrival in his introduction, and this is clearly one of the most important experiences of his journey. The "empty bunks" inside the hut belong "to friends who were no longer there," he writes. "Yet there was still a feeling of imminent reunion, of excitement tinged with tragedy and awe, a feeling, almost, of coming home" (*F* ix). The arrival at the hut conjures up memories of the texts Swan has read, the film he has seen, and expectations of being met inside by familiar faces and music playing.

Mear's first impression of the hut is somewhat different and his description provides a contrast to Swan's sense of home-coming.

> The debris of an expedition is scattered about, discarded fragments which time has transformed into historical relics. I peered through the only window in the long east wall, into a russet shaded world of another age that was to open itself to us over the coming year. (*F* 54)

The expedition mentioned here is unspecified, but the past the second travellers have come to 'see' is perceived to exist within the hut. It is seen as revealing links to the past because of its unaltered state and is not 'contaminated' by civilisation, and this perception is extended to embrace the whole area. Although repeatedly visited since Scott's stay, the hut in Mear's description displays "relics" of "another age," giving the impression that the second travellers' experience is exclusive to them. Mear continues:

> My first impression on entering Scott's hut was that we were intruding into the home of someone whose absence was only temporary. There is a strange lack of dust. Often it was colder inside than out, yet the hut felt strong and secure, as though at any moment the door would burst open and with a stamping of heavy boots upon the wooden floor the occupants would return. It was impossible to feel at ease in the shadowy hall, and though the atmosphere was not malevolent, the feeling of reproach never left me while I pried into its dark corners. None of us, during the eleven months at Cape Evans, ever mustered enough courage to sleep a night there. The hut is filled with possessions. These were not the sanitised objects found in a

museum. Like favourite shoes which take on the shape of the feet that wear them, every item was pregnant with ownership. (*F* 71)

Again, in contrast to Swan's reaction when entering the hut, Mear does not connect the place to familiarity, but like Swan, he feels a presence or, at any rate, a temporary absence inside. The tragedy and the hardships of the previous expedition seem to permeate the atmosphere of the hut, giving it an almost ghostlike quality, and the objects inside are seen as still belonging to someone. This can be contrasted with Rankin's experiences in the Stevenson museums, discussed in chapter six, where he describes objects as orphaned and far removed from their original context. Objects, furniture and clothes in museum settings are framed and represented in a way that depersonalise them. The items in Scott's hut are not arranged in order to display or present the time period or their owners, but are simply left there, heightening the sense of perceived authenticity.[19] The landscape, bleak and with few landmarks, offers few opportunities to compare past and present. The most accessible way to establish a connection is instead through the human-made huts. The landscape is, in this sense, intangible whereas the huts and the remnants of shelters provide points of contact between first and second journey.

Close to the Cape Evans hut, the 1985 expedition establishes its wintering base. In this section of the text, there are repeated insertions of entries from other expedition members' diaries making the narrative polyphonic and stressing the journey as a multi-membered project. This feature can be sporadically found throughout the text, but it is here that it becomes most apparent. The five men who winter at the Cape, although they share some traits, such as a penchant for adventure, are very different. They all have different views as to why the journey should be undertaken, how it will be carried out, and what is important.[20] This part of the text also evidences the postmodern propensity for self-examination and the openness about worries and misgivings. The long period of darkness is especially trying in such confined quarters and all fallings out

---

[19] Surprisingly, Mear observes that "[o]nly Scott's enclosed 'den' is a disappointment. [...] The few things that remain are not Scott's. It is as though he wished to remain an enigma" (*F* 75).

[20] Thomson notes that few narratives are open about the friction and tension brought about by the unusual conditions and mentions Frederick Cook's account of the *Belgica* expedition (of which Amundsen was part) as one of very few exceptions (34).

are faithfully reported. During Scott's expedition the rest of the men also kept journals, more or less consistently. Scott's journals, however, stand on their own, and the hierarchy dividing him from the rest of the men is evident. The polyphonic quality is not to be found. Fears, worries and anxieties are further present in the first text as a result of the tragic end to the expedition and the (illusory) immediacy of Scott's last written-down thoughts.

The decision that Mear and Swan will be in the expedition walking south is an early one, made outside the text itself. Who will be the third man in the party, however, is beginning to be discussed only after the return from Cape Crozier.[21] The reasons for having three in the party have to do with safety and, thus, they do not imitate Scott's party of five. The heavy fuel supply must be divided among them and there must also be a possibility of turning back, decisions which reflect a sudden distancing from the previous stress on dangers. Personality issues also feature into the final selection of men. Mear describes himself as a counterweight to Swan's obsession and feels that he has to have someone to come between them in case communications break down. The choice finally falls on Wood, leaving Tolson and Stroud to remain at the Cape.

In view of their difficulties tolerating each other, the decision that Swan and Mear are to be included is strange to say the least, but it is nevertheless presented as indisputable. "All Robert had to do was pull his sledge, and that was how he and I wanted it to be. Each of us had our roles on this expedition—his, to provide the drive to get us to Antarctica, and mine, to get him to the Pole," Mear writes (*F* 200). Scott was also criticised for his choice of men to go with him on the last stretch to the Pole. Thomson makes the comment that "[b]y 3 January Scott had made and announced his final selection. It suddenly veered away from his basic plan, and has been a matter of controversy ever since" (271). Loyalty and friendship seem to have been more important than actual physical fitness.

---

[21] The expedition to Cape Crozier in search of Emperor Penguins imitates a similar trip in the middle of winter, 1911. Edward Wilson, Henry Bowers and Apsley Cherry-Garrard went, and almost perished in the dark and the cold. The adventure is described in Cherry-Garrard's *The Worst Journey in the World* (1922). This trip becomes crucial also to the second expedition and "the idea of repeating [it] an intriguing possibility." Mear continues: "Indeed, the prospect was as attractive in my mind as the Polar walk itself, for it became apparent that no one had visited Cape Crozier in the depth of winter since Wilson, Bowers and Cherry-Garrard" (*F* 95). This project, a second journey within the second journey, is described in Mear and Swan, chapters nine and ten: "The Winter Journey," and "Cape Crozier," 94-120.

"This is a game of course," Thomson continues, "and a grisly one, but it is a game Scott played before the result was known, and we should remember that Scott chose men not always for the most practical reasons, but to demonstrate his idea of a man" (273). Men representing loyalty and friendship, Thomson speculates, were thus chosen above those who were more physically fit or possessed other character traits which could have been useful on the walk south. A similar motive; that through choice promote desirable characteristics, is not articulated in the second journey narrative, but the resulting decisions remain odd. Included as an appendix in *In the Footsteps of Scott* is a psychological report whose findings suggest that a different composition might have been preferred. Both Mear and Swan are described as being very dominant, self-assured and independent-minded. While these character traits also work for them, it is clear that two such individuals in the same group may cause problems.[22] Swan has not been active during the winter; he has neither tried anything new nor familiarised himself with the environment. This seems like a persuasive reason for excluding him from the group. The most important reason for his inclusion is rather his obsession with Scott and the fact that he is initially responsible for the project. In light of Swan's romantic view of Scott and his willingness to die in his footsteps, the choice to include him in the group is at once curious and obvious.

THE WALK SOUTH

The multifaceted nature of the departure, as well as the connections to Scott, become very clear on Friday 25th October when the five expedition members leave Cape Evans to travel together to Hut Point. The focus is clearly on the departure from Scott's hut from where the original expedition left in November 1911. Swan ends his introduction with the following passage:

> I lay down on Scott's bunk and looked at the ceiling. 'Well, that's what you looked at the morning you set off,' I thought. Then I left the hut with tears

---

[22] It is further said about Mear that he is "hostile," "authoritarian" and that he runs the risk of being "rejected in group activities." Swan is characterised as one of those individuals who "may evoke antipathies and distrust," and who "slow group process and upset group morale." Wood, the third member of the party, is characterised as someone who dislikes or is even unable to work in a group. The report is written by naval clinical psychologist Elizabeth Holmes-Johnson who worked at the McMurdo Station in 1985. See Mear and Swan, appendix 5 292-4.

streaming down my face. I felt I was saying both greetings and farewell, for I had a sense as I stumbled outside that the spirit of those people would be with me, Scott, Bowers, Wilson and the others, and that we would all be going to the Pole together. (*F* xiii)

The identification with Scott presented here, as well as the companionship with the rest of the party, may strike the reader as overly romanticised, but it again ties into Swan's wish to re-introduce Scott, the hero, as well as to experience a connection with the first journey.

The second travellers leave the base at McMurdo on 3 November and here we come across one of the first quotations from Scott's journal in which he talks of the "sweltering day" (*J* 327) of his departure. They thus appropriately depart on the same day as Scott did 74 years earlier. On the 6th of November Tolson and Stroud are left. The breaking up of the group and the drama inherent in the start of the 'real' project is documented, the two groups "enact[ing] the parting several times before John's [Tolson] camera, shaking hands repeatedly until the real moment was pushed away, lost in the falseness of the repetition" (*F* 143). Another repetition starts as the walkers set out alone. Swan, Mear, and Wood have one sled each instead of the one that Scott, Bowers and Wilson pulled together.

> We travelled alone, each in his own world, each with his own problem, each harnessed to his own sledge, and with no one to blame but himself if it did not move. [. . .] Imagine the frustration when, returning from the Pole, short of food and time, Scott's party hauled their single sled across the snows of the Polar Plateau. [. . .] Imagine the brewing suspicions that the others are not pulling as hard as they might. [. . .] I know that if we three had been forced to work under conditions that demanded such tolerance we would not have gone a hundred miles. This as much as anything is a measure of the moral strength of Scott's men. (*F* 149-50)

The sentiments expressed here indicate that the original journey is not emulated in every detail. The use of three sledges increases the second travellers' speed, it reduces the antagonism between them and takes away one aspect of Scott's narrative which is found in its most memorable passages; the last pages where he, exhausted and undernourished, voices suspicions about the others or is forced to outright say that he is not helped by one or some of them. Simultaneously, the differences indicated work to stress Scott as hero, one of the expressed aims of the second journey.

A chance meeting with an American geological party comes as a great disappointment to the 1985 group. Mear, in the lead, sees the figures first, "ponder[ing] what this awful event might mean" (*F* 169). They have been informed, even at the preparation stage of the journey, that a field camp is to be set up. Mear writes:

> Even that had been a blow to the isolation we sought. Now to have the isolation destroyed by this unexpected encounter made the 400 miles we had walked an exercise without point or reward. Isolation is Antarctica's most fragile resource; only Shackleton had savoured it untarnished, for Scott had carried with him the knowledge that he was not the first to set foot upon the Beardmore Glacier. Our journey too, we knew, added to man's encroachment upon this last great wilderness, and we were selfish in our desire to experience something of what remains of the continent's remoteness. In an instant, the presence of that figure had caused the sense of isolation I had felt to evaporate, as if it had never existed. (*F* 169-70)

To be the first, or at any rate to be alone, is a desire that surfaces repeatedly in connection with second journeys and the presence of other travellers at times even causes travellers to abstain from journeys. Antarctica, however, differs significantly from other geographical destinations. The isolation, and the authenticity this isolation seems to guarantee, has been the one thing taken for granted by the second travellers, and when it is unexpectedly shattered, this seems to negate the very purpose of the journey.

In addition, the interrupted solitude draws Mear's thoughts to his own expedition's intrusion into the pristine wilderness and the threats to its uniqueness the expedition members represent. The result of this insight and the discovery of the American scientists have emotional consequences. Mear reports that he and his companions are "on the verge of tears" (*F* 172) and that part of the aim of the second journey is (temporarily) thwarted.

> [T]he encounter had destroyed the mystery and doubt that had hung over the remaining 480 miles. Gone was the knowledge that we were engaged upon an unsupported journey of a magnitude that was unique, and the loss

> removed a good deal of the purpose that, for me, justified our undertaking. (*F* 174-75)[23]

In the absence of the isolation they have sought other features of the landscape become central in the second journey narrative and are often described as emphasising the smallness of the human form. In this way, the authors reclaim a sense of vulnerability.

The environment sets its own rules for the crossing of the area. It has a continuous impact on second journeys and seasonal and other changes repeatedly thwart itineraries and plans. Here, however, the divergence from the first journey presents less of a problem. To follow either Shackleton or Scott (who took different routes across the Beardmore Glacier) would be pointless; instead the second party strives to find the shortest, straightest path through this section. When it is finally crossed, Mear notes: "Now we could begin to make direct comparisons between our own progress and that of our predecessors. The end of our first day on the glacier saw us two days behind Scott and five behind Shackleton" (*F* 178). Again, the first text(s) are pushed aside in favour of more straightforward geographical comparisons or contrasts.

The second travellers camp in the evening opposite a hill that Scott named Monument Rock.

> It was here that Edgar Evans, frostbitten, concussed and terribly exhausted, died of hypothermia. I filmed and photographed Robert holding the silver Polar Medal that was awarded posthumously to Evans, and it did feel that we had returned it, for a time, to where it rightfully belonged. (*F* 179)

The view of the first travellers as national heroes surfaces again, on two levels. Heroism is firstly illustrated by the fact that Evans was awarded the medal, secondly, there is the romanticised notion that the second travellers temporarily return it as if to Evans himself, immortalised at the site of his death.

A complexity arises from the fact that Scott's journey is in essence two. The second travellers measure their progress against Scott's journey *to* the

---

[23] The unwanted meeting with the scientists does not result in a complete distancing from them. Mear, Swan, and Wood use their facilities to wash themselves and launder their clothes and the first evening is spent in a cook tent "christened The Gateway Inn" where the walkers sate their huger by large portions of "steak, lobster tails and broccoli, excellent coffee, Earl Grey tea and Amaretto" (*F* 172-3).

Pole, but the passage quoted above pertains to his unsuccessful return journey. This double focus is retained throughout the second journey. Earlier on, and almost in passing, the following is said:

> By the end of the fifteenth day of our journey we had travelled 142.32 miles. During the morning we had passed the point where Scott's One Ton Camp had been sited, and we camped that evening 2.5 miles short of where Wilson, Bowers and Scott had erected their tent for the last time, only 11 miles short of the depot. (F 151)

This is the last entry of the day and considering the emphasis on the tragic fate of the first expedition, particularly in the introduction to the second journey narrative, a more thorough discussion might be expected, centring on the 1985 walkers' physical proximity to what has become the essence of the first journey: the simple, harrowing descriptions of lives fading away. The next day, and in a similarly unemotional tone, Mear notes: "Somewhere about here . . . Oates walked to his death, but this place makes no acknowledgements of such events" (F 154). The sections of the first text which stress the heroism of the first travellers are, despite these brief mentionings, pushed into the background of the second narrative as the landscape itself and the strenuous walk take precedence.

The days on the glacier are comparatively comfortable, however, and the second travellers experience few problems crossing the crevasses.

> There was only the threat of injury, for without a radio, we were as alone as it is possible to be. At midnight we were woken by the sound of an aircraft. An American Hercules bound for the Pole flew directly over us at 24,000 feet, another reminder of the smallness of the modern world. It thundered into our world and then was gone. If we had been in trouble, those aboard would not have known, and it served only to reinforce our sense of isolation. (F 186)

The desired sense of isolation, previously shattered by the chance meeting with the American geologists, is thus restored, ironically through the reminder of the outside world in the form of an airplane. This restored sense of isolation is necessary to emphasise, it seems, since they cannot find sufficient occasions for danger.

At the beginning of January, the second travellers are affected by the proximity to the Pole. Although the members of the party long for the privacy that the arrival at the Amundsen-Scott base will paradoxically entail, they are also apprehensive about it. "How would we cope with the return to civilisation, and what would we find to replace an adventure which had consumed so much of our lives?" Mear asks (*F* 204). The success of the project is thus, even here, balanced with a sense of emptiness. Scott and his men reached the Pole on 17 January, a month later than Amundsen. They too, were apprehensive about reaching it, but for different reasons. Two days earlier Scott wrote in his diary: "We left our depot today with nine days' provisions, so that it ought to be a certain thing now, and the only appalling possibility the sight of the Norwegian flag forestalling ours" (*J* 394). The following day, Bowers discovered the Norwegians' black flag in the distance. Scott wrote:

> This told us the whole story. The Norwegians have forestalled us and are first at the Pole. It is a terrible disappointment, and I am very sorry for my loyal companions. Many thoughts come and much discussion have we had. Tomorrow we must march on to the Pole and then hasten home with all the speed we can compass. All the day-dreams must go; it will be a wearisome return. (*J* 395)

The second travellers spot the Pole from a distance also, but now it is discernible by the buildings erected by the Americans at the Scott-Amundsen Base; buildings that very concretely move the place into the twentieth century. Mear comments: "As we approached the object I was amused to think how like Kubrick's monolith it looked standing in eerie isolation, hard black against a yellow sun made soft by the crystal-filled air" (*F* 223). The monolith in the film *2001: A Space Odyssey*, its smooth surface and angularity signalling the work of a higher intelligence, is completely out of place in the initial world Stanley Kubrick shows the audience; a world not yet contaminated by manmade objects. The image of the monolith can then be contrasted to Mear's thoughts about months spent emulating a journey made in the past and is, in view of the "artificial light" (*F* 227) and the advanced technology awaiting them at the base, an apt one.

When the first travellers reached the Pole on 17 January, Scott wrote: "THE POLE. Yes, but under very different circumstances from those expected" (*J* 395). The discovery of the black flag, the symbol of Amundsen's victory, has been put forth as one of the reasons why Scott's party never made it back. The journey is difficult during the best of conditions, but to return with the sense of failure may have broken the morale of the group and turned the difficult into the impossible. Mear underlines the randomness when he compares their arrival at the Pole to Scott's. News reaches them that their ship, the *Southern Quest*, has been crushed by pack ice, which will make their return difficult. "In such circumstances how can one doubt the hand of fate, a power that predetermines events with a synchronicity that speaks of more than coincidence. Like Scott, 'The Pole. Yes, but under very different circumstances from those expected'" (*F* 227-28). The equation Mear makes here between Scott's circumstances and those of the 1985 expedition is tenuous to say the least. His invocation of fate and a predetermining power that make the meaning of events surpass mere coincidence seems hyperbolic in the last, strenuous attempt to provide or find a link between first and second journeys.

The second travellers have travelled faster than planned, they have supplies to spare and they are welcomed at the base. Instead of seeing this atmosphere as positive, Mear describes the confusion he experiences inside, the loud noises of 'civilisation,' and how he withdraws from the others, missing the isolation of the continent he has crossed and feeling distinctly different. "I stood before the bathroom mirror and stared at a face that was my own but which wore the mask seen before in sepia images of early Antarctic exploration" (*F* 229). This statement works in a manifold capacity. It illustrates Mear's desire to make a distinction between himself and the scientists at the base, between the expedition's 'us' and civilisation's 'them.' It signals his initial identification with the first travellers and with the tradition of exploration. It is also an attempt to connect with the heroism of earlier travellers, which is seen to be achieved by the 1985 party through reiterating the itinerary, despite the different outcomes of the first and the second journey.

The Return

In January 1912, the weather became progressively worse as Scott commenced the tiring return from the Pole. Miscalculations in supplies and the mysterious shortage of fuel at the depots weakened the men. They suffered increasingly from frostbite and became steadily more exhausted. Despite their weakened condition, the members of the party collected rock samples, going out of their way to do so. At no time did they contemplate leaving these samples behind, meeting as they did one of the scientific pretexts for the journey.

Much space in the *Journals* is taken up by the worsened condition of Evans. On 16 February it is said: "Evans has nearly broken down in the brain, we think. He is absolutely changed from his normal, self-reliant self" (*J* 415). The following day Edgar Evans died. On the 18th, Scott began the last of his small notebooks. From this point onwards, the entries are brief and marked by fatigue and misgivings. The icy surface continues to be bad, making it difficult and tiring to ski. Towards the end of February the temperature drops, sometimes below -40°C, and they barely make it to the depots. Scott's misgivings shine through in the entries and he repeatedly questions their possibilities of surviving.

Around March 16, Scott has lost track of dates and this is also when Oates walks out into the blizzard, which will kill him. Scott writes:

> I take this opportunity of saying that we have stuck to our sick companions to the last. In case of Edgar Evans, when absolutely out of food and he lay insensible, the safety of the remainder seemed to demand his abandonment, but Providence mercifully removed him at this critical moment. He died a natural death, and we did not leave him till two hours after his death. We knew that poor Oates was walking to his death, but though we tried to dissuade him, we knew it was the act of a brave man and an English gentleman. We all hope to meet the end with a similar spirit, and assuredly the end is not far. (*J* 430)

The view that their attention to the sick has slowed them down also surfaces in the message to the public and in several farewell letters. The last entries are written on 29 March.

The 1985 expedition plans to be flown out of Antarctica in a privately hired Cessna. Behind this decision lies in part the desire to make their journey independent of help, but also international politics. As Thomson points out concerning the first journey "[c]laims of priority litter this story" (29) and this is most certainly the case also seventy-four years later. Argentinean and American interests in the area prevent co-operation even if Mear is careful to point out that encounters with individuals are distinguished by "a generosity entirely in keeping with the spirit of international co-operation that has long been the great tradition of Antarctica" (*F* 236). On an official level, the case is very different, causing deleterious effects at the bases.[24] The hostility mainly arises from the fact that the U. S. government feels that the expedition's members would have had to be saved had they been in jeopardy. If the meteorological conditions had been bad, this, in turn, might have jeopardised the Americans' safety.

When unexpected news comes that the expedition members are unable to use the Cessna as transportation from the Pole it is decided that an American plane will come to the rescue. The director of the National Science Foundation's Polar Program, Peter Wilkniss tells the walkers the following:

> 'I have nothing against you people personally, but you were warned. We made it clear before, and I want to tell you now, that we have a policy of no assistance to private expeditions which it is my business to enforce. There is no place in the Antarctic for adventures such as yours any more, and we are going to make that point. You will be flown to McMurdo now, where you will join the rest of your people. Arrangements will be made for your immediate evacuation to Christchurch.' (*F* 241)

Mear rewards the events following their arrival at the Pole with a significant amount of space in his text and introduces the idea that they provide links to Scott's return journey. When describing the departure from Antarctica, Mear indicates that it made "a mockery of the 70 days of toil it had taken us to the South Geographic Pole" (*F*, 242). In this sense, the journey of the 1985 expedition is a failure like Scott's. Whereas Scott failed because help was absent, the second travellers fail because the unwanted help is forced upon them as the authorities of another nation evacuate them, and this makes the comparison limp. Scott repeatedly returns to the fact that the party was aware of the dangers inherent in the Antarctic journey: "We took risks, we knew we took them," he writes in the message to the public (*J* 442). Although Swan and Mear underline the same voluntary aspect and the awareness of the difficulties they may meet, to take risks is no longer allowed. "We had wanted to play the game by the old rules," Mear states, "and now, just when it seemed we had come

---

[24] The following telex, for instance, illustrates the confusion and the double loyalties at the bases. "Perhaps one of the most significant effects to the U. S. Antarctic program is that the incident has affected morale at McMurdo and South Pole stations. With emotions running high, both communities have experienced debates among those supporting the expedition and those supporting U. S policy" (*F* 238).

through, the game was called off . . . because it was no longer reasonable to remain isolated from the arbitrary set of rules imposed by the presence of American [interests]" (*F* 239). As Wilkniss previously has put it, "there is no place for adventures such as [the 1985 expedition's] anymore" (*F* 241). That is, the members of the 1985 expedition have travelled in Scott's footsteps, but they will be the last to do so. What surfaces here is the second journey's construction of the appropriate contexts as "against and in opposition to the current of the time" (Matos 224). This is a crucial feature and one that is to varying degrees repeated throughout the second journey discourse. Alexander and Rankin are not thoroughly opposed to modern means of transport, but Swan and Mear are. The walk to the South Pole as their clearly delineated project[25] provides the raison d'être for the endeavour, despite the fact that there are more convenient ways of getting to the Pole. If the context "in opposition to the current time" is jeopardised, then that defeats the entire purpose of the project.

ANOTHER TALE TO TELL?

In an epilogue, Swan uses his feelings of homecoming and recognition at Scott's Cape Evans hut as a reason to make further comparisons between the two expeditions.

> I remembered the feeling I had had on my very first visit—the feeling of belonging, almost of coming home. It made me think how closely we had indeed travelled in the footsteps of Scott. Memories flooded back of all the parallels that contrived to bring our story so close to his. (*F* 270)

Among these parallels, he mentions that he was once allowed to sleep in Scott's bunk on board the *Discovery*, that the *Southern Quest* had been escorted out of the harbour by the same tug that had guided the *Terra Nova* and that the warehouses where the preparations for both expeditions were made were situated close to each other. These are external, even trivial, things that may or may not lend significance to otherwise un-noteworthy events, but his contention is that the experiences of the two walks to the Pole have been similar indeed. The similarities do

---

[25] The planned ride in the Cessna would take place after this, after the essential second journey is over.

not end with external things, however. "I was overcome with an intense satisfaction," Swan writes,

> a quiet elation at what we had accomplished: not simply the Pole, though that in itself was a great prize for us. Perhaps—I dared to think—we had also come close to achieving what Scott had described as 'the height of that fine conception which is realised when a party of men go forth to face hardships, dangers and difficulties with their own unaided efforts'. (*F* 271)

The "hardships" and "dangers" are continuously used to heighten the authenticity of the project. In the emphasis put upon these notions lies a desire to emulate not only the first journey itself, but to reach the heroic ideal Scott and his contemporaries were influenced by. "I hope," Swan finally contends, paraphrasing the closing words of Cherry-Garrard's *The Worst Journey in the World*, "that others may find the inspiration in our story to stretch themselves beyond their own horizons" (*F* 271). This again signals the second travellers' stress on the unusually heroic, on feats inspiring others to overcome obstacles, much in the same manner as Scott looked upon himself and his men as examples of endurance and moral strength.

The continued emphasis on independence works similarly to underline the heroism inherent in the project. Independence, that is, of modern means of communication and transport. When the desire to remain independent fails, when the expedition is evacuated, this is paradoxically presented as another obstacle to overcome, and as such yet another parallel to Scott's return, no matter how tenuous this link may be. The traditional image of the heroic traveller has undergone changes. In commenting on these changes, adapting the heroic ideal to contemporary conditions, the second travellers mediate Scott's text, choosing from it those definitions of heroism that translate over time, adapting them to the new circumstances.

Although the multiple references to the first text are not present to the same extent as in the following case studies, it is clear that Scott's journey is the most powerful intertext in *In the Footsteps of Scott*. His observations are measured against contemporary conditions, and the 1985 walk across the ice to the Pole is used as a way to demonstrate how external events worked together to make the first journey a failure.

However, the very geography inhibits clear, intertextual references. Mear writes:

> We built our own landmarks across the featureless plain and placed them within imaginable distance. [. . .] Periodically, there would arise ahead a date, a distance or a position, that loomed large in history. Robert said that this first half of the journey was like returning in time, day by day following each page in Scott's journal. Yet never on the Barrier was there any feature upon which to hang the memory of those events which are preserved only in the legend that has grown out of the account in Scott's diaries. (*F* 146)

Although Mear's statement invokes Scott's *Journals*, the landscape itself makes comparisons between first and second journey difficult. The harsh, meteorological conditions, instrumental in Scott's failure and characteristic of the last part of his text, can naturally not be duplicated. Despite these differences, the nature and the landscape traversed that posed insurmountable obstacles to Scott and his men are relatively unchanged. The 1985 travellers' attitude towards it is altered, however, with contemporary emphasis on preservation and ecology. The isolation the continent offers is one of the key attractions for the 1985 expedition and when it is shattered it compromises the justification for the entire undertaking.

The absence of isolation, the presence of several nations with conflicting interests on the continent, and the political implications of this presence paradoxically work to underline the exclusivity of the second journey project. If their journey is the first in the footsteps of Scott, political interests will simultaneously, it is suggested, ensure that it is the last. As subsequent events illustrate, this is not the case. In the winter of 2008-9, for example, the 1911 race to the Pole was repeated by a British and a Norwegian team (and repeated in more than one sense, since the Norwegians won).[26] An all female expedition with the aim to reach the South Pole is planned for 2011. The expedition is marketed as "In the

---

[26] *The Daily Telegraph* ran a number of articles about this race concluding on 22 January, 2009, by reporting that: "It was a case of history repeating itself when the Norwegian Team Missing Link arrived at the Geographic South Pole at 7pm on Wednesday. The team had completed the 481-mile Amundsen Omega 3 South Pole Race in 17 days and 11 hours. Rune Malterud and Stian Aker linked arms high in the air as they walked to the Pole and proudly planted the Norwegian flag just as their ancestor Amunsden had done on January 17, 1912, with Captain Scott behind him." Andrew Pierce "Ben Fogle and James Cracknell beaten to South Pole by Norwegian team."

Footsteps of Amundsen 2011" and has clear environmental and educational aspirations. These examples illustrate that the jealously guarded areas of Antarctica are becoming increasingly available to travellers and that the area might be losing some of its connotations to extreme isolation and dangers. In the mid 1980s, however, with his experiences in Antarctica behind him, Swan's disbelief in the possibilities of other travellers undertaking a similar journey is quite natural. His concluding hope that their story might make others excel must therefore, within the context of the second journey, be interpreted symbolically.

Chapter Five. Women Travellers: Following Kingsley in West Africa

> *What happens when Penelope voyages?*
> *What discourse, what figures, what maps do we use?*
> Karen R. Lawrence, *Penelope Voyages*

The second journey which forms the basis of this case study is Caroline Alexander's journey in the footsteps of Mary Kingsley, and the resulting book *One Dry Season*, published in 1989. Kingsley's text, *Travels in West Africa*, the first journey in this case, was published in 1897. In her second journey narrative, Alexander creates a double focus, partly on Kingsley, partly on the geographical destination as such. The foregrounding of place creates a difference between first and second journey, because whereas Kingsley was interested in West Africa, Alexander has a pronounced interest in Gabon. Like Robert Swan and Roger Mear's second journey project, Alexander's travelogue illustrates the emulation of one clearly delineated movement in the past by a contemporary traveller, however, the scientific pretext is removed from this journey, and both Alexander and Kingsley are unsponsored and, more or less, amateur travellers. The two, single voices as represented in *One Dry Season* and the *Travels* draw attention to the travellers' relative isolation, and their amateur status means that they both, to varying degrees, struggle with discourses which traditionally have structured and influenced journeying. The fact that both travellers are women and that their texts offer opportunities to engage in the ongoing discussions about women's participation in, or subversion of, the imperial project as well as the situation for contemporary women travellers are added foci.

Female travel writers have been neglected in criticism for a long time and there has been a reluctance to incorporate them into the canon of travel literature. Although this is changing, it is a slow process. For instance, in *Classic Travel Stories*, published as recently as 1994, there are

66 stories about travel. Three of these are written by women. When female travel narratives *are* published, they are instead often grouped together in anthologies presenting women's texts only.[1] Anthologies can facilitate the process of differentiating between women travel writers; when women are presented side by side, the differences between them become clear. Patrick Holland and Graham Huggan observe that anthologies featuring only women travellers "risk essentializing women's travel writing, seeing it as inevitably 'feminist' or preoccupied with 'the private sphere'" (113). However, they further state that there is a contemporary market demand for these kinds of anthologies, a "tendency to look for connections between different women's travel narratives—to see women's travel writing as a repository of shared female experience" (Holland and Huggan 113), which again stresses the perception that female travel writing can or should be unified.

Although there is a significant development towards more comprehensive studies, the traditional division between female and male travellers has resulted in unbalanced or prejudiced texts. An example of the difficulty with which women's texts enter a male-dominated genre is found in the index of Eric Leed's *The Mind of the Traveler*, which actually contains the entry 'women.' "Women," it says, "*See* Genderization of travel; Incorporation; Sessility; Sexual hospitality" (328). There is, not surprisingly, no entry under 'men.' In the table of contents one finds that Leed's fourth chapter is dedicated to "Space and Gender: Women's Mediations," and divided into "The Erotics of Arrival," "Sexual Hospitality and Prostitution," and "The Force that Moves Nations." The chapter as a whole spans seventeen pages. The examples Sara Mills uses in a more recent article, to add to this discussion, are Edward Said's *Orientalism*, in which only one woman traveller is discussed, Paul Fussell's contention that women travellers should not be considered "since their writing is second rate" and Mary Louise Pratt's *Imperial Eyes* which, like Leed's text, devotes a chapter to women travellers "where they are treated as a distinct category of writers" ("Knowledge, Gender, and Empire" 48n). As a tentative reason as to "why women's travel writing has been so completely

---

[1] As examples can be mentioned Alexandra Allen, *Travelling Ladies* (1980), Leo Hamalian, *Ladies on the Loose* (1981*)*, and Marry Morris and Larry O'Connor *The Illustrated Virago Book of Women Travellers* (2003).

ignored in general accounts or why, when general accounts are written, women's texts are ghettoized into a separate chapter," Mills mentions the "assumption underlying much of the theoretical work on travel writing ... that men's and women's texts are fundamentally different" ("Knowledge, Gender, and Empire" 35). A more fruitful way of discussing women's texts would be to balance a discussion of separate issues with an incorporation of these narratives into general discussions. This balancing act, as well as recent theories concerning female travellers will be the focus of the first part of this chapter. I too "ghettoise" women's travel narratives into a separate chapter. However, my aim is to connect the discussions about female travellers to the overall arguments concerning authenticity and intertextuality: the basis of my thesis concerning the second journey, thereby suggesting the benefits of more general discussions.

Gendered Discourses

In the vast majority of travel narratives, women have been associated with sessility, with fixed places to depart from and return to, with passivity rather than agency. "In the history of patriarchal civilizations—and, as yet, there are no other kinds—humanity has worn the mask of masculinity, and travel has been a performance of this persona," as Leed puts it (*The Mind of the Traveller* 220). That is to say that when considering travel as an important feature of life, or even life itself as a journey, it is hardly surprising that the traveller in the patriarchal society, even when the journey is fictional, is a man. Naturally there exist female travellers; the earliest recorded instances date from the fourth century, and it is safe to assume that female journeys have been undertaken long before that despite the lack of textual evidence. Continuously, women have also been featured as accompanying their husbands or other male relatives rather than as subjects travelling on their own, that is, as observers rather than agents.

Karen Lawrence's discussions concerning the Odyssey-myth and the perceived connection between women's wanderings and sexual promiscuity reveal another male-centred theory. One traditional belief, expressed though this myth, was that women journeyed to meet other men, but that men rather travelled to escape women. The question, then, is if these stereotypes can be conflated to reveal similar motives behind male and female travelling. Lawrence argues that many women *did* travel to escape, not perhaps from men as individuals, but "from the oppressions of patriarchy" (104). In Kingsley's nineteenth-century narrative, there are several indications that the patriarchal structures of Victorian England were confining, and that the journey represented one opportunity to escape and remould an identity not solely based on gender. The physical relocation enables Kingsley to, at times, adopt a male stance, but her occasional subversions need to be seen in relation to her compliance with and sustaining of a feminine discourse. In Alexander's text, a negotiation of gendered discourses is more difficult to detect; a result, perhaps, of the fact that the contemporary reader of her travelogue is positioned within the same, or similar, discourses. However, the lack of a textual oscillation between male and female identities suggests that the contemporary travelling persona has a less gender specific identity and, more specifically, that Alexander's pretexts for travelling are not formed in opposition to a current norm.

The gendered discourses governing travel (and other) narratives, resulting in a long standing resistance to incorporating women into more general discussions about travel, have been influenced by the view regarding women as representing sessility and men as representing outward action and movement. Even if this resistance has lessened in the last decades, emphasis has remained on the perceived fundamental differences between male and female travelling. In this sense, stress has often been put on the notion that women travellers saw and experienced different things and expressed themselves in different ways than their male counterparts. At the same time as this gives us valuable insights into the complicated structures of identity-making, subversions and (both figurative and literal) border-crossings, it prevents the incorporation of women travellers in theoretical discussions concerning travel literature. By insisting on difference it becomes difficult to view women's travels in relation to men's. Mary Russell's description of the manner in which women travel illustrates this tendency to make a sharp division between male and female travel writing and to romanticise female travelling, though not necessarily the accomplishments arising from it.

> [T]he uniqueness of [women's] exploits lies not so much in the doing as in the *manner* of their accomplishment. Travellers can be roughly divided

into two types. There are those who set out with their sights firmly fixed on a distant destination. [. . .] The journey is a quest, the travellers searchers who cannot rest until they have reached their goal. [. . .] There is a second sort of traveller, however—those who weave in and out among the lives of the people they encounter on the way, picking up, during their odyssey, a stitch here and a pattern there so that they return wearing cloaks embroidered with the rainbow of the world. It is this group which is dominated by women—the travellers who dawdle along the road, pausing to stop and stare and ruminate upon the idiosyncrasies of life. (Russell 211, original italics)

The sharp contrast drawn does more than to suggest that men and women travel under different circumstances. It also suggests the effects gendered discourses have on the attitude to the journey (the determination of male travellers and the haphazard motivations of female travellers) and on the itinerary as such (the set goals men are said to have and the whimsical, non-linear routes women supposedly take). The stereotypically essentialist qualities that are depicted emphasise the perceived difficulties in discussing male and female travelling on equal terms. Further, a continued juxtaposition between determinedness and '"dawdling" makes it difficult to situate the travelling subject within historical, social and cultural contexts.

Imperial discourses further reflect the differences, perceived as foundational, between male and female travellers. Colonialism has long been regarded as the establishment of an essentially masculine identity, rather than a national identity; a view which needs to be re-evaluated. Early theoretical works on imperialism have avoided commenting on women's participation, seeing them as, at the very most, marginal to the process, a position that oversimplifies the colonial project.[2] More recent works suggest important developments. Mills, for example, stresses that women's texts should be incorporated into the more general theories dealing with colonial literature. She also warns that the texts should not be seen as representations of individual struggles against Victorian conventions, and dismisses the view of early women travellers as "'indomitable' and 'eccentric'" (*Discourses of Difference* 1-4). To regard

---

[2] Equally misguiding, naturally, is to see all male travellers as exclusively goal oriented, and I want to stress that it is as important to see men as individual travellers and to situate each travelling subject in its historical, political, social, financial and cultural contexts.

them as such automatically disqualifies them from participating in larger discursive structures and makes them difficult to receive and analyse. Acknowledging the fact that women, although at times rejecting the proposed terms of subjectivity, may also have worked within and complied with the patriarchal structure (Mills, *Discourses of Difference* 67-107) illustrates the notion of discourse itself, in which resistance always is a necessary part of power. Mills argues that both male and female travellers have much to gain by an approach in which they, irrespective of gender, are incorporated into discussions because

> just as women's travel texts are often read as if they were only about the individual and not about colonial expansion, so certain male writings are read as if they were only about colonial adventure, when in truth they are also about proving individual manhood, and a particular type of colonial manhood at that. ("Knowledge, Gender, and Empire" 37)

When included in discussions about colonisation, the works of female authors paradoxically reveal why they have been difficult to situate there in the first place. As women were marginalised in their own societies they often display in their texts a tendency to identify with other marginalised groups and they "were unable to adopt the imperialist voice with the ease with which male writers did" (Mills, *Discourses of Difference* 3). This resulted in few opportunities for the reader to assert the colonial enterprise's success. Additional problems are found in the fact that the women of the colonial period were sometimes travelling under the guise of men, or adopting a male standpoint, but on returning they became unprofessional lady travellers, and were not included in travel anthologies of the time.

Travelling in the time period of High Imperialism, Kingsley needs to be situated within the colonial discourse. Although Kingsley *is* uneasy at times when using the imperialist voice, she also comfortably adopts it when articulating her support for Britain's domination in Africa, to mention one example. Kingsley's oscillation between discourses and, indeed, voices make monolithic interpretations of her texts problematic. Placing Alexander among postcolonial authors is easier. She is not out to explore 'unknown' areas of West Africa, but rather to explore Kingsley's text and, by extension, the region *through* Kingsley's text. The condescending, albeit often benevolent view of people found in Kingsley's text is supplanted with postcolonial, non-hierarchical descriptions.

Kingsley's published works were highly acclaimed, but were seen rather as unusual accomplishments by a woman, by an 'eccentric creature,' than anything else. Features often lauded in the *Travels* and in her subsequent work *West African Studies* (1899) were also often of an anthropological and ethnographic nature, and the travel-aspect is thereby downplayed. Anthropological work was thought of as a field more suitable for female authors and seen as almost solely based on subjectivity; first hand experiences become more important than resources or in-depth knowledge, and a lack of training and education was seen as beneficial, something that made contact with the foreign environment easier (Birkett 174). The contemporary travelogue is free from the need to give readers access to information of an anthropological nature, and the gendered discourse is less pronounced. However, Kingsley's curiosity in anthropological matters and the results of her research have consequences for Alexander's project. In the village of Onga (a place Kingsley never visits), Alexander finds herself "being absorbed passively into" the everyday life and wonders what Kingsley would have done in the same place and what questions she might have asked. "Are Bateké women allowed to eat antelope? Do they rejoice or despair at the birth of twins? I would not know what to do with such knowledge".[3] The filter of the first text in this case results not only in an approach to place, but in a vague idea of what anthropological information *should* go into the second journey narrative.

The stress on anthropology and ethnology is one way for both Kingsley and her contemporary readers to circumvent the fact that her journey was of an exploratory nature. Four additional aspects illuminate how Kinsley further negotiates the discourse of exploration: subversion through irony, the choice of destination, the attitude towards what is seen and in the manner in which truth claims are formulated. Firstly, Pratt observes that Kingsley "builds her own meaning-making apparatus out of the raw materials of the monarchich male discourse of domination and

---

[3] Caroline Alexander, *One Dry Season: In the Footsteps of Mary Kingsley* 211. All subsequent page-references to this primary source will be preceded by the letter *O*.

intervention . . . [t]hrough irony and inversion" (213). That is, the discourse of exploration Kingsley has access to is male and consequently uncomfortable, even impossible, for her to fully use. This difficulty is evident in how she downplays her own achievements and uses irony when recounting her experiences. A clear, ironic resistance to the discourse can be seen in the way Kingsley positions herself when it comes to her research. The irony here is directed towards the need to take accurate measurements and she recounts a story in her characteristic, understated manner:

> I should think that crocodile was eight feet long; but don't go and say I measured him, or that this is my outside measurement for crocodiles. I have measured them when they have been killed by other people, fifteen, eighteen, and twenty-one feet odd. This was only a pushing young creature who had not learnt manners.[4]

This is a claim to authority and scientific veracity that is subverted by the tone of writing.[5] Secondly, the landscape itself plays into the inversion of the exploration discourse as the region Kingsley chose consisted of swamps, of little use to both Europeans and Africans and as such meagre grounds for contestation. Thirdly, the viewing position of the "monarch-of-all-I-survey," another feature of the discourse, is also subverted in Kingsley's text and "[f]ar from taking possession of what she sees, she *steals* past" (Pratt 214, original italics). That is, rather than dominating what is seen and thereby making claims to it which becomes the representational consequence of the 'monarch trope,' Kingsley employs an understated rhetoric by which no such claims are made. A fourth aspect illustrative of the resistance to the discourse of exploration is found in Kingsley's few claims to originality. As an example, she claims to be "the first white traveller" on the river Karkola (*T* 242n), but this example is

---

[4] Mary Kingsley, *Travels in West Africa: Congo Français, Corisco and Cameroons* 90. All subsequent page references to this primary source will be preceded by the letter *T*.

[5] Prior to her journey, Kingsley is informed of the measure mania of the day and advised to "take measurements ... and always take them from the adult male" (*T* 244-5). Lawrence observes that this "admonition succinctly embodies the Western cultural assumption that the male is the generic norm" (124). It should be noted that Kingsley at times also employs irony when recounting other traveller's descriptions and claims. The Ogooué river, she writes, "is mainly known in England from the works of Mr. Du Chaillu, who, however, had the misfortune on both of his expeditions to miss actually discovering it" (*T* 103).

expressed in a footnote and similar claims are represented as curious asides.

The very language used to describe exploration as well as imperialist ventures is gendered, posing problems both for Kingsley and for readers of her text. The history of exploration and colonialism is invariably expressed in terms that sexualise the colonised Other, as well as the explored and conquered country. We read of penetrations into virgin territory, we are given the image of colonised areas as females that are in the end controlled and possessed by the white man, images that may sit uncomfortably with female travellers, and presumably many men. The sexualisation of the colonised place is important also when seen in the light of the heroic traveller. The "sexual imagery," Alison Blunt and Gillian Rose argue, was used "to create and sustain the heroic stature of male colonizers who conquered and penetrated dangerous, unknown continents, often characterized by the fertility of both indigenous vegetation and women" ("Introduction" 10).[6] Although the alignment with the male heroic figure at times presents a problem for Kingsley, her text initially concurs with narratives describing the African continent as an alluring, yet potentially dangerous female. For example, she refers to West Africa as "a *Belle Dame sans merci*" (*T* 11, original italics). As the travelogue develops, however, it is clear "that brands of masculinity are exposed as facade or performance but also that femininity, too, is shown to participate in the masquerade" (Lawrence 150). Lawrence ascribes this exposure of both masculinity and femininity to the "theatrical dimension in cultural encounters" (151), that is, the textually staged performances of both the traveller and the encountered Other.

The sexualised imagery used to describe the African continent is in travelogues often paired with detailed descriptions of males and females which, although not always sexualised, draw attention to the encountered individuals' physical attributes. In anthropological accounts, there is a

---

[6] Maps are also important in this context and "[t]he feminization of colonized landscapes can illustrate the positionality inherent in viewing/reading landscapes — and maps purporting to represent them — as both visual and written. The association of indigenous women with colonized land legitimated perceptions of both women and land as objects of colonization. [...] The construction of a 'sexual space' paralleled the construction of space to be colonized, and the desire for colonial control was often expressed in terms of sexual control" (Blunt and Rose, "Introduction: Women's Colonial and Postcolonial Geographies" 10).

clearly assigned function of these kinds of descriptions, whereas in Alexander's contemporary account there is not. She writes:

> It is typical of travel books written up until not so very long ago to make unabashed pronouncements concerning a "native's" physique: a number of memoirs written by the wives of colonial officials, for example, comment admiringly on the "magnificent physiques of the male African," and the reader is embarrassed for the author's inadvertent revelation of more private thoughts. With full consciousness of all the implications, I state that I looked up to see standing in the doorway a young African man with a magnificent physique. (*O* 230)

In a typically postmodern way (and echoing Kingsley's jocular tone) Alexander here draws attention not only to her personal reactions to the handsome man, but to how the reader of her text might react. By drawing attention to this probable reaction, she can also forestall it.

Textually staging a performance of the self is an aspect of autobiographical writing and autobiography, too, is a discourse in which gender plays a significant role. The representative Western male has traditionally been at the core of the autobiographical work and a division has often been made between 'major' and 'minor' works within the genre, the latter term frequently used to describe female writings. Mills contends that even works by women not expressly stated as being autobiographical were labelled as such and that this "should be seen as an attempt to deny women the status of creators of cultural artefacts" (*Discourses of Difference* 12). That is, when a text is viewed as a testament to personal experience, and then especially a woman's personal experience, it is seen as losing any claims it might have had to scientific veracity and general authority. In a colonial context it becomes particularly difficult to view women's texts from the period as unequivocally supporting or denouncing the imperial project as they have been seen as part of a personal discourse rather than an imperial one.

The autobiographical conventions of the travel genre prevented women from representing themselves in their own words. Female autobiography abounds with negotiations of prevalent standards and the truth-value is uncertain, not because women's texts are inferior, but because they are written within a tradition that does not recognise the female subject or even allows female language. Leigh Gilmore uses the word "autobiographics" to illustrate an aim to create a "map" to guide the reader, theorist or critic, to their destination. She claims that the world of women's autobiographies is unmapped and even unrecognisable when regarded from the viewpoint of prevailing literary standards and theories. The existing map claims to be a representation of reality, yet it is a reality that excludes large parts of humanity and makes its landscapes unrecognisable. "Clearly," Gilmore argues,

> the map has been drawn to represent "reality" differently from how feminist critics of autobiography, dubious of "realism," would draw it. A map is, above all, an argument for realism; it is a truth-scape, made for an audience that, without it, is "nowhere." It offers a way to re-cognize what one is otherwise unable to know. (7)

When this created, and in many ways false, map is imposed on women's travel texts it compromises the reality described in them. The aim becomes, then, to create new maps, to draw new lines within which to place women's travel narratives.

Issues connected to the division between major and minor autobiographical works are also connected to the fact that women in the colonial period (and earlier periods) were discouraged from expressing themselves in the public (written) form, which was thought sexually improper. One result of this was that many women used pseudonyms.[7] Another result is seen in the use of the diary form which, although being considered as inferior, was appealing to many female travellers as it was not as public as other types of writing, even in the published form. Kingsley has been informed, she states "that publishing a diary is a form of literary crime [but that] no one expects literature in a book of travel." She then defends the diary form, stating that

> there are things to be said in favour of the diary form, particularly when it is kept in a little known and wild region, for the reader gets therein notice of things that, although unimportant in themselves, yet go to make up the conditions of life under which men and things exist. (*T* 100)

After these introductory lines as to why she chooses to employ the form after all, she "*descends* to diary" (*T* 106, emphasis added). The passage

---

[7] Initially in the publication process, Kingsley suggested that she would publish her work anonymously (*O* 278).

quoted not only outlines the excuses for using this form, but downplays the findings described in the diary; the "unimportant" things which only combined can make a contribution to increased knowledge.

The diary form of *Travels in West Africa* is, of course, a textual construct, and although communicating a sense of immediacy the text is, as most travelogues, rather a mediated version of the traveller's experience. With different text-types come different layers of subjectivity:

> Kingsley based *Travels in West Africa* on diaries and letters she wrote to friends. On one level, this reveals different, layered sites of authorship: Kingsley wrote about West Africa while in England but used her own writings from West Africa as source material. On another level, it is clearly problematic to think of travel writing as autobiographical, but this seems increasingly possible when sources like these have been used. The use of information from such private and personal sources is made more explicitly known in travel writing by women than by men, paradoxically reinforcing notions of an individual author yet at the same time, by highlighting personal and potentially more emotional contexts, undermining the authority of that author as neutral observer. (Blunt 62)

Via diminished neutrality and emotional contexts the female travel text's general observations and statements are rendered untrustworthy, which is a damaging effect in a genre in which issues of fact and fiction are crucial. The diary form, formally illustrating as it does a subjective view of experiences, is viewed differently when discussing texts written by men and texts written by women. Seen in contrast to Robert Falcon Scott's use of the diary form, and the second expedition's employment of the journal form, one difference between male and female travel texts becomes very clear. In the first case study, the use of the diary form actually heightens the perceived sense of authenticity, whereas here it is mostly avoided. Keeping this difference in mind it is thus tempting to see Kingsley's choice of the word 'descending' as an astute, self-reflexive observation.

Alexander's travelogue is divided into chapters with geographical headings but, as is the case with most travelogues, it follows her day-to-day experiences in a chronological fashion. The immediacy as it is constructed in Kingsley's text is not as prevalent, however, as Alexander frequently interrupts her narrative with departures in other textual and geographical directions. As an example can be mentioned her extensive discussions about Dr Nassau and her own research into his writings and journals. Regardless of if this research is carried out before or after her journey, it is not part of the chronological structure of *One Dry Season*. The diary form (however subtly employed) is interrupted and Alexander draws attention to the multitude of sources which come into the creation of her text.

In connection with the autobiographical feature of the travel text we can notice two "selves" within the same text—the traveller outside the text, and the travelling persona presented *in* the text. At times, during her journey, Alexander approaches an increased understanding of Kingsley's 'outside' self; however, the first traveller's negotiations with patriarchal, Victorian discourses and with the restraints put on her because of the autobiographical element often work effectively against such recognitions. The resulting textual persona, whom Alexander calls "the Kingsley character of the *Travels*" (*O* 279) remains illusive and distant.

DEPARTURE: THE VOYAGE OUT

This form of the second journey is in part characterised by the traveller's pronounced interest in place. Alexander's reason for going to West Africa initially originates in a fascination with Gabon, rather than from any familiarity with Kingsley's narrative. During a previous African journey she is told that Gabon is a "still quite wild" country" (*O* 3). During the years to come she gathers odd bits of information without being convinced she will ever get the opportunity to visit the area, and then, unexpectedly, she finds the *Travels* in the library. "I was startled to see names I recognized" she writes (*O* 4), realising that Kingsley had travelled in Gabon.[8] She is impressed by this fact as well as by the style of the book: "the author's voice sparkled from the pages" (*O* 6). She thus finds a tangible reason for a journey she has yearned to make: an attempt to retrace Kingsley's route. The decision to use the *Travels* as a map is further influenced by the concluding words in Kingsley's introduction. "Your superior culture-instincts may militate against your enjoying West Africa," Kingsley writes, "but if you go there you will find things as I have said" (*T* xxi). Without further ado, and without commenting on the "superior culture-instincts," Alexander decides "to take Miss Kingsley up

---

[8] During the time of Kingsley's journey the region was known as the Gaboon territory of the French Congo.

on her offer" (*O* 6). The first journey, that is, works both as inspiration and invitation. Kingsley's voice speaks to Alexander and initiates a journey which does not have the sponsoring or the official motives that the other second travellers analysed in the case studies have.

The subtitle of Alexander's book, *In the Footsteps of Mary Kingsley*, further reflects the second traveller's initial aim to retrace Kingsley's route as closely as possible. Alexander's marked interest in place, however, limits the possibility of doing just that, and her physical mapping of Kingsley's journey is restricted to the initial place of interest: Gabon. However, she states that she is particularly interested "in those features . . . that had remained the most unchanged since the time of [Kingsley's] journey" (*O* 11) which illustrates the drive common to second journeys to establish a connection with an authentic past. In terms of the itinerary, Alexander does not duplicate the first stretch of Kingsley's journey by boat from Liverpool via the Canary Islands and along the coast to Libreville. She states that:

> Determined to parallel Kingsley's journey as closely as possible, I planned, like her, to stay in missions and villages during the course of my travels. I set my departure date for late May so as to arrive, as she had, at the beginning of the long dry season, which extends from June until the October rains. I was not so great a purist, however, that I felt obliged to mirror her journey in every respect: having suffered past unhappy experiences at sea, I thought I could probably forgo the lengthy boat trip, and so whereas Kingsley had arrived in the Gaboon five months after leaving Liverpool, I took the midnight plane from Paris. (*O* 12-13)

This statement indicates that there are rules to be followed when carrying out the second journey. The season itself is of importance as rains and draughts dictate not only how landscapes appear but which areas can be accessed. Avoiding hotels and large cities and towns is a strategy to attain a higher degree of authenticity and get access to information from both missionaries and indigenous inhabitants. However, Alexander, by not being "so great a purist," foregoes some of these rules by not copying the boat journey. Her preparations for the journey are not mentioned, and her narrative starts, in fact, after the first hundred pages of Kingsley's text.[9] The plane ride between Paris and Libreville thus situates Alexander in an environment, and at a stage of the journey, that Kingsley had travelled several months to reach.

"As it was my intent", Alexander writes, "to see if I would 'find things as Kingsley had said,' my immediate interest lay in those features of Gabon that had remained the most unchanged since the time of her journey" (O 11). These "unchanged" aspects are immediately contrasted to the major changes in the region. Alexander's contention is that one of the most important changes is in the fact that the Fang population (Fan as Kingsley has it) has grown from being a comparatively insignificant people (migrating into Gabon in Kingsley's time) into being one of its most important. "[I]n the spirit of the project I had undertaken," Alexander writes, "I supposed that I was glad that they were still rumored to be cannibals" (O 12). Although the concept of the cannibal may be seen as a Western construct, Alexander's comment signals a return, although somewhat sarcastic, to the role of traveller-as-hero, stressing the adventurous aspect of the journey. As such it is also an attempt to identify more closely with the adventurous conditions Kingsley indicates via *her* descriptions of the journey.[10]

Kingsley's reasons for travelling to West Africa initially seem as haphazard as Alexander's, and as such more striking considering her background and the time-frame within which she travelled. When Kingsley's parents died in the winter of 1892, she was left with a sense of indirection, but only a few weeks later she went to the Canary Islands and the year after on her first trip to West Africa. Of this journey, no coherent narrative exists, but bits and pieces of information surface repeatedly in the *Travels*. In its first chapter she states that, in 1893, she was left with a

---

[9] Alexander's interest in place also excludes the last stretch of the journey, the ascent of Mount Cameroon. It should also be noted that Kingsley's journey, as it is indicated on the map in the *Travels*, starts at Libreville, and does not include the route from Liverpool.

[10] Alexander somehow reaches the conclusion that much has remained the same, but it appears somewhat superficial as she states that she is primarily "encouraged by finding most of the place names in the *Travels* on modern maps, if with glossier francophone spellings" (O 12). The change in spelling, due to the French colonisation of Gabon becomes troublesome when comparing the two texts. When quoting Kingsley I naturally use her spelling of the place name; in the general discussion, the modern, French spelling. Hence, Kingsley's Ogowé is modern day Ogooué, Rembwé is Remboué, Lambarene is Lambaréné, Rembo Vongo is Rémbo Ouango, Lake Ncovi is Lake Nkonié and Njole is Ndjolé.

little time to pass as she liked and that she had a small amount of money to spend. Her other alternative was South America, a tempting destination but rumoured to be even more dangerous in terms of fevers than Africa. "I hardened my heart" Kingsley writes, "and closed with West Africa" (*T* 1).[11] An unmarried, dutiful, Victorian woman should have a more tangible aim for her journey than a mere desire to visit West Africa, or so it was thought. Reminiscences of a loved one, senses of duty or religious purpose would be justifiable reasons for women to travel. None of these pretexts are to be found in Kingsley's narrative and she does not state her explicit reason for choosing West Africa until some hundred pages into the text. There she reveals that she has chosen the destination because of her chances "of getting a collection of fishes from a river north of the Congo" (*T* 103), an enterprise supported by the British Museum of Natural History.

Alexander briefly outlines Kingsley's background to establish more subtle reasons for the first journey and what emerges in this biographical section of *One Dry Season* is a "complicated situation" within the family, characterised by the expectations placed on Kingsley to care both for her parents and her brother and severe limitations to her own educational opportunities and freedom. Kingsley deeply admired her father Charles and was inspired by his amateur anthropological research, to the extent, Alexander suggests, that his death prompted Kingsley to undertake her own journey "because it was what her father would have done" (*O* 11).[12] The complexity of the family situation was exacerbated by the contrast between Charles Kingsley's mobility and his wife Mary Bailey's sequestered existence due to illness. The contrast produced a complex view of female family members, a view, Dea Birkett observes, common to many female travellers in the Victorian era. Their upbringing "clearly pointed to the way in which the role of wife and mother could injure a women [sic] both physically and mentally; happy, stable and long-lasting

---

[11] Due to the potential dangers of the established image of Africa, well-meaning friends attempted to dissuade Kingsley from making the trip at all. One said that "[w]hen you have made up your mind to go to West Africa the very best thing you can do is to get it unmade again and go to Scotland instead" (*T* 4). By another friend she is given a review of a book of phrases that may come in handy, but which unsettles her as the first sentence reads: "Help, I am drowning" (*T* 5).

[12] As a private physician George Kingsley was required to accompany his patients to exotic, foreign countries and many of his trips were marked by his interest in ethnology, anthropology and folk medicine.

marriages and family life were rarely within their childhood experience" (Birkett 18). The differences between the life-styles of the father and the mother, and the tensions within the family that these differences produced often led to the denial of the importance of other female family members, and to a neglect of mentioning them at all. The exclusion of women from family histories made many female travellers turn to literature, to travelogues from which they formed their own views of the world and in which they could picture an identity for themselves. These are then the same travel texts that mention few or no women, and that in many cases employ highly sexualised imagery.[13] The Africa that Kingsley subsequently encounters during her journey is not always in accordance with the adventurous world (or at any rate the descriptions thereof) she had come across in the reading of outdated travelogues. Her emphasis on dangers and difference originates partly in this fact.

The stress on dangers and adventures is a discursive commonplace in nineteenth century travelogues focused on Africa as the continent at this time was known in Europe as the Dark Continent of Stanley's adventures, and West Africa was often referred to as 'the white man's grave.' Kingsley does not describe the first journey in further detail, but concludes that "I did not know the Coast, and the Coast did not know me, and we mutually terrified each other" (*T* 5). The cultural clashes indicated here, and the fear they produce, are seldom stressed in the *Travels*, however. Despite descriptions of dangers represented by the area itself, the climate, the rivers and the forests, the lasting impression is rather that Africa does not intimidate Kingsley. Alexander specifically refers to human threats in the few instances in which fear surfaces in her travelogue. When the boat from Port Gentil to Lambaréné is forced to stop and its passengers are subjected to an unexpected check by soldiers, hers is also a "modern" fear:

> The images of horror offered by the modern world could not have been guessed at by the traveler of Kingsley's day—the brutal pulling out of the patient line, the interrogation in the yellow light, the detention witnessed only by the black river and indifferent forest. (*O* 33)

---

[13] Kingsley fed not only on travelogues written by male explorers, but also on scientific and anthropological texts, for example E. B. Taylor's *Primitive Culture*. She also cherished her subscription of *The English Mechanic* (Höjer 25).

Although the landscape, and specifically the forest, here plays a threatening role simply by its indifference, the threat comes from the randomness of the stop and the powerlessness the passengers experience. Alexander returns to the image of the forest as being an anonymous spectator in several instances and also underlines the inapproachability of it, especially in the dark; the forest is likened to "a walled city after curfew [which shows] only a black, impenetrable front" (*O* 61). In other instances, however, the landscape is described as being tamed and controlled and it is rather in encounters with predominantly male individuals Alexander voices feelings of fear or worry.[14]

To both Kingsley and Alexander, the first contact with West Africa in the coastal areas present challenges, albeit for different reasons. To Kingsley, the colonial world, the transposed Europe meant a curtailing of her literal and figurative mobility as the excursions she takes part in are organised and of a sightseeing nature (far removed from the authentic experiences she sought) and as her gender and single status are emphasised in the settlements. Birkett argues that there was "rarely a well defined female place" within the early colonial settlements. After being reluctantly incorporated into the colonial society the women travellers "became embodiments of fossilized Victorian middle-class values abroad, their place within the colonial hierarchies of race and sex as fixed as that of the colonial subjects" (77). The presence of women within the colonial setting made the colonisers into a family, complete with mothers, daughters, sisters and wives. As Vron Ware convincingly argues, this also presented the colonisers with a justification to defend this family (162). Because of their unmarried state, single women travellers found themselves quite out of place. They could not convincingly set an example, one of the moral duties women were seen to fulfil. They were furthermore denied complete access to, and incorporation into the established, transposed and traditional society. They were also perceived as unable to explore the country on their own. Thus, the colonial settlements did not

---

[14] The most frightening incident on Alexander's journey takes place as she is about to leave Booué and is convinced to wait for the train in a house belonging to former member of the French Foreign Legion with the foreboding name of Le Couteau, the Knife. Not only does his house turn out to be far away from the train station, but a series of bizarre and progressively more threatening incidents force Alexander to invent people waiting for her and fabricate a destination instead of telling him the truth (*O* 187-92).

have a defined place for single female travellers, and in many respects it was within this world that their status was called into question.[15]

Alexander's time in Libreville, her first point of contact with Gabon, is spent preparing for her journey and includes visits to the library and communication with various groups who can be of assistance. There is a sense of suspended movement in this part of Alexander's text and although her physical movement is not circumscribed, Libreville becomes a place of waiting, of preparation for the "real" journey which is to come. She also voices feelings of disappointments which are tied to her second journey project. Although the Pastor of the Baraka mission is very knowledgeable concerning local history, he does not recognise the name of Mary Kingsley and Alexander finds few points of contact between her own and Kingsley's journey. She concludes that her time in Libreville causes an

> uneasy feeling of being at a loose end: the character of Libreville has changed so drastically since Kingsley's visit that there were few points at which I could make meaningful comparisons. [. . .] I had encountered neither the past nor the present in which I was specifically interested. (*O* 22)

Ironically, this is fitting since Kingsley did not find the Africa she sought in Libreville either. Instead, she went through the formal aspects of travelling such as registering and spent several days aimlessly shell hunting in the bay. Alexander here presents her initial intentions to compare the past with the present but the changes, however natural, that have taken place in Libreville lead her to exclude even the possibility of making comparisons. Instead, she voices a feeling of wanting to leave the Westernised coastal city behind in search for more adventurous paths, away from 'civilisation.'

---

[15] The ambivalent, or outright oppositional, attitude towards her single status is internalised and surfaces in the way Kingsley describes colonial women as childlike and lovely, thereby contrasting them to herself whom she perceives as unattractive. (Her accounts of the West African women, it needs to be pointed out, also take their place among conventional, sexualised descriptions.) Her very style of writing is stricter when she is describing the colonial settlements and becomes progressively more relaxed when she moves away into the country. When describing the coastal cities Kingsley focuses on points of "general interest" (*T*, 26) and catalogues various features of the place encountered: animals, foods, handicrafts, etc. This is then to be seen in contrast to her vivacious descriptions of the interior of Africa, past the confines of the colonial settlements, that abound with emotive adjectives.

In the colonial surroundings, 'civilisation' to Kingsley also entails a curtailing of her identity as a free human being. It serves as a continuous reminder of her low status as a single female traveller and circumscribes her initiative to independent action. In the ports of call she becomes acutely aware of the fact that she is removed from the 'wild' and 'exotic' culture she is seeking. The limitations placed on her because of her gender in the colonial settlements become particularly pronounced when seen in relation to her status as she moves past these areas and where the importance is to a greater extent transferred to her racial identity as a (white) European. The altered means of identification do not preclude the fact that Kingsley, like many women travellers, sometimes assumes a masculine stance or is, by the colonised peoples as well as by herself, endowed with what can be termed as male status. Kingsley is repeatedly called "sir" by her native crew (*T* 502), and refers to herself as a man (*T* 276). She also assumes a male position as she identifies with the traditionally male occupations of traders, scientists and explorers.[16] She has no choice but to assume this male position since there are few or no female traders, scientists or explorers with whom to identify.[17] That is, although the scientific and explorational discourses are textually resisted through irony and inversion, Kingsley aligns herself with them on a practical and concrete level.

While the identification with the male tradition of exploration facilitates the practical aspects of travelling (introductions, authority in foreign societies etc.), one may also discern two additional reasons for this identification. Firstly, assuming the role of the explorer supplies reasons for travelling at all. The originality and "first routes" associated with

---

[16] The paradox produced by the expectations of both ladylike and 'male,' heroic behaviour is also visible in the public press reviewing Kingsley's work. "Gender and nationality seem inseparable, and the construction of an 'English lady' seems to epitomize notions of appropriate feminine conduct transgressed by Kingsley" Blunt observes in connection with an article contrasting the "English lady" with the experiences that Kingsley has "manfully borne" (Blunt 116).

[17] The adoption of a male standpoint is also visible in what people expect of her in terms of decision-making, strength and force. She is, for instance, recognised by the Fans as belonging to a "section of the human race with whom it is better to drink than to fight. We knew that we would each have killed the other, if sufficient inducement were offered" (*T* 264). Throughout the overland journey to the Remboué, the mood changes, but simultaneously, Kingsley's self-confidence grows. She takes charge, she leads her men, she feels responsibility for them, she trades, she interrupts, she even dares to express herself in terms that at home would have been considered incorrect in potentially dangerous situations (*T* 255-307).

exploration are in Kingsley's case seen in the ascent of Mount Cameroon on a route previously untried by a European, and her overland journey to the Remboué. Secondly, when nationality becomes more important than the traveller's gender, the risks of sexual harassment are diminished and issues concerning the female traveller's single status are of less importance. This latter possibility is, however, theoretical. Although almost a century separates the two journeys, Alexander remarks that the most often asked question during her travels concerns the whereabouts of her husband, a question that Kingsley also is asked without being able to offer a 'satisfying' answer. The moral example that European women during the colonial period were expected to set is removed from the second journey; however, Alexander's status as a single female still raises questions concerning her own, individual moral standards. At times lies and fabrications are easier than relaying the truth and Alexander invents a husband who full of faith awaits her return (*O* 250).

In Kingsley's text, the oscillation between masculine and feminine discourses makes problematic the autobiographical element. Who is the persona narrating the events? Does the narrating voice belong to Kingsley, the female traveller? Are the descriptions influenced by the male, heroic stance? Are the statements subverted by irony? These kinds of questions cannot be asked concerning Alexander's narrative. Despite questions concerning her unmarried state and the sometimes uneasy feeling in situations where gender is of increased importance, she does not adopt the guise of a man, either practically or textually. The status of the solitary, female traveller has changed significantly in the century separating the journeys and the textual persona is not constructed as a response to a current norm where gender is concerned.

The identification with a male persona discernible in the first text is not uncomplicated. The images gathered from Kingsley's childhood reading may have made her see herself as an adventurer rather than a participant in the imperial project, but the inspiration stems from somewhat dated visions of male travellers. The changes she encountered in the landscape and in the subjected people were not welcomed, in a somewhat similar manner as the century's developments prevent Alexander from discovering Kingsley's West Africa. Kingsley's need to maintain the differences between self and Other may be seen as a result of the desire to remain a Westerner foremost, to retain the freedom that follows with the notion that race rather than gender is important, because when the colonised becomes more like the coloniser gender will be what separates them and Kingsley will become a woman again. The fact that the colonial project at times provided women with an opportunity to in this way escape or remould their identities carries racist connotations. Birkett writes:

> Often finding their inclusion as women in their male heritage uneasy and unsatisfying . . . women discovered a more attractive, inclusive history as *white* people in an age of increasing European intervention and colonization in distant lands. (19, emphasis added)

The racial characteristic of 'whiteness' is part of Kingsley's identity-making on her journey, but as Ware points out, there is some resistance even in contemporary theory to deal with these issues. "Feminism," she argues, "has tended to deal with the representation of white women in terms of gender, class and sexuality without also acknowledging the dynamics of race" (18). Kingsley's text illustrates a process of creating a persona that rests upon dissolution of gender and identification with a racial group.

At the time of Alexander's journey, things have changed considerably and she draws attention to the fact that invitations from strangers to take part in excursions would, in Kingsley's time "have been very difficult to extend, let alone accept" and that the contemporary possibility of doing both puts her in a "far more fortunate" situation (*O* 55). In Alexander's text we find no alignment with male travellers; her gender, or indeed her 'whiteness,' are not expressed issues. Despite this, she is given advantages that she has not sought—a cabin on board a boat, and protection from male Peace Corps volunteers. When Alexander hitches a ride on a truck, for example, her "place was felt to belong in the front of the cabin," she writes, "not because I was sick, certainly not because I was a woman, but because I was white" (*O* 205). In the postcolonial society she is travelling through, she too is seen in terms of the colour of her skin. The racial characteristic of her 'whiteness' gives her unwanted advantages, while her femininity remains unimportant. Whereas Kingsley needs racial difference, since this is the means with which she can overcome the limitations put upon her by her gender, Alexander's awareness of the special treatment she receives becomes a source of embarrassment. A more specific national identity has also been assigned to what is perceived as a naturalised Other. Alexander describes a meeting with women in a village and contends that "[t]hey seemed most intrigued by me not being French and therefore truly foreign" (*O* 35). Being white, but not French, is here seen as a sign of difference, and language seems to be of greater importance when determining what is truly foreign, who is the Other.

Passage: Into Africa

The prospect of danger and adventure, in Kingsley's text seen as primarily residing in the interior of Africa, provided early female travellers with a possibility to prove their own ability to control the situation. Dangers and challenges were actively sought, and if the women travelled alone, their single status on the journey was in itself a way to make heroic achievements. On the one hand, this corresponds to the search for authenticity, as it is perceived to be attainable away from civilisation; on the other hand, the adventure element can be seen from a crass economical standpoint, since heroic tales appealed to the public.[18] The heroic persona however connects with a host of male myths and as such it adds yet another male discourse in which Kingsley finds herself writing, and sometimes writing against.

Moving from the clearly assigned female position in the colonial, coastal areas to a less gender specific, and at times more male, position is a gradual process in Kingsley's text. In facing the imagined or real dangers of West Africa and being alone in the landscape, Kingsley's previous self dissolves. On her way to the Okota rapids, she and her crew are stranded. In the aftermath of the struggle to survive the violent waters, she contemplates a night scene. Characteristically she takes this dissolution of self as a sign of her inability to become inspired by nature.

> Do not imagine it gave rise, in what I am pleased to call my mind, to those complicated, poetical reflections natural beauty seems to bring out in other people's minds. It never works that way with me; I just lose all sense of

---

[18] This fact remains, Mills argues, and "has led to the reprinting of certain examples of women's travel writing that accord with the masculinist norms of the adventure narrative; therefore, those texts that contain strong adventuring heroes are reprinted, whereas those where the character is a more retiring feminine one are rarely reprinted" ("Knowledge, Gender, and Empire" 37).

> human individuality, all memory of human life, with its grief and worry and doubt, and become part of the atmosphere. (*T* 178)

This observation is made when she has recently left the colonial environment and ventured out, 'alone,' in the company of her native crew. From this dissolution of the woman she has been she can rebuild an identity of her own, an identity both wished for and needed, since she is the captain and leader of the project. From this point onwards, her text reflects greater self-reliance, initiative and action.

On the fifth of June, Kingsley left Libreville on the *Mové*, to embark upon what she sees as the 'real' journey away from the coastal colonial areas. In 1895, the Ogooué River was reached by way of Nazareth Bay and led on to Lambaréné. At the time of Alexander's journey there is an overland road connecting Libreville and Lambaréné, but "[i]f one is perverse enough to wish to go by boat, the journey must be divided into two stages" (*O* 27). Determined to imitate Kingsley's journey as closely as possible, Alexander chooses the latter "perverse" possibility, only to be confronted on board the boat with a video screen showing "a nonstop series of Tom and Jerry cartoons" (*O* 27). The authenticity sought by imitating the means of travelling is thus deferred by the decidedly modern intrusion of animations on a television screen.

Alexander reaches Port Gentil from where she takes the *Ekwata* up river to Lambaréné. The Ogooué becomes, as she observes, "the backbone of Mary Kingsley's travels" (*O* 30) and when reaching it, Alexander is "prepared to sit as Mary Kingsley had done and watch the water part and flow as my little steamer made its picturesque way upriver between banks of towering forest that held so many collective memories" (*O* 31). Kingsley had a pleasant journey, with excellent accommodation, delicious food and good company, whereas Alexander's experiences include heavily intoxicated male passengers who prevent all women from claiming places on the roof where a bar has been established. These differences between the two journeys prove too great to be ignored and effectively spoil all chances of the second traveller's main objective: emulation.

The Ogooué forest, which Kingsley described in a manner that earned admiration from her contemporaries, does not have the same impact on Alexander. The latter concludes that their different impressions "might have arisen as much from [their] respective circumstances as from [their] different temperaments" (*O* 36). To Alexander "the forest manifested not passion so much as an inscrutable front, jealously screening what it felt alien eyes had no business seeing" (*O* 36). This image of the second traveller as an intruder in the forest can then be contrasted to Kingsley's description. Not satisfied with just mentioning the forest, her narrative abounds with descriptions of different trees, plants, insects, colours and shades of light.

> Doubtless it is wrong to call it a symphony, yet I know no other word to describe the scenery of the Ogowé. It is as full of life and beauty and passion as any symphony Beethoven ever wrote: the parts changing, interweaving and returning. (*T* 129)[19]

The passion is here made manifest in the romantic image of the forest, which Alexander perceives as a hindrance and as a possible threat. The emotion which gleams through the pages in Kingsley's text continues to elude Alexander as the boat makes its way up the river and as she watches the "increasingly deforested shores" (*O* 37). The approach to and appreciation of the landscape is not the only difference between first and second text and Alexander voices a suspicion that perhaps Kingsley has not been entirely forthcoming when relating her experiences. Alexander is specifically referring to the debilitating effects of the heat which makes her report her own worries and misgivings. The self-awareness and the openness concerning discomforts are discursive elements in the contemporary travelogue, but in Alexander's view the heat is so oppressive and its effects so powerful that the suspicions that Kingsley might have downplayed certain elements become guiding.

In the Lambaréné area, Alexander enlists two European Peace Corps volunteers, Brent and Kurt, to help her reach the nearby lakes. The trip becomes quite adventurous as their jeep gets stuck and the travellers lose their way and are forced to camp out in the forest. In this section, Alexander's tone is light and breezy as if mimicking Kingsley's style, despite few references to the first text.[20] The excursion in the company of

---

[19] The quotation from Kingsley can be found paraphrased in Alexander's later book where she observes "the difficulties inherent in attempting to revive the symphony and song of an experience" (*The Way to Xanadu* 167). See also chapter three.

[20] At one point, Alexander sarcastically subverts the tradition, commonly found in travelogues, to instruct future travellers in what to bring to an area. Between them, "two Peace Corps workers with two full years

the Peace Corps workers seems to free Alexander from the strict emulation of Kingsley's itinerary, and several other travellers and sources of inspiration enter her text. Alexander decides to visit the nearby Samba Falls as it is a place like "(t)he Zambesie, Congo, Shanghai, Zomba [she] would seek out merely for their names" (*O* 73). That is, although Samba Falls are mentioned in the *Travels*, it is the mere name that conjures up a desire to visit them. Kingsley was unable to do so because of the river Ogooué's low water level and the "description of the falls was in all likelihood taken from that of their 'discoverer,' Paul du Chaillu" (*O* 73). This serves as an illustration of the tendency within travel literature to substitute experiences with previously encountered descriptions, here exemplified in the first journey. As Alexander is travelling during the dry season as well, she cannot go to Samba Falls by boat, but instead she has the opportunity of going there by land. Alexander states that she "felt Mary Kingsley *would* have gone to the falls if she had been able" (*O* 76, original italics). She is furthermore tempted by another traveller, Trader Horn, whose book has previously captivated her and whose description of the falls for her "epitomized . . . the glamour of African exploration" (*O* 80). The several layers of intertextuality in the second journey are articulated here, as Alexander moves away from Kingsley's text.

Samba Falls are not reached easily, it soon turns out, and planning for the trip there causes Alexander various problems. Her misgivings about ever getting to them is paired with despondency concerning Fougamou (the village where she makes the preparations) and "an acute sense of vulnerability" (*O* 86) as she has a fever and is suddenly far from medical help. Several people profess to know about the whereabouts of the Falls, but "no one seemed to know exactly how to reach them" (*O* 92). When she finally, with the help of her guide Bakary, is able to locate a fisherman by the name of André who will be able to take them, she is not overwhelmed with confidence as he appears to be drunk, is said to be "a little mad" and insists on bringing a gun (*O* 94). The excursion to the Falls paradoxically, since Kingsley in all probability never saw them, results in one of the first instances in *One Dry Season* where Alexander describes a connection with

---

in the bush of equatorial Africa, and a seasoned traveler, who had come to Gabon expressly to make treks of this kind" bring on their excursion raw chickens, rocket flares and mosquito coils, all of which are rendered useless because no one has thought to bring matches (*O* 60).

the first traveller: "[w]ithout contrivance and against all expectation, I had entered the world I had dreamed of, and fleetingly made contact with the past" (*O* 97). This experience of Alexander's is accomplished by moving away from Kingsley's narrative as she does not follow strictly in Kingsley's footsteps, but the feelings communicated by the first traveller are perceived as attainable to a higher degree when the temporal distance between the two journeys is reinforced by a spatial distance, allowing Alexander to concentrate on her own journey.

Kingsley rode on the steamer the *Éclaireur* up the Ogooué to Ndjolé, the most interior of the French posts, established in 1883 by Count de Brazza, where she briefly stayed at the nearby Talagouga Mission. In Ndjolé she visited the house of Dr Robert Nassau, which already was in ruins. "[B]ut in front of it, as an illustration of the transitory nature of European life in West Africa, is the grave of Mrs. Nassau, among the great white blocks of quartz rocks, its plain stone looking the one firm, permanent, human-made-thing about the place," Kingsley writes (*T* 154). Alexander traces Kingsley's footsteps to this point and segues into a rather detailed description of Dr Nassau's life in Africa, his marriage to Mary Foster, and Mary's death in childbirth. Outlined also are the problems Nassau experiences following his wife's death, which involve tensions between different European factions and, at the time, scandalous rumours about a romantic relationship with a Gabonese woman. Kingsley briefly mentions Nassau in the *Travels* and was indebted to his long experience in the area in some of her own discussions about customs and fetish. Alexander's interest in Nassau's journals have their starting point in her interest in Kingsley as Nassau is "our only eyewitness to Mary Kingsley in Gabon [and as] his journal provides a more precise record of her activities in Libreville at the beginning and end of her journey that she herself gives" (*O* 126). However, reading Kingsley through Nassau's texts is rather turned into an opposite approach as she tries to ascertain the reasons behind the relatively few references to Nassau in the *Travels*. Her reading of Nassau's journal reveals that the two had a much more extensive contact with each other than Kingsley's text reveals and her conclusion is that Kingsley kept his name largely out of her text because of the scandal his name was associated with. These turned tables do not preclude a greater understanding of Kingsley, however, as "[t]he behind-the-scene glimpse of Mary Kingsley in the Nassau story further warmed me to her: her friendship with Nassau, I believe, reveals a wise and gentle insight, a softer edge to her usual public voice" (*O* 142).

Returning from this textual foray into another life-story, Alexander uses Kingsley's descriptions to find Dr Nassau's house. Despite the fact that the buildings are crumbling already at the time of Kingsley's visit, the overgrown landscape, with the ruins of the house barely discernible, causes Alexander to experience "an unexpected panic" as she cannot locate, nor picture, the buildings as they once were (*O* 148). Because of this perceived failure, it becomes a matter of utmost importance to Alexander to find Mrs Nassau's grave. A frantic search begins. Alexander describes this search as "an obsession" and states that "I was goaded by an irrational sense of failed responsibility, by a belief that I alone could rescue this site, and its vanished people, from complete oblivion" (*O* 148). Exactly how this rescue-mission is to work is not explained, but the responsibility she feels is also directed towards Kingsley. Alexander searches for tangible features found in Kingsley's text such as landmarks or monuments of which the grave is an example. She has previously experienced feelings of failure, not only when it comes to retracing Kingsley's exact steps, but also in the attempt to re-experience Kingsley's reactions to the surroundings. Alexander's search for the grave is in vain, however. She later learns that it has been moved from its original place to a cemetery on Talagouga Island, and that she must have seen it without recognising the name on the stone. Translated into a new context it becomes unrecognisable. Alexander's update of Kingsley's descriptions thus reveals that "the original mission house is not in ruins, it is gone. And . . . the one firm, permanent, human-made thing about the place, no longer exists" (*O* 152).

The excursion to the presumed site of the grave is followed by another experience that also serves to illustrate that time influences features of the landscape as well as artefacts. Alexander describes an old monastery and a church in which "the jungle had come peering in each window, groping with its sinuous tendrils into this private darkness, and leaf by leaf consigning it to a forgotten secrecy" (*O* 150). The succeeding line of perceived failures leads her to wonder "[w]hat kind of outlook is shaped by an environment in which natural forces claim a man's artifacts within his lifetime?" (*O* 151) Nature, growing and consuming the traces of the past is perceived as a threat, as invading and intruding into what Alexander sees as private and secret. In this sense, nature is working as a shield between Alexander and the recognitions she desires, between her present and Kingsley's past. Again, however, it is not only Kingsley's past which is conjured up through Alexander's physical presence in the area. At night she is unable to sleep and wonders why and "when at last I knew, the answer startled me. I was waiting for word to come that Mrs. Nassau, her lifeblood dripping away over seven days, had finally died" (*O* 151-52). Combined with invasive and threatening aspects of the landscape, the vulnerability and worries expressed through Mary Foster's diary provoke an emotional response in Alexander which is more seldom produced by Kingsley's narrative.

As she progresses through the interior of West Africa, however, Kingsley's descriptions also change to reveal a more vulnerable side to her textual self. Her description of her trip to the Okota rapids, while characterised by its adventurous, eventful mode, replete with her ironic understatements, also contains disclosures of a more personal nature. She mentions her own vulnerability and notes worries and doubts that are rare elsewhere in her text. She also reports the dissuading comments she receives from missionaries she meets. The comments work in a twofold capacity: they underline the adventurous nature of her project, and they explain and naturalise her own sense of worry. This particular adventure has a special significance for Alexander and is one that she has planned for some time.

> I had an image of myself making my way through white water, accompanied by perhaps two boatmen in a little outboard boat, and occasionally being called upon to fend off from dangerous rocks with an extra paddle. My mother had suggested to me that I might want to take a life jacket, but I had disdained her advice: my trip was to be as adventurous as Kingsley's. (*O* 157)

The repetition in this case is envisioned as one which entails both a physical and a psychological re-enactment of Kingsley's experience, or, at any rate, an approximation of it. Alexander's expectations come to naught, however and her painstakingly arranged journey becomes a disappointment to her. The physical re-enactment fails because the means of travelling are too modernised, the motorised boat being able to fight the currents that left the first traveller stranded. Alexander infers that "Kingsley and her crew had been forced to engage with their surroundings; I observed them passively at a distance" (*O* 159). The sense of adventure is not accomplished, despite the lack of a life jacket, and neither is the emotional response to the sights. The Alemba rapid, which struck Kingsley as particularly magnificent, does not leave the same impression on Alexander. "[H]ad it not been for these unmistakable features," she writes of the landmarks, "I could not have believed that I was following Kingsley's route" (*O* 158). She goes on to state that "[a]t no point were my impressions more at odds with hers than when I witnessed the Alemba, which . . . was hardly a phenomenon of nature I would call haunting" (*O* 160). She voices her suspicions that perhaps Kingsley exaggerated her experience or, perhaps, did not see the falls at all. This statement needs not be contradicted, but it is important to emphasise that this is Kingsley's first trip outside the organised and regulated colonial areas. The experiences thus illustrate a literal as well as a symbolic emancipation from the colonial society, which may account for the presumed exaggerations.

Alexander contrasts her "tourist's day outing" with Kingsley's "memorable adventure" and decides it is "all together too shameful to leave matters as they [stand]" (*O* 164). She then comes across an entry in her ("generally unreliable") guidebook informing her that there are other rapids to be found in the Upper Ogooué offering the traveller a possibility of "experiencing a river journey as it was conducted 'as of old'" (*O* 164). Alexander decides to undertake an adventure of her own design. She feels that she is "breaking new territory" (*O* 166) as Kingsley never got further inland than Ndjolé. For a brief period, her narrative illustrates a new direction due to the possibilities of 'unfiltered' experiences. In Lopé, however, Alexander meets an English researcher, Caroline Fernandez, who is well acquainted with the *Travels*. "Don't think *I* haven't thought of redoing her trip," she tells Alexander. "My father has always told me I should" (*O* 169, original italics). This comment, and Fernandez's way of life, described as "[p]ioneerlike, in the tradition of the first European settlers," leads Alexander to doubt the purpose of her own journey:

I suddenly felt vague and insubstantial. Once again, I seemed to be skimming over the surface of someone else's deeper experience. Mary Kingsley had inspired Caroline Fernandez to come and stake her claim in Africa, and I began to feel that I might have slyly usurped a project that was hers by right. (*O* 171-2)

The meeting with Caroline Fernandez and the renewed sense of indirection are essential as a series of disappointments follow. Alexander has experienced few points of contact between herself and Kingsley, and the few recognitions from the first narrative lead her to see her journey, indeed herself, as "vague and insubstantial." In this sense, although her wording is different, she equates herself with a tourist, and suspects that a more profound understanding of Kingsley can be gained only by someone who has moved beyond the front region to the authentic experiences.

The differences between first and second journey become increasingly pronounced while, ironically, the tone of writing in *One Dry Season* comes closer to Kingsley's. The breezy, jocular way with which the Hotel Cascades in Booué is described (as "a kind of Gabonese Fawlty Towers") and the narration of an increasingly bizarre dinner are cases in point (*O* 175-77). Alexander's guide Gregoire, a European man who never leaves home without a gun and proudly shows her pictures of the endangered animals he has shot similarly becomes a caricature (*O* 178-80). The experiences at the hotel and in the company of Gregoire are narrated in ways which stand in marked contrast to the previously articulated sense of insubstantiality and vulnerability and can be read as a defence mechanism which, briefly, draws attention to Alexander's own construction of a distanced, sarcastic textual persona. They can also be contrasted to Alexander's epiphany upon finally reaching the Booué rapids. "At one glorious moment, I saw Mary Kingsley's white lilies growing among the rocks on long, floating stems," she writes. "Only the blue-haloed rocks were lacking" (*O* 184). She thus appropriates Kingsley's experiences as her own in order to make a comparison even if this takes place outside Kingsley's route, and experiences a fleeting moment of recognition which allows her to return to her hotel "triumphantly happy" (*O* 185).

After her adventure in the rapids, Kingsley returned to Lambaréné where she spent several weeks preoccupied with her ethnological research. When she eventually was to leave, she abandoned the Ogooué and traveled north on the Rèmbo Ouango (the 'small river') the northern arm of the Ogooué. She was accompanied by men from the Ajumba tribe, whom she re-named after their specific traits in the imperialist tradition, Gray Shirt, Singlet, Silence and Pagan, as well as a native interpreter, by the name of Ngouta. By canoe they reached a Fan village by the shores of Lake Ncovi. The Fans in this area were elephant hunters, but as they were also reputed to be cannibals, Kingsley expresses an initial fear that only gradually subsides. Five men of the Fan people will lead her and her crew through the forest to "a big Fan town called Efoua, where no white man or black trader had yet been" (*T* 253). This is, of course, the same people that during Alexander's trip are still rumoured to be cannibals. Kingsley's vulnerability as a solitary female traveller is accentuated by this danger, but it is counterbalanced by the opportunity to be the 'first.'

During the night Kingsley cannot sleep. She leaves the village and takes her canoe out on the lake where she feels peaceful and content. In Franceville, almost a century later, Alexander meets a Peace Corps volunteer who has read the *Travels*, and who particularly remembers this passage; Kingsley canoeing by herself in the dark. Asked if there has been an equivalent moment of peace and beauty on her trip, Alexander has "to confess that there had not" (*O* 208). Neither can she claim to be the 'first' in the manner Kingsley, at least textually, is able to.

As many readers of the *Travels*, Alexander includes the journey through the forest from Lake Nkonié to the Remboué among the greatest adventures of the book, but she also notes the subtle change in mood. The atmosphere becomes more threatening and she suggests that "this adventure was in its reality more frightening and unnerving than is directly conveyed" (*O* 218). Kingsley encountered elephants, gorillas, ticks and leeches, she detected signs of nearby leopards and the walk itself was strenuous and dangerous as they made their way through the underbrush, the swamps and the bogs. A number of accidents also occurred, Kingsley herself falling into a hole lined with spikes and realising the often quoted "blessing of a good thick skirt" (*T* 270). Although she travelled in the company of Fans, their reputation and the fear Fan country instilled in the traveller surface in Kingsley's text. When they reached Efoua she was given a hut to sleep in and found there, in a bag above her head, remnants of human beings (*T* 273). Although communicated in Kingsley's characteristic humorous tone, it serves as a reminder of the danger, and gives the passage the 'appropriate' touch of adventure.

Alexander observes that the route Kingsley took was "the most difficult—indeed almost senseless" and she cannot understand why the "generally protective and helpful European community [. . .] *allowed* [her] to go this way in the first place" (*O* 221, original italics). She presents the convincing theory that perhaps "the itinerary chosen by Kingsley's Fang guides was tailored to suit their own trading interests" (*O* 223). Alexander has severe problems tracing Kingsley's footsteps on this leg of the journey, and experiences the same difficulties in acquiring information about the exact location of villages and roads as once did Kingsley. By water she gets as far as Lake Azingo, but the overland journey becomes impossible to emulate. "Ultimately," she writes,

> I suspect that Kingsley and I learned the same lesson, namely that it is one's choice of guides that determines one's itinerary. I made many plans that came to nought; Mary Kingsley's overland trek may never have been planned—but at least it happened. (*O* 244)

Alexander's journey comes to a safe and uneventful end by boat to Akondjo, where she hopes she will find someone who has at least heard of Kingsley. This hope too is in vain. "It has to be," she writes,

> that there is a path from Lake Azingo to Akondjo; and it has to be that someone knows the way. It has to be that in all Gabon there is someone who has heard of Mary Kingsley. But it has to remain for someone else to find him [sic]. (*O* 263)

The second journey is thus markedly different from the first. The desired emulations have proven difficult to carry out, and the traces of Kingsley, however natural this may seem to the reader, have vanished. The return in Alexander's case means the re-entry into the modern, hectic world of Libreville. She does not find it worthwhile to try to emulate Kingsley's boat trip to Corisco Island, and it is furthermore "outside the province of [her] predetermined territory" (*O* 267). Her initial interest in place thus surfaces again, although many of Kingsley's further adventures, especially the ascent of Mount Cameroon, seem worth repeating. Alexander comments on the fact that Kingsley had her mountain-experience as well as the twelve-week boat ride back to England ahead of her when she reached Libreville, a fact that "undercut[s]" Alexander's "sense of having come to journey's end" (*O* 270). That is, the desired connection between the two travellers is again subverted. The physical journey in Kingsley's footsteps has come to an end and the sense of completion of the project remains absent.

Homeward Bound: Negotiating the Return

As the many instances of thwarted recognitions illustrate, Alexander has, throughout her journey experienced problems in recapturing Kingsley's experiences and in emulating both routes and emotional responses. After leaving Gabon, Alexander recapitulates events succeeding Kingsley's return to Britain and it is with some irony that the reception of Kingsley's works and the re-association with British society is what leads to Alexander's increased understanding of the first traveller. The biographical element of the second journey, entailing research into Kingsley's background, also leads to a deepened understanding of Kingsley's textual persona, "the Kingsley character" (*O* 279), in particular.

One of the main problems Kingsley encountered upon her return was the re-adjustment to the restrictive world of Victorian women. During her journey, she identified both with Africa and Africans as well as with the white, male, heroic explorer; roles that were no longer available. Her comments in letters signal her "inability to feel 'at home' and her references to West Africa as 'home' reveal the destabilization of both 'home' and away" (Blunt 124). She was seen, by many, as an exceptionally independent woman, and was for this reason, again by many, more or less expected to support female suffrage and other emancipatory movements. Kingsley resisted this equation, however, and denied any affinity with proto-feminist groups. From a contemporary perspective, comments such as although "[a] great woman, either mentally or physically will excel an indifferent man . . . no woman ever equals a really great man" (*T* 659) can be seen to jar slightly with Kingsley's own accomplishments. However, many women travellers resisted being seen as representative of a larger cause or making statements concerning women in general. The fact that women generally were dissuaded from taking part in public discourses can be discerned as one reason for this resistance. Many also undertook their journeys for personal reasons (in contrast to mainly male participants in explorational and colonial endeavours) and for that reason resisted making pronouncements for larger groups.

The spatial element of travel in itself meant that Kingsley's efforts were appreciated and accepted to a certain extent. Blunt observes that "[b]ecause her social transgressions were spatially distant and only possible when traveling away from 'home,' domestic constructions of the inferiority of women could remain unthreatened" (Blunt 137-38). Upon her return, and reluctantly entering the public sphere, informing the public of West African affairs by lectures, political lobbying and extensive correspondence, the lack of a spatial distance between her identity and her exploits became more and more pronounced.

The entrance into the public sphere demanded of Kingsley that she legitimise her journey by assigning to it scientific and professional motives; motives based in her assumed 'male' identity. In her general discussion on this phenomenon, Blunt concludes that

> [t]he desire to be distanced from suffragists and 'new women' could thus stem from the need for women travel writers to legitimize their travels and writings in the masculine, public realm of scientific research, professionalism and politics that arose from their construction as feminine on their return 'home' (157).

When stressing the need to analyse women's travel texts within discursive frameworks, it also becomes important to stress the frameworks in which they refused to participate, and retain the double focus: the reasons for travelling made attractive by the possibility of assuming a new 'male' identity, as well as the re-creation of the female identity upon the return and the subsequent writing process. Kingsley's position in several different discourses: the feminine, the colonial and the male; scientific and heroic, public and private may in part account for the difficulties in discovering Kingsley that Alexander repeatedly voices.

Alexander's awareness of Kingsley's difficulties in situating herself within these discourses means, however, an increased appreciation for the textual persona. "All these considerations—the selective editing of personal experiences and a vehement resistance to being typecast as an intrepid lady explorer—eventually combined with her naturally vivid style and sense of humor to create the Kingsley character of the *Travels*" (*O* 279). Insecurities, fears and forms of resistance which on the actual journey produce a distance between first and second traveller, superseding the temporal one, are in hindsight, then, re-evaluated. Alexander's deeper understanding of the conflicting discourses, her understanding of constraints, and the heightened realisation of the first text's constructedness thus lead her to a greater appreciation of Kingsley, both inside and outside the *Travels*.

At the same time as the first text evidences omissions, silences, or other types of tensions, it also, to Alexander, reads in ways that make her momentarily forget that "Kingsley was a woman of a specific, bygone era" (*O* 272). This, she argues is not only a matter of stylistics and the 'modern' sense of humour Kingsley employs in her descriptions, "but also because Kingsley encounters little that is 'dateable' in European terms in the course of her travels—jungles and rivers are timeless and for the most part still need to be traversed on foot and by boat" (*O* 272). Alexander's expressed aim to stay at missions and in villages, and to attempt to recreate Kingsley's trip in terms of transportation comes into play here and the recognitions she has experienced on her journey very often coincide with her presence in forests and on lakes and rivers, where modern day Gabon does not intrude. Both Kingsley's and Alexander's descriptions in these instances are 'undateable.' Alexander continues

> This essential insulation from a sense of specific time had persisted throughout my actual retracing of Kingsley's route. Clearly I had been aware of important differences between our journeys, but this had never overwhelmed the sense of stepping back into 'times past' that so often—at least for a visitor from the West—characterizes travel in Africa (*O* 272).

This pronouncement does not mean that Alexander sees Africa as a static place where few changes have occurred, but rather that the continent, and in her case Gabon, presents such a difference to the Western traveller that he or she may have difficulties precisely dating experiences. Alexander's knowledge about Gabon makes her highly aware of changes as groups of people have willingly or involuntarily relocated and as the decreased trade between villages means lessened opportunities for contact and exchange of information. Alexander discusses the latter change with emphasis on her own selfishness. It would benefit her own project if information concerning routes through the forest were continuously updated, but, in postcolonial fashion, she does not judge whether the development is for the better or for the worse.

What does cause a problem for her, however, is the lack of memories of Kingsley in the area, a lack also connected to developments in the villages of Gabon. She states that

> [t]hroughout my travel in Gabon, I had hoped that somewhere I might come across someone who had heard of Mary Kingsley through stories that had been passed down by his or her ancestors. Oral traditions are tenacious, and Kingsley had made her trip not so very long ago; it was not impossible that somewhere a great-grandchild of one of her boatmen or porters might have heard of this unusual white woman traveling alone several generations ago. But individuals, villages, and whole tribes shift and scatter; the same factors that had caused the disappearance of the interior forest trails have also ensured that people today do not necessarily live in the villages of their ancestors. (*O* 261)

Repeatedly, she asks people she meets if any of them can recall having been told the story of the white woman travelling through their areas, but the reply is in all instances negative. The *Travels* themselves fill a concrete function on Alexander's journey, especially in situations in which information is sought, but in these situations as well, Alexander has some problems in communicating the nature and purpose of her trip. The copy of the book is held up high, passed around "as a kind of emblem of authority" and it induces curiosity in several individuals, but many of them confuse the picture of Kingsley on the front cover with Alexander (*O* 226). The idea of a retracing of the route is not always understood, and in a telling example Alexander recounts a meeting with a man who in vain tries to wrap his head around the concept. He finally arrives at the question: "'what I want to know is, *if* you *already* made this trip ninety years ago, *why* are you doing it *again*?'" (*O* 237, original italics) which makes Alexander realise that her project is not as self-evident as she initially has thought. Alexander's impressions of the *Travels* are such that she assumes the text's popularity transgresses all geographical and linguistic borders. Tellingly, the people she meets who *have* heard of Kingsley and read her travelogue are all European.

It was never Kingsley's intention to remain in England for any longer period of time; Africa, she felt, was her true home. In a lecture to the Imperial Institute in February 1900, with plans set to leave for Africa again, she concluded with the words; "Goodbye, . . . and fare you well, for I am homeward bound" ("West Africa from an Ethnographical Point of View," cited in *O* 281).[21] In letters and in lectures, Kingsley's attraction to Africa becomes even more apparent than in the travel narrative. Her descriptions often draw attention to the complexity and the double nature of the continent, echoed in her double identity as an adventurous explorer and a Victorian woman. She also continues to caution her readers that Africa may not appeal to, or suit everyone. "The charm of West Africa is a painful one," she says in a lecture:

> It gives you pleasure to fall under it when you are out there, but when you are back here it gives you pain, by calling you. It sends up before your eyes a vision . . . and everything that is round you grows poor and thin in the face of that vision, and you want to go back to the Coast that is calling you, saying, as the African says to the departing soul of his dying friend, 'Come back, this is your home.' ("A Lecture on West Africa," cited in Blunt 131)

In the introduction to the *Travels* she mentions her "ability to be more comfortable there than in England" (*T* xxi), and a similar statement can be found in a passage in which she describes the forests of Africa:

> Unless you are interested in it and fall under its charm, it is the most awful life in death imaginable. It is like being shut up in a library whose books you cannot read, all the while tormented, terrified and bored. And if you do fall under its spell, it takes all the colour out of other kinds of living. (*T* 102)[22]

The Africa that Kingsley felt at home in and longed to return to does not produce the same effect for Alexander. Although Alexander expresses interest in place as an initial reason for travelling, there are perceptible differences in how she describes the area. Kingsley's repeated comments on how West Africa calls her back find no equivalents in Alexander's narrative, and the personality with which Kingsley endows the continent does not exist in the second journey. The lack of a personified area does

---

[21] In March the same year, Kingsley went to South Africa where she volunteered to nurse Boer prisoners of war. She contracted enteric fever there, which led to heart failure, and she died on the third of June, aged thirty-seven. She was buried at sea with full naval and military honours, off the coast of Simonstown.
[22] Lawrence observes that "Kingsley's rather conventional metaphor of Africa as unreadable text is offered as an alternative to the topos of seduction—unless a man [sic] is spellbound and seduced, he [sic] will feel as though he [sic] is imprisoned in a library, tormented by the totally opaque foreign text" (134).

more than illustrate the differences between the texts, it also signals Alexander's postcolonial perspective. West Africa is no longer 'available' for colonisation and conquest. Gabon is an autonomous part of the continent in which Alexander is a guest. In this she naturally stands in marked contrast to Kingsley's position as an advisor on how to manage the colony.

There is a sense of disappointment at the end of Alexander's book, an anticlimax, as she has not been able to find Kingsley in West Africa. Even in those instances where she has been able to retrace the actual route, she has not been able, as was her intention, no matter how impossible this intention might be, to repeat or verify Kingsley's experiences. The expectations aroused in the second traveller often remain unfulfilled, as Henderson has noted, precisely because the "texts tend to prevail over the material world of real places, real people: past sight dominates present site" (Henderson 230-31). This, as shown, is a fact that Alexander repeatedly comments on in the search for Kingsley's authentic experiences; she goes to great lengths to imitate the first journey only to discover that the previous narrative renders the second journey pale in comparison.

Henderson has further observed "the potential for disappointment is so great that it becomes virtually a convention of the genre itself," (235) which is especially poignant in this case. The colonial West Africa of the nineteenth century naturally no longer exists, and the hundred years of development have made the retracing of Kingsley's footsteps impossible. The comparisons carried out by the second traveller extend further than the tangible, concrete changes. Alexander has sought to 'find' Kingsley as she appears before her reader by her very style of writing; the "greatest revelation" of the book, as Alexander writes (*O* 5). Her expressed inability to achieve this goal may be partly due to the conventions of the genre with its great potential for disappointment, but also to the complex structure of Kingsley's identity as travel writer and public figure after the return to England. The problems with finding Kingsley only through her writing can be seen in relation to the presence of Robert Falcon Scott in the hut at Cape Evans and the framing of Robert Louis Stevenson in the public spaces of the museums. That is, Robert Swan, Roger Mear, and Nicholas Rankin all encounter places or sites containing tangible objects belonging to 'their' first travellers, and it is in these sites that moments of sometimes very intense recognitions occur. There is no equivalent 'Kingsley-site'.

Towards the end of her trip, Alexander visits Cape Esturias, an excursion which illustrates her awareness of potential disappointments and failures. In Cape Esturias, "now a holiday resort with a hotel and weekend bungalows," Alexander has difficulties locating the site; a Catholic church Kingsley visited after her trip to Corisco Island (*O* 267). Kingsley describes the church at the Roman Catholic Mission as "sweet and clean, giving evidence of the loving care with which it is tended" (*T* 422). When Alexander finds it, however, it is charred by fire and its remaining walls are covered with graffiti. Her disappointment is instant:

> I had embarked on this abbreviated version of Kingsley's trip with the awareness that the most I could expect was to see the same scenery as had Kingsley, but that I would have no approximation of her experience. Still, ... now I realized that I had after all looked forward to some kind of emotional climax. [. . .] [T]ry as I did I could make no connection; there was nothing evocative on this scorched and desecrated site, where even the view of the sea and western horizon was obscured by the overgrowth of grass. (*O* 270)

The awareness articulated here does not preclude the disappointment when points of contact between the two journeys cannot be established. Kingsley's 'sweet and clean' site is 'scorched and desecrated' and nature, growing and changing, works as a shield between the second traveller and the desired recognition.

The journey itself has illustrated the difficulties in recapturing experiences, but it has also led Alexander to reflect on the constructedness not only of text but also of memories. At the end of the chapter outlining her excursion to Samba Falls she makes the following reflection:

> How, I wonder, in years to come, might I tell the story of my little expedition? Already, Fougamou's row of desolate houses has subsided into the mental landscape of other nameless villages, and my initial depression has been virtually forgotten. The route to Samba Falls, as I choose to recall it, leads one deep into primeval forest, through the palatial grandeur of a bamboo grove, past a deserted mission and haunted valley, and by pirogue down a silent river channel. Samba is first glimpsed across a broad expanse of fast-flowing, dangerous water, perilously approached at risk of life, and beheld at last through spray and mist and jungle creepers: the scene is tinged with the green shade of the forest, and there is no noise for miles around save the thunder of its falling waters. (*O* 108)

One retelling of the memories is already accomplished; found on the pages which precede this reflection. In that section, Alexander has been forthcoming with her experiences of disappointment and vulnerability and, despite one fleeting contact with Kingsley's past, the excursion has not had the desired result. But this is not the only version of events, Alexander suggests. Time will cause her to improve the memory, remove unwanted obstacles and create a very different story. It becomes a matter of how one "chooses to recall" experiences and how one elects to represent them, in writing, to oneself or relating them to others. In the version Alexander chooses, the disappointments fade away, and Samba Falls retains the magic they had when she first came across the name.

The reflection illustrates Alexander's overall, final conclusion to her second journey project: that finding Kingsley in West Africa is an impossibility. Despite the 'undateable' landscape and the close emulations of details of her trip, the essence of Kingsley is not there, because it was never there. Just as Alexander's representation is a construction (of memories, of the textual persona), so is Kingsley's. The sparkle in Kingsley's voice is not necessarily extinguished by this realisation, but it needs to be heard with an eye, or an ear in this case, to the fact that it is a textual construct. Kingsley's initial encouragement to the reader, "if you go there you will find things as I have said," pertains to the realities she outlined in her text, not the emotional responses to them. The accommodated paraphrase "if you go there you will find things as *we* have said" (*O* 283, original italics), with which Alexander captions her experiences, must then be read against this background and with the awareness that memories and representations are chosen among many.

Chapter Six. The Biographical Journey: On Stevenson's Trail

A voyage is a piece of autobiography at best.
Robert Louis Stevenson, *Travels with a Donkey in the Cevennes*

Before defining the biographical form of the second journey in greater detail, it needs to be stressed that all second journeys, to a certain extent, are biographical projects, and contain autobiographical elements as well. Robert Falcon Scott's background and the circumstances surrounding his journey are explored by Robert Swan and Roger Mear, and Caroline Alexander's journey following Mary Kingsley includes discussions of biographical facts and Kingsley's situation as a solitary, female traveller, unusual at the time. The biographical feature is, however, more prominent in this third form.

The second journeys in the footsteps of Kingsley and Scott focus on one first text, on one defined period in the first travellers' lives, whereas Nicholas Rankin in *Dead Man's Chest: Travels after Robert Louis Stevenson* (1987) concentrates on a life quest that starts at the birthplace of the first traveller and ends at Stevenson's grave. The biographical project aims to present the time period in which the first traveller lived, but also includes anecdotes and commentary of a more peripheral nature. This second traveller extensively uses secondary sources, such as letters and memoirs written by others, in order to give a more nuanced image of the first traveller. The aim of the biographical second journey is to comprehensively illuminate the first traveller's whole life by a contemporary journey in his or her footsteps. This biographical text illustrates yet another form within the second journey genre.

Although *Dead Man's Chest* is an official project as Rankin is "asked ... to go off and write about the travels of RLS"[1] his interest in Stevenson coincides with a meeting with Jorge Louis Borges. In the prologue to the book, Rankin brings Stevenson's *Fables* to read to Borges. The choice of reading material is influenced by the Argentine author's 1960 essay "Borges and I" in which he states that he "like[s] hourglasses, maps, eighteenth century typography, the roots of words, the taste of coffee and the prose of Stevenson"(Borges 246) As Rankin parts with Borges he is given "a small pockmarked pinkish stone from an ancient city [. . .] [a] touchstone," and he remembers this gift as he sets out on Stevenson's trail, the *Fable* ending with the words "I will go forth into the world with my pebble in my pocket"(*D* 5).

The life and writings of Robert Louis Stevenson have proved to be treasure troves for several second travellers, as well as for more traditional biographers.[2] A reason for this may be that Stevenson himself was a highly autobiographical writer; that is, there is a wealth of material by and about him which makes him a well suited, though challenging, subject for biographies. Ian Bell observes that "[h]is own life fascinated him, and he returned to it time and again in essays, poems, stories, and letters like a dog to a beloved bone. It is an odd sensation to realise that the reader over your shoulder is your subject" (xx-xxi). Rankin mentions these autobiographical qualities as reasons why some of Stevenson's texts have attracted so many readers. "The traveller," he says, "is often the true subject . . . and is of more interest to us than the terrain."(*D* 116) There is, then, a wealth of material to choose from concerning Stevenson, which may in part account for the numerous biographies already written about him.

Further, Stevenson's life is greatly suited for second journey emulations. He travelled extensively throughout his life to find a climate that would improve his health, and he wrote about most of his journeys. His family took summer vacations in his childhood to the European continent; he went alone to England and France. He followed Fanny

---

[1] Nicholas Rankin, *Dead Man's Chest: Travels after Robert Louis Stevenson* 5. All further references to this primary source will be given within brackets in the text, preceded by the letter *D*.

[2] As examples of the multitude of Stevenson biographies can be mentioned Joseph Chamberlain Furnas' *Voyage to Windward* (1952) and Jenni Calder's *Robert Louis Stevenson: A Life Study* (1980).

Vandegrift to California, returned to Scotland, went to France again, convalesced at Lake Saranac, returned to California and travelled from there to the Pacific Islands. Rankin comments on Stevenson's entire literary production, but I will concentrate on the discussions that concern the travel narratives, most notably *An Inland Voyage* (1878), *Travels with a Donkey in the Cevennes* (1879), *From the Clyde to California* (1985)[3] and *In the South Seas* (1900).

Although Rankin's text remains central to my discussion, I have included discussions concerning other similar texts, that is other second journeys, to give an idea of Stevenson's allure to biographers and, indeed, to second travellers. Works similar to Rankin's—or works originating in the same idea—both precede and follow his text. In celebration of the hundredth anniversary of Stevenson's death, for example, biographer Hunter Davies travels in Stevenson's footsteps in an attempt "to catch glimpses of him by visiting places associated with him in the past." Davies quickly realises, however, that others, too, have thought of the same project:

> Here is one by a certain Laura Stubbs called *Stevenson's Shrine* [...]. So, I am ninety years late in thinking of that angle, though she did only go to Samoa, not to the other sites. But here is a 1915 volume called *On the Trail of Stevenson*, by an American, Clayton Hamilton. [. . .] Hamilton did visit the sites in Edinburgh, England, Belgium and France—but not Samoa. (ix-x)

The quotation evidences that second journeys in the footsteps of Stevenson are numerous, but also, with a few exceptions,[4] projects dating back several years. This is interesting because second journeys otherwise predominantly take shape towards the end of the twentieth century. Stevenson's prolific travelling is of course perfectly suited for second journeys, and Rankin's journey in 1984 includes a multitude of comparisons, taking into account the century that has elapsed between the travels.

---

[3] *From the Clyde to California* is a text compiling *The Amateur Emigrant* (posthumously published in 1895) and *Across the Plains* (1892).

[4] Most notable among these exceptions are Richard Holmes' 1985 *Footsteps: Adventures of a Romantic Biographer* which will be discussed later, and Gavin Bell's 1995 *In Search of Tusitala: Travels in the Pacific After Robert Louis Stevenson*. Both journeys focus on clearly delineated periods of Stevenson's life; his trip across the Cévennes and his time in the Pacific, respectively.

In an effort to bring something new to *his* narrative, Davies lets each biographical chapter be followed by a contemporary description of places. The form of the biographical chapters—letters addressed to 'Dear Louis'—strives to signal a more intimate relationship between the biographer and his subject. This strategy may seem far-fetched as a device to distinguish this book from others like it, and many of the observations Davies makes are anticipated in Rankin's book, which makes *The Teller of Tales* slightly redundant.

This case study centres on issues connected to biography writing, autobiographical elements within biography writing, and on how second journeys can be seen as offering new options within the genre of biography. Authenticity is problematised within biography writing as such and will be analysed from this perspective. Stevenson's romantic notions about travelling, but also the clashes with reality that follow will be analysed and seen in relation to Rankin's views and experiences, and to how his romantic ideas about his second journey produce disappointments and feelings of failure. Discussions of *Travels with a Donkey in the Cevennes* and *From the Clyde to California* are especially important in this context, as they represent very different approaches to travel. The former is marked by romanticised notions about solitude and adventure. The route through the Cévennes, a remote and, in Stevenson's view, romantic destination, has been made accessible to, and marketed for, contemporary tourists and this has had consequences for the authenticity of the second journey project. Rankin does not undertake this journey, but Richard Holmes' second journey *Footsteps: Adventures of a Romantic Biographer* offers an alternative discussion to analyse. Stevenson's emigrant journey, finally, as well as his destination, illustrates powerful clashes between his expectations and reality, something that causes problems for Rankin.

There are tensions in Rankin's text between what he perceives as 'lively' ways of remembering and the static collections of memorabilia he comes across, and notions of heritage, tourist attractions, museums and contemporary developments in California and the Pacific come into play. The lively ways of remembering are by Rankin seen as authentic representations of Stevenson, while many of the museums and memorabilia collections are regarded as 'fake.' In this context, the second journey becomes a kind of evolving, moving museum. The tension between the second journey and public spaces like museums and tourist attractions, and what this public quality does to the desired authenticity will also be discussed.

BIOGRAPHY AND AUTHENTICITY

The notion of authenticity, so prominent yet so problematic to second travellers, has continuously been discussed within biography writing, and questions about the 'invention' of truth have been raised. In an illuminating essay, Holmes outlines four problematic areas: ethics, authenticity, celebrity and empathy. The first issue concerns what is permissible to write, where to draw the line. This is an increasingly problematic area in contemporary culture, where the boundaries between public and private life, between fact and fiction, are shifting. *If* a line is drawn, what happens to what is perceived as the 'truth'? Authenticity is problematised by the fact that the sources biographers rely on, such as memoirs, letters, journals or personal interviews with family members and friends, can be seen as unreliable since they include elements that are "reinvented" or even "fictional" (Holmes, "Biography" 17). The issue of celebrity concerns the fact that the art of biography is always slanted, aimed as it is towards major figures in history, avoiding the mundane or the ordinary. The final problem area is similarly slanted. "Why is a biographer drawn to particular subjects, what element of suppressed autobiography is involved, and how does this affect the possibilities of an 'objectively' truthful account?" Holmes asks ("Biography" 19). In Rankin's case, his admiration for Stevenson is apparent and the insertion of autobiographical material in a second journey is naturalised since the second traveller is present in the text, being the journeying subject. The second traveller is allowed to foreground his or her own experiences, since this is part of the project. The second journey, therefore, is not, indeed cannot be, objective.

There are, thus, two sides of auto/biography that are difficult to reconcile in more traditional forms of biography writing. Jürgen Schlaeger notes:

> Autobiographers have to be true to themselves and true to the image they would like to present to the public or to posterity. Very often these two

> obligations are extremely difficult to reconcile. The persuasiveness of the result almost wholly depends on the authenticity and authority of the self that speaks. Biography, on the other hand is a discourse of *usurpation*. The truth-criterion does not consist in the authenticity of an inside view but in the consistency of the narrative and the explanatory power of the arguments. (59, emphasis added)

Biography and autobiography are similarly considered to be non-fiction, but autobiography is, however naïvely, considered to possess greater authority because of the inside, first-hand view.[5] This is problematised by the inherent difficulty of being objective about oneself. An interesting possibility is opened up, however, by autobiography's greater authority, in that the insertion of autobiographical material may lend greater authority also to the biographical element.

The second journey offers an opportunity to avoid this clash between opposing forces. The second traveller's aim in the biographical second journey is to attempt a new take on a traditional genre, and it is accomplished by using the contemporary, second journey as a narrative vehicle. The consistency of the narrative required of successful biography writing is accomplished through the natural progression of the journey. That is, the author does not have to labour to create a convincing narrative structure for the biographical project; the consistency is rather provided by the second journey's progression. This movement is then authenticated through the second traveller's physical presence at the destinations described. There is no question that the 'self' should be absent; if this was the case, the contemporary journey could not be narrated. The second texts' 'selves,' the autobiographical 'I's,' are writing within a tradition—the travel genre—in which fears, misgivings and disappointments from being virtually non-existent in the earlier forms are becoming norms. The expressions of these feelings lend authenticity (if not what has traditionally been seen as authority) to the material. The second journey form can thus be viewed as an option for biography-writers, since they do not have to struggle to cover or hide themselves in the text. The second journey becomes, in effect, a natural combination of biography and autobiography. The "usurpation" mentioned as defining biography writing (Schlaeger 59) may also be seen in less invasive terms since the first

---

[5] For a discussion about authority within autobiography studies, see Thomas Couser, "Authority" 34-47.

travellers' life and journey(s) are seen as intertexts rather than as sole points of interest, as in more traditional forms of biography.[6]

Holmes has theorised about biography writing, but he has also written a number of biographies. In his acclaimed *Footsteps*, his musings are all the more pertinent to this case study, since one chapter is devoted to his 1964 journey across the Cévennes, following Stevenson's *Travels with a Donkey*. Holmes' trip is not originally meant to result in a Stevenson biography, but as his journal is formed "one totally unforeseen thing" occurs: "the growth of a friendship with Stevenson" (*Footsteps* 66). He designates this friendship and at times even identification with Stevenson as "an essential motive for following in the footsteps, for attempting to re-create the pathway, the journey, of someone else's life through the physical past" (*Footsteps* 67). The stress on the physical movement within biography writing thus makes the second journey seem like a natural option for Holmes. The growing relationship between biographer and subject is not unproblematic, however, and Holmes describes the process with words such as "trespass," "invasion," and "haunting," (*Footsteps* 66) connecting to the previous definition of biography as "a discourse of usurpation" (Schlaeger 59).

The one-sided intrusion into Stevenson's life then gradually gives way to a feeling of mutuality, as the past is perceived as beginning to influence the present. This process forms the basis of Holmes' idea of what biography is: "a continuous living dialogue between the two [biographer and subject] as they move over the same historical ground, the same trail of events" (*Footsteps* 66). For Holmes, this initiation to biography means that he comes to see it as "a kind of pursuit, a tracking of the physical trail of someone's path through the past, a following of footsteps" (*Footsteps* 27). That is, a physical movement rather than merely a gathering of facts and the writing of the book. To catch the subject of the quest is difficult, he argues, but "if you were lucky, you might write about the *pursuit* of that fleeting figure in such a way as to bring it alive in the present" (*Footsteps* 27, emphasis added). He consequently argues that capturing a figure frozen in a specific time is impossible. It is by moving along the same

---

[6] Stevenson's fictional writings, as well as all anecdotes and stories that Rankin finds interesting, are discussed without notes or references. The quotations are left unexplained and he leaves only a small bibliography, thereby fusing all Stevenson's writings into one.

path, by trying to experience similar things, and by writing about this very movement, that a connection between the first and the second traveller can be established. He continues:

> The past does retain a physical presence for the biographer—in landscapes, buildings, photographs, and above all the actual trace of handwriting on original letters or journals. [. . .] But this physical presence is none the less extremely deceptive. The material surfaces of life are continually breaking down, sloughing off, changing, almost as fast as human skin. A building is restored, a bridge is rebuilt or replaced, a road is widened or rerouted, a forest is cut down, a wooded hill is built over, a village green becomes a town centre. (*Footsteps* 67-68)

As Holmes moves across the same ground, the instability, not only of the surroundings but also of the subject, becomes clear. Although he emphasises the fact that the pursuit may be difficult and the subject illusory and unwilling to let itself be caught, he announces his objective to be "to produce the living effect" (*Footsteps* 27). This is an interesting choice of words, and I will return to Holmes' image of the vivid subject when discussing Rankin's view of successful representations of Stevenson. However, Holmes' conclusion is less clear-cut than is suggested by the quotation. "There was no way of following him, no way of meeting him," he notes when discovering that a new bridge has replaced the old one Stevenson used. However self-evident this impossibility is, Holmes' disappointment is so great that it puts him "in the blackest gloom" (*Footsteps* 26).

Travels

Throughout his life, due to incessant illness, Stevenson was continuously moving, seeking a climate or a place that would improve his health. As Ian Bell puts it, "[s]ickness shaped Stevenson, formed his emotions, scented his art, and obliged him to acquire the habit, willing though he was, of travel" (xvii). Aside from journeys in and around the coast of Scotland in his childhood, his family took several trips to England, and to the European continent. He travelled alone to London when he came of age and returned repeatedly to France. Two of these journeys resulted in travelogues, *An Inland Voyage*, which became his first published book, and *Travels with a Donkey in the Cevennes*. These two journeys, the first a canoe-trip with his friend Walter Simpson on the canals along the

Belgian-French border, the second a solitary journey across a remote area in France, correspond well to Stevenson's romantic notions about travel. Destinations are also marked by this romantic view, as can be seen in Stevenson's view of what was to become his family's last home, the Pacific Islands. The journey to the 'exotic' Pacific is described as a romantic adventure in Stevenson's *In the South Seas*. Although he had ideas and dreams about what the islands would be like, they "touched a virginity of sense" in him, they were places he had read and heard about but never visited (Stevenson, *RLS in the South Seas: An Intimate Photographic Record* 36). This notion of a place as 'new,' as appealing to senses hitherto 'unused,' is an illustration of Stevenson's desire to get off the beaten track; and the rumours of cannibalism among the islanders correspond to his longing for adventure. The ideas of novelty and adventure are combined in *Travels with a Donkey*, where he equates solitude and originality with adventure. This is an equation that surfaces also in Rankin's text.

Rankin observes that "[p]artly because of its distance, partly because of its exotic and fragmentarily reported cultures, the Pacific has been seen as a 'romantic' place by Europeans" (*D* 241). This is a view that persists in the contemporary commodification of the destinations, catering to the tourist industry. Stevenson had heard about the Pacific since childhood, building up a desire to go there. These stories and reports were naturally influenced by the colonial, political climate, and did not accurately reflect the destinations. Stevenson's romanticised notion about the Other, about the 'foreign' and the 'exotic' were to alter and change during the time he actually spent in the Pacific. This serves to illustrate yet again that earlier narratives, be they letters, newspaper reports or stories, influence also the first journeys, creating, in the mind of the traveller, an image of what the destination will be like. As is the case with second travellers, the image is then modified in the meeting with reality. Although Stevenson's later writings, then, to a certain extent, contradict the romanticised notions he has had of the Pacific Islands, Rankin is influenced by the past images of Stevenson's, and becomes disillusioned and disappointed when they are proven false.

Rankin's journey in Stevenson's footsteps starts, predictably, in Stevenson's native Edinburgh, reached from London by railway on the Intercity Nightrider. The trip is advertised with emphasis on the notion of romance, the poster projecting an image of a highwayman in front of a starlit sky and a castle. "The reality was grimy sit-up carriages of single men and plural beer-cans," Rankin writes, "but the advertisement wrapped it in a purple cloak of bogus adventure, equating Travel with Romance" (*D* 6). This is a Stevensonian equation as well, and therefore fitting for the first in a long series of journeys, and the "grimy" reality of the railway trip does little to modify Rankin's view of Edinburgh. The romantic notion Rankin has of the city influences his perceptions of it, and he expresses recognition at many of the places described in Stevenson's fiction.

Despite the absence of statues, or streets named after Stevenson, there is no doubt that Edinburgh is his honoured hometown. Reconstructions of Stevenson's old homes are under way and there is a Robert Louis Stevenson Heritage Trail winding its way through the streets. "[A] tourist package," Rankin argues, "but also proof of RLS's enduring popularity" (*D* 14). While the public nature of destinations on the Stevenson Trail seems to undermine their authenticity, they still work to ensure Stevenson's enduring popularity and the balance between exclusivity and popularity is central in Rankin's text. Similar to the trail, Rankin's project aims to re-introduce Stevenson and keep the interest in him alive. In this sense, while criticising the inauthenticity of the tourist package, Rankin too helps popularise Stevenson.

Mrs McFie, the contemporary inhabitant of 19 Heriot Row, where Stevenson grew up, "loved the man," Rankin writes, "and living in his home gave her responsibilities" (*D* 15). The house is still considered to be Stevenson's; keeping it as a private home prevents it from "degenerat[ing] into offices, or becom[ing] an arid museum" (*D* 15). That is, by preserving the house but using it as it was intended to be used—as a home rather than an "arid" frame for Stevenson—Mrs McFie and Rankin view it as a more vivid representation of Stevenson's childhood. The house is also perceived as still holding some of Stevenson's spirit, and Mrs McFie, being sympathetic to Rankin's need to travel in Stevenson's footsteps says: "'If you're going to all those places,' . . . 'you really must spend a night in this house'" (*D* 16).[7] By spending two nights in a room that used to belong to Stevenson's nurse, Rankin thus gets what he and his hostess perceive as the appropriate start on his journey.

In contrast to Heriot Row, preserved as it is thought to have been in Stevenson's childhood, other places along the Robert Louis Stevenson Heritage Trail have undergone changes that in some instances make them unrecognisable. It is only the notice boards connected to the Trail itself, which signpost them as significant for the traveller or literary tourist. There are also some sites which are not marked on the Trail, but noticeable and recognised only by a traveller, such as Rankin, with further knowledge of Stevenson's background and literary production. In this first chapter, the issue of context surfaces as Rankin describes the return to beginnings, to Stevenson's childhood home and to places he visited and described in a melancholy tone. Rankin draws attention to the problem of drawing too far-fetched or too simplistic conclusions about the author whose work(s) the second journey concentrates on. The situating of each traveller into his or her contemporary historical, cultural and personal context is crucial to the re-rendering of the first journey. Rankin seems to be acutely aware of this.

During his visit to Colinton he ponders over the garden in which Stevenson used to play as a young boy. Rankin is looking for tangible proof of Stevenson's physical existence in that garden; initials carved in a wall or even a toy. He concludes, however, that this is "an absurdly literal quest" (*D* 31) and is helped to this conclusion by Stevenson himself as in the last poem in *A Child's Garden of Verses*, Stevenson emphasises the fact that the bodies and souls of long gone people are irretrievably lost. Stevenson shares Rankin's wish to communicate with the memory of the imagined person, but expresses the futility of such a wish, even if the circumstances of the setting and the milieu provide the emotionally 'correct' context. Stevenson writes of someone looking out "[t]hrough the windows of this book" and who is trying to see a child out there.

> But do not think you can at all,
> By knocking on the window, call

---

[7] When Davies visits, a decade later, he too is invited to "stay the night, to get the real atmosphere" by Mrs McFie, by now Lady Dunpark (Davies 44).

> That child to hear you. He intent
> Is all on his play-business bent.
> He does not hear; he will not look,
> Nor yet be lured out of this book.
> For, long ago, the truth to say,
> He has grown up and gone away,
> And it is but a child of air
> That lingers in the garden there
> (Stevenson, "To Any Reader," *A Child's Garden of Verses* 125)

Being physically present in the surroundings and having Stevenson's texts at hand, Rankin is reminded of things that inspired Stevenson, but what he hoped to see, hoped to recognise from Stevenson's writings, has changed. Although realising that this is inevitable, it produces a sense of disappointment. Jacinta Matos observes that Rankin "is aware that there is no direct access to the past, nor an empirically restorable 'reality,' but only . . . encoded configurations of it" (225). I concur with the view that Rankin is aware of the formulaic ramifications of the second journey, but he nevertheless, with some surprise, returns to this specific kind of disappointment repeatedly in *Dead Man's Chest*.

Most of the things Stevenson saw and described in France, following the narrative in *An Inland Voyage*, have also changed—for the worse, is the impression left by Rankin. Away from the cities, however, features of the landscape are less dateable, and it is again possible to feel the desired connection with the past. Rankin describes paths in the forest as "winding into a denser green world unchanged from when Stevenson described it." He concludes that "[d]eep in a European hardwood forest, it is still easy to forget where you are and what century you are in" (*D* 90). France, or at least parts of France, offers an atmosphere closer to Stevenson's descriptions than Edinburgh does. Although buildings Stevenson described have long gone, some features, some constructions, are still left, leaving the impression in the mind of the second traveller that the past can somehow be captured. "[Y]ou can walk over the bridge that generations of art-students . . . have painted, and sit on a bench in the willow-hung park on the opposite bank, to look back over the same flowing river" (*D* 97) Rankin says of Grez. He follows in Simpson's and Stevenson's wake to Mauberge and goes paddling along the same stretch of the river as they did. "At Landrecies, the weather hadn't changed in 108 years," he states. "The rain was 'simply bedlamite' for Simpson and Stevenson too" (*D* 106). This may seem a naïve strategy to establish a connection between first and second journey, but the fact remains that it is in solitude, away from 'civilisation' reminding him of where and indeed *when* he is, that Rankin's emulation of the first journey, to him, is most successful. External things, in this case the rain, help the authenticating process, and the experience is exclusively Rankin's. This can then be contrasted to the disappointment and feelings of failure he experiences in more public spaces devoted to Stevenson's memory, which will be discussed later.

An Inland Voyage was written at a time in Stevenson's life when he had met and fallen in love with Fanny Vandegrift[8] (then going under her married name of Osbourne). The couple had several obstacles to face. Fanny was married in California, she was ten years Stevenson's senior, which made his parents suspicious, and she had two children. Stevenson's travelogue is marked by worries about the situation, but nevertheless ends on a more hopeful note. Rankin has also noted this and ends this section of his text as follows. "I felt oppressed by war and rain and took the train back, in search of Fanny Osbourne and the love with which RLS ended his book" (*D* 111).[9] But back in Paris, Rankin is hard pressed to find the romance that coloured this part of Stevenson's and Fanny's lives, since the area in which they stayed is situated below what is today the red-light district of the Place Pigalle.

Travels with a Donkey in the Cevennes

In September 1878, Stevenson returned to France, to the Cévennes region, to traverse the mountain range accompanied only by a donkey. His twelve-day trip took him across some of the most remote places of the area and he also climbed two of the mountaintops of the range. The journey has been seen partly as an attempt on Stevenson's part to break free from his family. It also contains many reflections on the religious doubts and oppositions that echo Stevenson's own mixed feelings on the subject. By this time, Fanny had returned to California, and Stevenson's

---

[8] Fanny's last name is given alternately as Vandergrift, Van de Grift or Van der Grift. My use of the former is based on Rankin's use

[9] The final paragraph of Stevenson's text, what Rankin terms as a hopeful note, reads as follows: "You may paddle all day long; but it is when you come back at nightfall, and look in at the familiar room, that you find Love or Death awaiting you beside the stove; and the most beautiful adventures are not those we go to seek" (Stevenson, *An Inland Voyage* 178).

worries about this, his uncertainty about a future with her, have also been read into the narrative.[10] In addition to the hopelessness this situation suggests, Stevenson's parents' objections to the alliance troubled him. These are all issues that have been taken into consideration in discussions of *Travels with a Donkey*. Stevenson's loneliness and existential doubts give the impression of an initiation and the depth this lends to the narrative may in part account for the popularity the book enjoyed.

The past and continuous popularity of the travelogue leads Rankin to dismiss the opportunity to retrace it. Not only are there "[t]oo many people [who] have already followed RLS and his mouse-coloured donkey," there are, in Rankin's view, also too many arm-chair travellers with knowledge of the text who preclude the need to retell events again. Add to this a more clear-cut marketing towards tourists following hundred-year anniversary of the travelogue's publication in 1978, in which both French and Scottish tourist boards were involved in marking the route and publishing a 'bilingual French-English edition: *Sur les traces de STEVENSON—topoguide de l'itinéraire/In Stevenson's footsteps—a guide to his journey*'" (*D* 115, original italics). All these aspects combined make this leg of the journey less authentic in Rankin's view; a problematisation of authenticity which persists in his later discussions about museums. The view echoes Stevenson's romanticised notions of being first. In this section, Rankin is clearly distanced from the text—quite naturally so, since he himself is not travelling, and comments, instead, on Stevenson's ideas about travelling and on how his narrative style developed and matured into a distinct authorial voice.

I will instead turn to Holmes' second journey along Stevenson's route in the Cévennes, carried out in 1964, but published as a text in 1985. A few instances of this journey where Holmes hopes to 'meet' Stevenson and the disappointment with which he reacts when this proves to be impossible have previously been discussed. It should be noted, however, that although Holmes' text has clearly defined biographical aims it differs

---

[10] The book is introduced with a letter addressed to Sidney Colvin, Stevenson's friend and benefactor which has been taken as another indication of the fact that the text is highly autobiographical. "Every book is, in an intimate sense, a circular letter to the friends of him who writes it. They alone take his meaning; they find private messages, assurances of love, and expressions of gratitude, dropped for them in every corner" (Stevenson, *Travels with a Donkey in the Cevennes* xiii).

significantly from Rankin's work. It traces one journey only and is not a project charting the subject's whole life. In this sense it offers a variation on the biographical form of the second journey as I have defined it.

Romantic aspirations and romanticised notions of solitary travelling are visible already when Stevenson chose the Cévennes as a destination. This choice has puzzled several later critics, but it seems as if Stevenson, at this point, has a desire to travel off the beaten track. Almost proudly, he asserts that "[a] traveller of my sort was a thing hitherto unheard of in that district" (*Travels with a Donkey* 4). Perhaps as a result of this novelty, the people he meets are helpful, curious and interested in the traveller. The very idea of novelty, of being first, is also connected to adventure, the lack of which Stevenson laments. "I have been after an adventure all my life, a pure dispassionate adventure, such as befell early and heroic voyagers," he writes, as he wakes up after a mild storm, alone in the woods of Gévaudan. He is disoriented; "an inland castaway" and sees in this state "a fraction of [his] day-dreams realised" (*Travels with a Donkey* 50).

A sense of danger, however vague, and of physical exertion also serves as a distraction from the problems previously occupying Stevenson's mind. He expresses this idea in one of the most famous passages of the text, which illustrates the romanticised image he has of travel, of solitude and of adventure:

> The great affair is to move; to feel the needs and hitches of our life more nearly; to come down off this feather-bed of civilisation, and find the globe granite underfoot and strewn with cutting flints. Alas, as we get up in life, and are more preoccupied with our affairs, even a holiday is a thing that must be worked for. To hold a pack upon a pack-saddle against a gale out of the freezing north is no high industry, but it is one that serves to occupy and compose the mind. And when the present is so exacting, who can annoy himself about the future? (*Travels with a Donkey* 57)

This is a fairly traditional view of what travel ought to be; a contrast to the comforts of 'civilisation' which makes the subject aware of the realities of life and the joys and challenges of seemingly simple tasks. Stevenson formulates this ideal view of journeying in his solitary and "castaway" state, in 'uncivilised' nature, and the last sentence in the quotation can easily be interpreted as a comment on his personal concerns at the time.

For Holmes, travelling through the region in 1964, few things seem to have changed. His journey takes place before the transformations of the area into a tourist destination which Rankin laments. Roads following Stevenson's itinerary have not been built and it is possible for Holmes to undertake a solitary journey through a mostly uninhabited landscape. The people in Le Monastier, where Holmes' journey starts, strive to heighten the similarities between first and second journey but their attempts to persuade Holmes to rent a donkey are in vain. "The reality of Stevenson's presence in Le Monastier was uncanny. I asserted myself rather desperately. 'No, no, I do not desire a donkey. My companion of the route—is Monsieur Stevenson himself!'" (Holmes *Footsteps* 17).[11] This is an early formulation of Holmes' expressed desire to 'meet' Stevenson, to travel *with* him, to establish points of contact between his present and Stevenson's past. Nevertheless, he excludes the possibility of a more concrete emulation of Stevenson's journey—the company of the donkey.

A comparatively large part of Stevenson's narrative centres on his visit to the Trappist monastery of Our Lady of the Snows where he spends a pleasant evening. He cannot, however, support the monks' religious beliefs, which leads him to conclude: "And I blessed God that I was free to wander, free to hope, and free to love" (Stevenson *Travels with a Donkey* 81). Holmes, educated in Roman Catholic boarding schools, voices a similar desire. "Free thought, free travel, free love was what I wanted" (*Footsteps* 15). At the monastery, however, much has happened:

> The original buildings which Stevenson saw had been burnt down in 1912. His small guest wing for travellers and retreat-makers had been replaced by a brightly painted café-reception house astride the main drive, constructed as a Swiss chalet, with a self-service food bar and souvenir counter. (*Footsteps* 34)

These changes leave Holmes "dazed with disappointment," (*Footsteps* 34) most likely because this is such an important part of Stevenson's narrative. The quiet atmosphere, which enables Stevenson to find the time

---

[11] Considering Stevenson's trouble with his donkey Modestine, it is no wonder that Holmes opts to travel without a beast of burden. Readers have objected to Stevenson's treatment of Modestine; one of the more well known examples of her species. There are accounts of how Modestine's pace slows more and more, and how Stevenson, despite the fact that it is not in his nature to lay his "hand rudely on a female" has to resort to beating her to make her move faster or to move at all (*Travels with a Donkey* 13). Even Stevenson's contemporary critics have commented on his maltreatment of Modestine, one saying that "I must confess that I should have liked Mr. Stevenson better if he had beaten his donkey less unmercifully" (Allen xxvi, cited in Maixner, ed., 66).

to formulate himself, is difficult to find among wine-selling monks, tourists and souvenirs.

The brief stay at the monastery seems to Stevenson as an experience far removed from life outside and the narrative changes when he re-enters the 'world.' Being surrounded by people again, he retreats into recounting the history of the area. Holmes remarks that:

> The original journal becomes brief, disjointed, dreamlike and in places highly emotional. Though he travels with increasing speed and purpose he is sunk in his own thoughts, physically driving himself—and Modestine—towards the point of exhaustion. As I followed him, I was aware of a man possessed, shut in on himself, more and more difficult to make contact with. (*Footsteps* 49)

The difficulty of reaching Stevenson is underlined by the evasive nature of the first text and the distance between first and second traveller becomes apparent. Interestingly, Holmes has also gradually disappeared from his text. What started out as a highly personal account of his trip and his initiation to biography has become a more distanced retelling of the earlier journey. Instead of reporting on his own experiences, he concentrates on Stevenson, and speculates about possible influences and developments. The emotional turmoil Stevenson went through is, naturally, impossible to evoke in the second traveller, and the way Stevenson is trying to mask these feelings in his writing also puts a distance between the first and the second traveller. When Fanny enters the story, or, rather, when Holmes 'discovers' her in Stevenson's prose, the text is even further removed from the actual movement and the personal experiences. As she is not physically present in either journey, Holmes momentarily moves his narrative (but not himself) to California. This part of Holmes' text is thus markedly different from the rest of the narrative, which is more closely connected to the actual, physical movement and the second traveller's own experiences.

The last day in Saint Germaine de Calberte is marked by the re-emergence into civilisation. Stevenson's text becomes hurried—he is nearing the end of his journey and he is impatient for news from Fanny. "[P]erhaps it was not the place alone that so disposed my spirit. Perhaps some one was thinking of me in another country," he writes (*Travels with a Donkey* 168). At the same place, Holmes "immediately [feels] alone" he states, because

> Stevenson had departed. I cooked my last coffee with strange sensations of mixed relief and abandonment. Then as I packed up my rucksack a wild happiness filled me, and a sense of achievement. I had done it, I had followed him, I had made a mark. (*Footsteps* 63)

However vague and unexplained Holmes leaves this 'mark', the authentication process is completed as far as he is concerned. He has travelled in Stevenson's footsteps and seen many of the things Stevenson saw. He has occasionally been disappointed and realised some of the inherent impossibilities of the project, that is, to actually 'meet' Stevenson, but as Stevenson 'departs' it is also clear to Holmes that he *has* been there. There is of course a difference between Stevenson's actual presence and a presence in a more figurative sense, but Holmes does not expressly make this distinction. *Footsteps* is, in its entirety, as much a comment on a highly personal form of biography writing as it is an actual biography. Holmes' expressed desire to "produce the living effect" (*Footsteps* 27) repeatedly makes him use terms like 'meet,' 'depart,' and 'see' as if the subject he is discussing is actually there.[12]

The perceived continued existence of Holmes' subject does not only exist in his text. In 1964, the imprint Stevenson left on the area he travelled through is still there. People still talk about him, many are aware of where and how he travelled, and Holmes feels a sting of belatedness when he hears stories of people who have already undertaken the journey in Stevenson's fashion. The Trappist monks, Holmes notes, "knew all about Stevenson when I passed through: a hundred years, they told me, is not so long in the eyes of eternity" (*Footsteps* 34). The belatedness is emphasised by roads that have been overgrown, landmarks that have withered away and trees that have been cut down as 'civilisation' has come closer. Some later changes are less obvious, and Holmes observes that

> [t]he well-meaning attempt to conserve or recover the past can be more subtly destructive. Since the centenary of Stevenson's *Travels* I am told the whole route has been marked out . . . with a series of blazed stakes which

---

[12] *Footsteps* consists of four biographies of which Stevenson is the subject of the first. The subsequent chapters deal with Mary Wollstonecraft, Percy Bysshe Shelley and Gèrard de Nerval.

lead the pilgrim from one picturesque *point de vue* to the next, and bring him [sic] safely down each evening to some recommended hotel, Carte Touristique, hot bath, and Souvenirs Cévenols. I have not had the heart to go back and see. (*Footsteps* 68)[13]

This is written close to the publication of *Footsteps* in 1985, making it virtually simultaneous to Rankin's text. A return to this area, now that it has been made accessible to contemporary tourists, seems unnecessary both to Rankin and to Holmes. By the transformation of the area into what is perceived as a more public space, the desired authenticity of the kind that is connected with remoteness, with establishing a connection not readily accessible to others, vanishes. The transformation, the marketing of the itinerary, makes the emulation difficult in several ways. The idea is not to have the route marked out, since Stevenson's was not, nor to stay at hotels, since Stevenson camped out. Neither should points of view be signposted. Stevenson's articulated idea of what true travelling should be, his views on adventure and his uncertainty about where to stay the night, are thus transformed into a neatly packaged and marketed tourist-trip, far removed from the first journey.

FROM THE CLYDE TO CALIFORNIA

1879 becomes a year of change for Stevenson as he leaves Scotland against his family's wishes to seek an uncertain future with the still married Fanny in North America. His emigrant journey proves to be very different from his previous experiences, as his fellow travellers, far from his romanticised notions, are escaping poverty or are impelled to go for other reasons. The

---

[13] This observation, as well as Rankin's apprehensions, can be contrasted to Davies' experiences in 1993, when the awareness of Stevenson seems to have subsided. The following quotation illustrates the changes that have taken place. "Next morning, I went to pick up Mirabelle [the donkey he has decided to rent]. A young French couple were just leaving with their donkey, all saddled up. I made some jokes about hoping their donkey would not be as awkward as Modestine. They looked at me as if I was a lunatic. I presumed my schoolboy French had confused them, so I told them I was following the trail of RLS. Still they looked confused. They had never heard of you. In fact, according to Monsieur du Lac [the proprietor of the donkeys,] very few of his customers have heard of RLS. And he would like to keep it that way. Oh, come on, I said. You have eight donkeys which you hire out, with special cane luggage panniers, and you send people off with maps, names of hotels or camping sites, an unusual rural holiday, with literary connections — surely you must be cashing in on RLS's fame? 'Pouf,' he said, or sounds to that effect. 'Steff Enson, 'ee was very bad publicity for donkeys'" (Davies 77).

volumes[14] the journey resulted in mirror the enormous difference between emigration and other kinds of travelling.

Because of the externally imposed changes Stevenson experienced, it is convenient to see this journey with all its boundary-crossings as symbolising a number of changes within the man. "[T]he crossing of such a significant boundary in himself between the unmarried man and the married state cast an extremely illuminating light on the other boundaries he was crossing," Andrew Noble remarks in his introduction to *From the Clyde to California*:

> This is a book concerned with crossing multiple, interconnected boundaries: from Scotland to America; from being an upper-middle-class, slightly spoiled writer to mixing with a far lower social stratum; from being single to becoming married. All such transitions involve not only deep change but the ambivalent pain of loss and gain implicit in such change. (6)

The more or less fixed social identity Stevenson had enjoyed in Scotland becomes unfocused. This unsettling of an identity, often found in travel literature, is then balanced with the opportunity to move more freely among the people he meets and through the places he visits. This, in turn, makes for interesting, creative opportunities.

Prior to this journey, Stevenson's views on emigration, and then particularly to North America, were excessively romantic. He saw the country as a land of opportunity and wealth, and "emigration ... as a great epic" (Noble 15). As Noble observes, however, he came to see the emigrant journey "as far more of a voyage of the damned than the elect" (17) as he became aware not only of the underlying reasons impelling people to escape or voluntarily leave their home country, but also of the enormous economic and social differences between passengers in first class and in steerage. The view of the United States changes as well, as he confronts the reality of unemployment and uncertainties. In addition to this, Stevenson was overwhelmed by the boundlessness, by the sheer size of the continent, and feelings of isolation and disorientation can be detected in his writing. Combined with the experiences on board the ship,

---

[14] The journey resulted in two texts, *The Amateur Emigrant* and *Across the Plains*, now usually printed as one volume as is the case with *From the Clyde to California*. Although written around the same time, Stevenson's father "hated" the latter "and withdrew it from publication" (Davies 278).

Stevenson felt depressed and gradually distanced himself from the romanticism he previously had articulated in connection with emigration and North America. The freedom to move about, the lack of a stable identity, may have provided creative opportunities, but it also leaves Stevenson temporarily without any clear sense of the place he has come from and what role he may fill in the new country.

The issues outlined above indicate the difficulties of an emulation. Rankin, naturally, cannot imitate the motives behind Stevenson's journey, but even the prosaic means of transportation have undergone significant changes. "I wanted to get a ship from Glasgow to New York to follow in his wake," Rankin writes, "but there were no passenger boats in 1984" (*D* 120). He continues: "Stevenson's ticket to America cost eight guineas on a 3500-ton emigrant ship. A hundred and five years later the cheapest fare was £99 on a mass-tourism jumbo jet. We both left on 7 August" (*D* 121). The extreme conditions and the experiences on board the emigrant ship that were so profound and influential can naturally no longer be duplicated, and these irreconcilable differences between the first and the second text make recognitions in this section of *Dead Man's Chest* especially problematic. The external but fundamental differences—the tourist air plane instead of the passenger boat, the jetlag instead of the time-consuming crossing of the Atlantic ocean—serve as reminders of the distance between the second traveller and his subject, and they are repeatedly reinforced during Rankin's journey across North America.

From New York, Stevenson made his way by train across the continent, but "[t]he railways have sadly declined in 1980s America" Rankin notes. "The country is so big that it is faster and frequently cheaper to take a plane, and so I flew to Chicago Midway" (*D* 129). The Windy City of 1984 proves to be very different from the Chicago Stevenson saw, and it is not until he is entering the Midwest on a train that Rankin has a sense, albeit fleetingly, that "Stevenson had been here before me" (*D* 133). Rankin then takes a Greyhound bus from Omaha, but this way of travelling also removes him too far away from Stevenson's experience:

> It was strange to wake up hours out of Omaha and see the parchment of Nebraska scrolling past, its colours uncertain through the tinted windows of a Greyhound bus on Route 80. Stevenson had travelled too slowly, and now I was going too fast, trapped in the irrevocable speed and unreality of

the modern tourist, a condition that some try to arrest with manic photographing. (*D* 137)

Although this is a link between the travellers: neither is pleased with the speed at which they are travelling, it is tenuous to say the least. The remark rather signals Rankin's sense of disappointment and what he perceives as a failure to relive Stevenson's experience. It has additional implications, however. The 'inauthenticity' of the touristic condition—to be transported rather than to travel, to share the experience in the public space of the bus, rather than in solitude along a route the second traveller is the only one to take—interrupts the desired connection. The lack of adventure in modern travelling also makes Rankin jealous of Stevenson's arduous journey a century earlier. "I envied Stevenson, perched on the 'dirty and insecure' train roof in the sunshine, in his shirtsleeves and Derby hat" (*D* 137). Then, half way through the continent, Rankin has a sense that he finally connects with Stevenson:

> In the middle of America Stevenson and I coincided. Between Kearney and North Platte it was 1540 miles back east to New York and 1540 miles on west to San Francisco. It was a hundred and five years to the day since RLS was there, and by the side of the road and the railway track there were still 'innumerable wild sunflowers, no bigger than a crown piece'. (*D* 137)

This tenuous connection despite the continued differences in speed and modes of transport is based on coinciding dates and undateable aspects of nature—the sunflowers which look exactly the same. The connection is also very brief, and interrupted by Rankin's contemplation concerning the enormous differences between his journey and Stevenson's. Where Stevenson described a society still in the making, Rankin comments on the "tackiness" of "human artifice" (*D* 138). To a greater extent than in other places of Stevenson's past that Rankin has visited, the differences, however natural, serve to increase his sense of failure. His disappointment is even discernible in the derogatory descriptions of the contemporary sites he is travelling through.

In the absence of points of contact with Stevenson, Rankin increasingly reverts to personal observations. The second journey narrative moves back and forth between Rankin's experiences, other stories of the West, and personal stories from other passengers. He talks about famous characters from the country's past, Chinese railroad workers, Native American peoples and nuclear test sites in Nevada. The lack of contact also leads Rankin to employ another strategy common in second journeys: to quote extensively from the first text. To a greater extent than in other parts of *Dead Man's Chest*, Rankin repeatedly returns to the first text, not so much to make comparisons as to substitute his own descriptions with Stevenson's. The filter through which the second traveller sees the place thus becomes visible to a much higher degree. As Alexander, who, when she is unable to make the desired connection with the past, that is when her present is too far removed from Kingsley's past, more frequently quotes from and uses the first narrative, Rankin uses Stevenson's texts and have them take precedence over the encountered and in many ways disappointing reality.

TOURISM AND MUSEUMS

The many prior texts and the streamlining for tourism that have taken place along Stevenson's route in the Cévennes cause Rankin to abstain from carrying out this journey. Ian Bell also notes that "the route itself has become part of the local tourist industry—a business R. L. S. would have deplored" and that "[t]here are occasional signs on the way that the author's name is being exploited, albeit gently" (116). In a similar vein, Holmes has "not had the heart to go back and see . . . [t]he well-meaning attempt to conserve or recover the past" (*Footsteps* 68) in the Cévennes. The problematic relationship between availability and authenticity is emphasised by these views. For Rankin, the accessibility of that particular route makes it uninteresting. It is, however, not only the actual, physical repetitions he dislikes, that is, routes marked out for the benefit of tourists, but also several of the Stevenson museums he visits, which are similarly aimed towards tourism.

James Clifford states that "[g]athering an individual's or a group's treasures and history in a museum overlaps with practices such as collecting memorabilia, making a photo album, or maintaining an altar" (218). Or, one might add in this context, writing a biography. The difference between the collections of Stevenson paraphernalia and what is more traditionally considered a museum exhibition is, however, significant. The Stevenson collections do not aim to present a culture in any comprehensive way, and do not have ethnographical, archaeological or anthropological objectives. The intention is rather to present one life story, illustrated with objects belonging to, or otherwise connected to, the subject. At the same time, the collections are part of the local culture. Stevenson's Monterey house for example, is part of a tour of historical Monterey aiming to present what the town used to be, thus exaggerating Stevenson's impact on this site.

Since Stevenson travelled extensively and lived in so many places, there is an ongoing struggle between museums and between collectors (*D* 171). The question is often what is the more quantitatively impressive than what is the more authentic; in other words, whose collection is the largest. And, as often is the case when a museum's objects are treated as "someone's cultural property" (Clifford 210), the question is whose property this is. Are objects from Stevenson's time in the Pacific part of the history of Monterey? Is a piece of furniture from Bournemouth authentic when transported to New York state? Issues concerning private collectors and ownership and what these issues do to the collections are also crucial to an understanding of the museum as an institution.

Taken together, the Stevenson collections, as well as other reminders of him, statues, plaques and monuments, fill various functions when the journeys in Stevenson's footsteps are considered as heritage trails. Museums are points of interest along the routes of travel, and second journeys (Rankin's text, but also in this context, tourism) follow this heritage trail. The objects are not presented in any discernible context, at least not one similar to other organising principles within museum settings. Instead they gain importance, or even meaning, by their association with Stevenson. His life is the frame within which the objects are ordered. In this context Rankin's text becomes a frame as well. Disparate stories and events gain meaning when placed within the frame of the book, within the narrative consistency that the second text supplies when presenting its subject.

Concrete examples of how Rankin's text frames Stevenson, and how Stevenson supplies the frame for various collections will follow, but let us return for a moment to the notion of (re)creation within tourism. In a study of how culture, and in this context constructed and/or ordered culture, shapes destinations, Barbara Kirshenblatt-Gimblett maintains that "[t]ourists travel to actual destinations to experience virtual places.

They set out for the very spot [of interest to them] only to find that the actual spot is remarkably mute" (9). This muteness results in a need for recreations, simulations and reconstructions. Ironically, inauthenticity makes the experience authentic. If we see the second journey as a recreation, its inauthenticity lends life to the first journey and makes them both authentic. The first journey is visualised by the second, and is given a new and contemporary actuality, while the second journey needs the first to exist at all.

The second journeys may also be seen in the light of heritage and the virtual worlds presented to visitors in some museums. Kirshenblatt-Gimblett argues that:

> Heritage and tourism are collaborative industries, heritage converting locations into destinations and tourism making them economically viable as exhibits of themselves. Locations become museums of themselves within a tourism economy. [Sites] "survive"—they are made economically viable—as representations of themselves. (151)

Kirshenblatt-Gimblett uses the example of Cluny, France, to illustrate a point which can also be applied to second journeys. Each year, hordes of tourists come to Cluny to see the famous church or, rather, the church that once was. In its place, in the midst of the destruction among the old foundations, tourists do get to see it if they visit the museum next to the site where a three-dimensional virtual church has been constructed. "The museum does for the site what it cannot do for itself," Kirshenblatt-Gimblett argues. "It is not a substitute for the site but part of it, for the interpretative interface shows what cannot otherwise be seen" (169). Translated into the second journey discourse, the first journey remains in the past and is gone, save for its existence as a text. The second journey, the replica, the virtual recreation or copy, then makes both the first text and its past accessible. The second journey makes the first visible in the same way as the model of the church makes the past seen.

The links and similarities between heritage sites, museums, and second journeys do not necessarily appear as striking to the second traveller. In *Dead Man's Chest*, Rankin is in general apprehensive about the constructedness of museums which he characterises as "fictions made of objects, not words" and therefore "strange" (*D* 154). That is, a written text, such as his own, is a natural fiction whereas a narrative told through the assemblage of objects is not. Rankin's tour of the Stevenson house in Monterey, complete with a guide, is an example of the strangeness of object-based fictions and is described as an experience which centres on a sense of displacement. The displayed mahogany table is a case in point as it has first gone from its place of assembly in the tropics to Stevenson's childhood home. It has then been taken apart and sent to Samoa where it was used "at Vailima, then shipped and stored again before ending up in Monterey, where it was touched and admired by ladies with blue hair" (*D* 154). The eclectic collection of human-made and natural objects, furniture, and clothes, assembled from different periods in Stevenson's life, makes Rankin ask: "What was 'the real thing' on the heritage trail of objects? Everything in the museum was both solidly real and quite unreal, because divorced from history and function" (*D* 154). He is excited to see the objects that have belonged to Stevenson, previously known to him only through photographs and written descriptions. The display of these objects, however, removes them from their contexts and places them within the public space of the museum, readily available to all visitors. This can be contrasted to Mrs McFie's house in Edinburgh, preserved as it was in Stevenson's childhood, but still used as a home. The "divorce" between "history and function" is not as final in the Edinburgh example as it is here, nor, it might be inferred, is it as final in his own text which contextualises Stevenson's life within another type of frame.

Davies also visits the Monterey Stevenson House, and leaves a rather more detailed description. He adds that photographs underscore some of the objects' authenticity. The use of photographs is rare, but can help 'translate' objects into recognisable contexts. In his ongoing work on museums as contact zones, as places for objects, ideas, peoples and cultures in transit, Clifford argues that "[g]iven the overriding focus in Western museums on objects—collected, preserved, and displayed, whether for their beauty, rarity, or typicality—a distinction between object and context, figure and ground, is crucial" (159-60). But photographs, especially in colour and prominently displayed, can give a sense of authenticity, surpassing the authenticity of the object itself. They can help the spectator see how the object was used. This is particularly useful in cases such as the Stevenson collections where one person (Stevenson) becomes the context, the frame, within which these disparate objects make sense.

The claims to authenticity within museum settings have traditionally been marked by a desire to present a context. It is, for example, common to present scenes from life and from nature complete with statues of people or animals suspended within this special setting, this constructed cultural context. In her work on the historical and philosophical background of authenticity, Regina Bendix argues that "[t]he intent is to startle a visitor for a brief time and to transmit the impression of actually being in another time and another place" (135). For Rankin, this intended removal does not work in Monterey. Stevenson's clothes are spread out as if waiting for their owner; the rooms are decorated to give the impression that the Stevenson family is still living in the house. What seems to negate this impression to Rankin is the obvious *gathering* of objects, this collection that puts objects together that never were together, in a house that Stevenson spent comparatively little time in. Rankin's knowledge of Stevenson and his access to family pictures and material not readily known to the rest of the visitors hence work as shields between him and an experience of authenticity.[15]

In Napa Valley, along the Silverado Trail, there are further reminders of Stevenson.[16] It is not only the Stevenson family's physical presence around Napa that remains in the form of a travelogue. One of Stevenson's greatest admirers, Norman H. Strouse, has constructed a "world of Stevensonian names" (*D* 171) in St Helena.[17] He has also founded the Silverado Museum, which holds a collection of Stevenson memorabilia. Although Rankin appreciates several of the paintings, photographs and the wealth of written material, he notes that some of the objects displayed are "orphaned" (*D* 172).[18] Again, the implication seems to be that they are

---

[15] It may also be argued that, in order to become an authority, Rankin has to distance himself from other tourists.

[16] After an unceremonious wedding in San Francisco, Stevenson and Fanny went here in May 1880 on their honeymoon, bringing Fanny's children. The diary Stevenson kept during his time in and around the valley was later published as *The Silverado Squatters*.

[17] Rankin says that upon retirement, Strouse "moved to the St Helena area to build a house called 'Skerryvore' on a part of Glass Mountain they had renamed 'Spy-Glass Knoll'" (*D* 171).

[18] An example of the broad scope of the collection is "a pair of gloves Henry James had left behind at the Stevensons' house in Bournemouth" (*D* 172) that is, the museum displays objects not specifically connected to Stevenson.

too far removed from their one-time owner. They have, furthermore, been moved there, taken from their original surroundings, and are thereby orphaned also in terms of contextual belonging. Instead of being used as illustrations of Stevenson's life, the objects are presented as autonomous parts within the collection. The collection then becomes more important than the context of each Stevenson-related object. Again connecting to the idea of Stevenson as a frame, the individual objects when presented only as such lose the meaning they were intended to have. The 'absence' of Stevenson in the house, the lack of the frame as it were, suggests Rankin's sense of the objects as "orphaned."

After taking part in several tours and visiting several museums, Rankin makes the following reflection:

> It was strange what cultures value: old arrowheads or bits and pieces of Stevenson in glass cabinets. Museums became mausoleums, and life was locked away. The wedding-rings of Fanny and Louis Stevenson were in a bank-vault that the curator was unwilling to open. (*D* 184)

The imagery of orphaned objects, implying the figurative or literal death of its parent's is here extended to an image of the museums themselves as symbolising death or an arrested life. Rankin then continues to say that, "the spirit of Stevenson was in his writing, not in his possessions—the books were the real dead man's chest" (*D* 184). His own quest for the man, its reward presented as a treasure found in Stevenson's writings, retains its authenticity. The museum of written words—Rankin's book—is presented as more authentic, and more 'alive' than the museum, in which the objects become more important than the man.[19] This idea of the text as "produc[ing] a living effect" (*Footsteps* 27) is also seen in Holmes' pronounced objective in biography writing.

Yet another Stevenson museum remains for Rankin to visit. After a few years on the European continent, the Stevensons went back to North America in 1887, this time accompanied by Maggie Stevenson, by now a widow. At Lake Saranac, the extended family took a house for the winter, hoping that the air would improve Stevenson's ever-deteriorating health. Rankin goes to find it. This cottage, too, has been converted into a

---

[19] It should be noted, however, that Rankin's narrative presents *one* journey, that is, all the journeys Stevenson made are moulded into one and, consequently, one that he never made.

museum, and a poster claims that it is "still preserved in its original state [and that in it] you will see the world's finest collection of Stevenson relics and personal mementoes" (*D* 228). By now, this is hardly an original statement, but Rankin's visit to the cottage makes him lay claim to a new level of authenticity. He is invited to sleep in the back room, which allows him to search the empty museum at night and to feel temporarily in charge of it when the regular guide is away. This exclusive experience makes him present a more positive view of the Saranac museum overall. The exclusivity is demonstrated by Rankin telling his readers that the boots on display are stuffed with "the *Sydney Daily Telegraph* of Thursday, 12 August 1897" (*D* 231). This is, of course, information that is not readily at hand to any visitor and the findings, unlike the ordered ones in the other museums, make this specific experience more genuine to Rankin. The Saranac Museum is, as the other examples mentioned, a public space, but within this public space, Rankin has an experience that is exclusively his, no matter how trivial the findings are.

After the cold winter at Lake Saranac, the Stevensons made one of their last journeys as a family, this time to the Pacific. Even though Stevenson had undertaken several journeys throughout his life, this was the one in which his expectations of novelty and adventure were met. Ian Bell describes Stevenson as the heroic explorer and adventurer "playing his part to the hilt, [and calling] out 'Land!'" He remarks that this is "the moment Stevenson had long sought and dreamt of, the first encounter from the sea with a strange, glorious new world" (210). Stevenson describes his first encounter with the Pacific as follows:

> The first experience can never be repeated. The first love, the first sunrise, the first South Sea island, are memories apart and touched by a virginity of sense. [. . .] [B]etwixt and to the southward, the first rays of sun displayed the needles of the Ua-pu. These pricked about the line of the horizon; like the pinnacles of some ornate and monstrous church they stood there, in the sparkling brightness of the morning, the fit signboard of a world of wonders. (Stevenson *RLS in the South Seas* 36-37)

This arrival is characterised by exclusivity and the experience takes place far off the beaten track. Comparisons with other monumental occasions in which senses are affected in new ways or for the first time combine with descriptions of land- and seascapes to paint a picture of a romantic and 'exotic' location which the traveller's previous experiences have not quite prepared him for. The contrast to Rankin's arrival in Hawaii is striking.

> It was a sunny Sunday afternoon. The middle-aged tourists on the flight from California, leathery necks poking out of fresh sportswear with Hawaiian Sunshine badges—Hi! I'm Samuel J. Ryan'—had done hollering and drinking. They sat with tables up and fastened seat-belts as the plane descended. (D 248)

This arrival to a destination which has considerably different connotations in the 1980s is made in the company of other tourists and does little to conjure up romantic ideas of travel. The easy availability of the destination precludes any sense of adventure and exclusivity. This is an experience Rankin shares with several people on the tourist plane, making it less 'exotic' and it is an experience that, in theory, can be repeated over and over.[20]

In the ensuing discussions, Rankin returns to the tensions between the past and a recreated version of this past, which he has previously noted in connection with museum exhibits. He writes that "Waikiki's favourite commercial adjectives are 'ancient', 'authentic' and 'traditional'," but that much of both the past and the present is "manufactured" (D 265). Of particular interest to him in this respect is one hut, bought by a Salvation Army Commander and moved north. It was then set "up as a tourist attraction, suitably embroidered with legends of Princess Ka'iulani and Robert Louis Stevenson" (D 265). When rain caused the grass walls of the hut to deteriorate, it was renovated which greatly changed its appearance. Rankin writes sarcastically:

> It is one of the authentic 'sights' of Honolulu—a fake replica of a house Stevenson was probably never in, standing behind the Waioli Tea Rooms at a place he never visited. Tourists happily take pictures of it and feel close to the spirit of the author of *Treasure Island*. (D 265)

This sense of fake authenticity is a recurring element in Rankin's text, but it is nowhere as clear as on Hawaii. Although he repeatedly tries to connect with the place, it is too commodified, too singularly focused on

---

[20] Tourists still can, and do, articulate Stevenson's sense of romantic wonder even if travelling on crowded jets.

marketability and tourism. Not even the trustworthy excursion into nature is to any avail as there are film crews there, trying to make Hawaii look like Ireland.

Western Samoa, on the other hand, provides freshness and a 'new' sight. Rankin feels "as if [he has] been given new spectacles, looking out at Samoa on that first sparkling morning" (*D* 298). Although notions connected to the new and the novel are fictions the use of them signals a significant departure from his earlier descriptions. Western Samoa is, at the time of Rankin's visit, considerably less aimed towards tourism than his previous destinations, and this may help account for the difference in his descriptions. This is not to say that Western Samoa has completely escaped the process of 'touristification,' so characteristic of Hawaii. The plans for Stevenson's old house at Vailima, for example, have been the cause of worry for many biographers and second travellers. In 1992, Ian Bell anxiously reports that

> Mormons have bought a twenty-year lease on Stevenson's old home and plan the 'Robert Louis Stevenson Museum/Preservation Foundation Inc.,' complete with souvenir shop and a cable car to the grave site on the summit of Vaea. Despised 'civilisation' reaches out to R. L. S. even in death. (xix)

Davies also remarks on these rumours, but can, after his visit, assure his readers that they are exaggerated. Rankin does not comment on this, but supplies no description of the house. Instead he writes that "[v]ery little has changed today beyond Vailima Stream. The forest is hot, silent and alive, the air is still, as if waiting" (*D* 326). Nature seems to offer the most sublime and authentic experience, a feature of second journeys that surfaces in most narratives. Rankin's reactions towards the Westernisation of the Pacific Islands are naturally of importance here, as they stand in such marked contrast to the unchanged forest, but he has previously experienced similar moments of recognition. Nature, in this sense, destabilises notions not only of where he is, but also, as it were, of *when* he is.

Rankin connects once more with the subject of his biography at Stevenson's grave on Vaea Mountain:

> I spent a lovely few hours up there. It rained a warm rain, and then the sun came out again and I stood on the raft of tomb and sang Stevenson's words to the old Jacobite tune:

> Sing me a song of a lad that is gone,
> Say, could that lad be I?
> Merry of soul he sailed on a day
> Over the sea to Skye
>
> ...
> Billow and breeze, islands and seas,
> Mountains of rain and sun,
> All that was good, all that was fair,
> All that was me is gone. (*D* 350)

As in a more traditional biography the narrative has thus moved from the subject's place of birth to its logical conclusion, the subject's grave. Here, however, it has taken on the form of an actual journey. Rankin ends his text rather abruptly; the second journey comes to an almost complete halt at the moment Stevenson 'leaves,' at the moment there are no places left to go. Rankin's journey back is not narrated, giving *Dead Man's Chest* its final, highly biographical touch: that Stevenson, not Rankin, has been the true subject of the text.

AFTER THE END

"I had seen the place of the name. Now it was time to take the lucky stone home and write the book you hold."(*D* 352) The last sentences in *Dead Man's Chest* bring us back to the prologue and the gift from Borges that Rankin has carried on his journey. Although the home is not textually reached, the sentences emphasise the circularity of the project, tracing Stevenson from his birthplace to his grave, and following the initial inspiration from Borges to the biography's textual completion.

Rankin has visited most of the places Stevenson went to and/or through, although not in the same order as Stevenson. Although the second journey *narrative* is chronologically ordered, the journey itself is not. His narrative is not an advertisement for different places (sometimes it is even the opposite,) rather it is an encouragement to the readers to find Stevenson's texts.[21]

When reporting on Stevenson's most productive periods, that is, when he wrote rather than travelled, Rankin repeatedly reverts to discussions

---

[21] Davies, in contrast, encourages his readers to carry out their own second journey. In the notes following his text he supplies information about the places he has visited, along the lines of traditional guidebooks, complete with opening hours, recommended hotels and accessibility to the public.

about style, reception and possible influences, de-emphasising his presence in the text. It is the travels that, literally as well as figuratively, move the text forward, and that enable the text to take its place among travel narratives and second journeys.

Travels with a Donkey and *From the Clyde to California* represent significantly different views on adventure, heroism, and travel and the image of the travelling hero, the traditionally male, heroic persona is somewhat different in Stevenson's texts than in Kingsley and Scott's narratives. Rankin also perceives and handles it differently than Swan and Mear and Alexander. In this context it is important to remember that many of Stevenson's journeys were projects that included his family—Fanny, her children Belle and Lloyd, Stevenson's mother Maggie. This may suggest that the heroic journey is altered; that we are concerned with a different kind of heroism than in the solitary, adventurous journeys.

In comparison to the multitude of places connected to Stevenson, *Dead Man's Chest* is presented as a more vivid project than the collections and the museums, since it connects the writer with the written word. In this sense, the souvenir of Stevenson (Rankin's book) is not orphaned but connected to the source, the frame. As Matos has observed "[t]he world of Rankin's book is, indeed, a world of texts" (225). The composite image we get of Stevenson is complex and the interweaving of people and contexts applies to the whole of Rankin's text. Matos states that "[t]he past, for him [Rankin], is not only the isolated figure or event that constitutes the motive for his own journey, but a vast field of interlocking elements and actions whose ramifications extend into the present" (225).

Rankin is clearly aware of the problems of recapturing a past. The randomness of historical representations is problematised in his descriptions of museums; and his disappointments and failures are played out against the backdrop of this awareness. Rankin does not preclude the complicated search for authenticity, however, and the desire for authenticity returns, again and again, both in the first and the second journey.

Concluding Remarks
—Where Do We Go From Here?

Immature poets imitate; mature poets steal; bad poets deface what they take, and good poets make it into something better, or at least into something different.
T.S. Eliot, *The Sacred Wood*

Today we see a booming interest in travel narratives. A visit to any bookstore reveals that we travel, and read about travel, as never before. Texts are reprinted and reissued and anthologies present collections of works within the genre. Online resources present not only texts and still images, but short films, and the sounds of faraway (or close) destinations. Applications such as weblogs ensure that a journey can be continuously chronicled, lending an immediacy to recounted events and experiences, and other types of software help the traveller to both plan for and envision the journey in advance. Travel, travel writing and tourism are also increasingly being discussed in the academic world from both cultural and literary perspectives, which suggests the erasing of previous divisions into 'high' and 'low' forms of textual expressions. Although the various forms travel writing takes today were difficult to envision in the mid-nineteenth century, the pessimism about the future the genre, as it was voiced primarily with the rise of mass tourism after World War II, can be seen as greatly exaggerated.

The exhaustion of both destinations and the genre of the travel book is exacerbated, however, by this multitude of forms (both in travelling and travel writing) and has produced new forms of both travelling and writing which illustrate the desire to find new places to go or, at any rate, a desire to be alone at the destination. The second journey, as I have defined it, reflects these general tendencies in contemporary travel and tourism, but exemplifies the renewal, of both the mode of travelling and of the text form. Second journey texts all illustrate an "employment of the retracing trope to transform the mapped space into new territory" (Alison Russell 10) as they reiterate previous journeys while adding new layers of meaning to the experience. The desire to find new places is not erased, but rather achieved through a return to the past. The desired experiences are transferred into the past. That is, spatial travel exists side by side with temporal travel, and rather than looking for an authentic place, the second traveller looks for an authentic time.

Second journeys combine traits from both travel and tourism; they illustrate a convergence of previously separate discourses. Postmodern travel writers in general seldom acknowledge the 'touristic' aspects of their journeys, and rather foreground self-reflexive comments and unstable subject positions, and break with traditionally chronological forms. Second journeys share some of these traits and authors using the form are often exceedingly open concerning fears, insecurities and misgivings, and draw attention to the constructedness of both their own, and the first journey texts. However, the links to contemporary tourism are strong in second journey narratives. Second travellers journey to recognise sights and sites described in the first journey; the first text works as a tourist's guidebook, alerting them to things of importance.

The originality of second journey projects is not (as in traditional travel writing) signalled through a suppression of previous voices; rather, the intertextuality found in second journey is of an open, transparent kind. Long quotations as well as open references, itineraries and titles all suggest the presence of the first text in the second; the intertext becomes both a pretext for and a pre-text to the second journey. However, to follow in a first traveller's footsteps in attempts to emulate his or her journey is not without problems and the filter of the first text can at times be perceived as obscuring experiences rather than heightening the authenticity of the project. The second travellers I have discussed all wrestle with feelings of disappointment and failure. In clearly voicing these feelings they distance themselves from traditional notions connecting travel with successful adventures and the journeying subject with heroism. Instead they connect to the more general postcolonial and postmodern developments within the travel genre in which the awareness of the self and the inability to represent encountered Others are continually being addressed.

Repetition with a difference, defined as one of the key features of intertextuality is highly visible in the second journeys. Especially so in that the second travellers, while emulating the traditional form and characteristics of the travel narrative, emphasise the 'un-originality' of their undertakings: the pronounced intention of repeating previous experiences. In addition, the postmodern desire to trans-contextualise the past, to rewrite it in the present context, is revealed by the contemporary repetition of a movement in the past. The gap between the past and the present is reduced, and the trans-contextualisations of the past experiences as well as the comparisons with the contemporary present 'rewrite' the first texts. The writers I have called second travellers thus openly embrace the idea of belatedness, of precursors. Their openly stated connection with earlier works, works functioning as 'maps' for the second traveller to follow, illustrates a new development in a genre in which originality and a sense of being first have always been emphasised. The creative and imitative acts that previously would have rendered the journeys inauthentic now serve, through the second journeys' open processes of emulation, as a postmodern authenticity. The rewriting of an earlier text can also be said to be particularly important in a postmodern "age of widespread cultural illiteracy [in which] the literary monuments of the past require continual revitalization" (Cowart 17). The first texts discussed in the three case studies are rescued from oblivion through the emulative process.

Second journeys illustrate the contemporary discourses its author moves within; discourses which govern constructions of self and Other, of home and away and of how destinations are seen. In addition, the filter that the first text constitutes illuminates past discourses. The first texts, the filters, are all produced within a fairly concentrated time period: from 1878 to 1911. The authors of these texts; Robert Louis Stevenson, Mary Kingsley and Robert Falcon Scott are thus writing during or shortly after the period of High Imperialism. A sense of nationality is particularly evident in the cases of Scott and Kingsley. Although Antarctica in both figurative and practical senses was unclaimed, Scott setting out to 'win' the South Pole for Britain must be seen as illustrative of a more symbolic colonialism. Kingsley, on the other hand, travelling through areas which were largely colonised and controlled by the British colonial administration, is taking part in the colonial process in a more literal sense, evident in how she offers advice on trading relations and the management of the colony. Colonial discourses are less evident in Stevenson's travel related texts and come as a result of his destinations. Neither France nor North America can be textually constructed as 'available' for colonisation and/or control in the same as as West Africa and Antarctica. The Pacific Islands is Stevenson's only destination which presents him with opportunities for textual claims, but his descriptions nevertheless seem structured more according to discourses of adventure, rather than to exploration and domination.

The second journeys which follow in these textual footsteps are all published in the 1980s which means that the authors comply with or resist similar discourses when it comes to representations and descriptions. The differences between them rather stem from the differences between the first texts. In the first case study, the continuous juxtapositions between first and second text illustrate a desire to uphold the traditional, male images of the hero. Antarctica as geographical area does yet not suffer from the same exhaustion as other destinations, as it is still relatively remote and difficult to access. The two texts, Scott's *Journals* and Roger Mear and Robert Swan's *In the Footsteps of Scott*, illustrate how Antarctica has been, and is, discursively constructed in ways which continually emphasise this remoteness and desolateness, which in turn feeds into the heroic qualities characterising the male explorers travelling through it. However, recent examples suggest that associations to this area are changing, illustrating a potential discursive shift. Members of the scientific and multi-membered second journey project lament the fact that an adventurous, potentially fatal recreation of Scott's journey has been made impossible by modern developments and technology. Hardships and dangers connected to the remoteness and isolation of the continent are nevertheless continuously stressed to heighten the authenticity of the project, and the emphasis on these notions reveals a desire to emulate not only the first journey itself, but to reach the heroic ideal influencing Scott and his contemporaries. One way of reaching this ideal is to mediate Scott's text, the second travellers choosing from it definitions of heroism that translate over time, adapting them to the new circumstances.

West Africa is discursively constructed as a place requiring another kind of heroism, particularly in the nineteenth century through images relayed through texts and tales. In contrast to Antarctica, however, this geographical destination was already 'conquered' through colonial and imperial processes, and the establishment of European settlements along the coast strengthens ideas of a transposed culture. Kingsley's *Travels in West Africa* illustrates a tendency towards adventurous exploration both in descriptions of experiences and in the emphasis on dangers posed by geography, but the identification with the role of the male hero is not unproblematic. Rather, it adds to the many discourses in which Kingsley already finds herself. It is, however, by literally and metaphorically distancing herself from Britain, or Britain transposed, that the authenticity of her project is achieved. Colonial discourses still permeate her narrative, evident in how she narrates both places and people. The postcolonial discourses structuring the journey in Kingsley's footsteps: Caroline Alexander's *One Dry Season*, result in different approaches to both landscape and people, but even more apparent is the representation of the travelling self as uncertain and doubtful, illustrating worries and misgivings that are largely absent from Kingsley's text. The juxtaposition of the two travel texts effectively illustrates the discursive constraints placed on Kingsley, as a Victorian woman and as a travel writer. By extension, Alexander's second journey draws attention to the wider implication of the constructedness of both texts and textual personae.

The biographical second journey, exemplified by Nicholas Rankin's *Dead Man's Chest*, aims to present a complex and 'true' picture of the subject: Stevenson. Although Rankin's repeatedly formulated sense of disappointment may be seen to stand in the way of such a picture, the complex and intertwined histories of the past and the present supply multidimensional images of both first and second traveller. This kind of second journey presents an option for contemporary biography writers since the narrative vehicle of the journey provides the text with a natural authority and removes the pressure to 'hide' themselves in the text with which biographers have traditionally wrestled. By relying on the same strategies of achieving authenticity as the other second journeys analysed in this study—by travelling to the places described in the first narrative, by attempting to emulate the experiences of the first traveller—authenticity may, in an extended sense, be lent to the entire biography project.

The three forms of the second journey discussed in this study are defined loosely and in this fact lies opportunities for further work. As the forms blend into each other it is possible to make more detailed definitions and to arrange the second journeys into a wider spectrum of texts. The complicated power structures underlying journeying are also interesting to consider for future studies of second journeys, especially when the journeys are undertaken by non-Western writers. The scope of this study has limited the possibilities of exploring this, but the case studies may perhaps suggest starting points for further discussions. More detailed analyses of the second journey's relationship to history, to map-making, to visual elements and to gender relations may also prove fruitful.

One of the focal points of second journey texts is authenticity and the numerous possibilities the writer has to attain it. In travel writing in general, authenticity is primarily seen as residing in the past, accessible only to previous generations of travellers. The lack of contemporary authentic places and experiences has been seen as signalling a decline, a sense that there is nothing left to write about or describe, that everything of worth has been seen and narrated in the past. In second journeys, the return to previous texts is certainly an expression of this contemporary, anxious sense of belatedness, but used to very different ends, as the recycling of itineraries indicates not exhaustion but a process of renewal. 'We have no choice but to rewrite' it has been said, but I see in the second journeys' emulations of previous travels none of the derogatory qualities signalled by this lack of choice. Second travellers do not simply imitate the experiences made by previous authors, and what they steal or borrow from the first texts is most often used to reinforce the natural distance between past and present. Because they return to previous texts and to paths already travelled, the journeying subject may discover not only the first traveller, but perhaps also him or herself. Through mediations or even failures it is possible for the traveller to begin to redefine his or her relationship to the world, thereby relaying experiences which, although not necessarily surpassing those of the earlier traveller, at least provide the reader with a different and alternative version.

Works Cited

Alexander, Caroline. *One Dry Season: In the Footsteps of Mary Kingsley*. London: Bloomsbury, 1989. Print.

– –. *The Way to Xanadu*. London: Weidenfeld & Nicolson, 1993. Print.

Allen, Alexandra. *Travelling Ladies*. London: Jupiter Books, 1980. Print.

Allen, Grant. Review in *Fortnightly Review*, (July 1979). *Robert Louis Stevenson: The Critical Heritage*. Ed., Paul Maixner. London: Routledge, 1971. xxvi. Print.

Barnes, Julian. *A History of the World in 10 1/2 Chapters*. London: Jonathan Cape, 1989. Print.

Bate, Walter Jackson. *The Burden of the Past and the English Poet*. Cambridge, Mass.: Harvard U P, 1970. Print.

Behdad, Ali. *Belated Travelers: Orientalism in the Age of Colonial Dissolution*. Durham: Duke U P, 1994. Print.

Bell, Gavin. *In Search of Tusitala: Travels in the Pacific After Robert Louis Stevenson*. London: Vintage Departures, 1995. Print.

Bell, Ian. *Dreams of Exile: Robert Louis Stevenson: A Biography*. New York: Henry Holt and Company, 1992. Print.

Bendix, Regina. *In Search of Authenticity: The Formation of Folklore Studies*. Madison, Wisconsin: The U of Wisconsin P, 1997. Print.

Birkett, Dea. *Spinsters Abroad: Victorian Lady Explorers*. Oxford: Basil Blackwell, 1989. Print.

Blanton, Casey. *Travel Writing: The Self and the World*. New York: Twayne Publishers, 1997. Print.

Blunt, Alison, and Rose, Gillian. "Introduction: Women's Colonial and Postcolonial Geographies." *Writing Women and Space: Colonial and Postcolonial Geographies*. Eds., Alison Blunt and Gillian Rose. London: The Guilford P, 1994. 1-25. Print.

Blunt, Alison. *Travel, Gender, and Imperialism: Mary Kingsley and West Africa*. New York: The Guilford P, 1994. Print.

Bongie, Chris. *Exotic Memories: Literature, Colonialism, and the Fin de Siècle*. Stanford: Stanford U P, 1991. Print.

Borges, Jorge Louis. "Borges and I." *Labyrinths: Selected Stories & Other Writings*. 1962; New York: New Directions, 2007. 246-47. Print.

Boswell, James. *A Journal of a Tour to the Hebrides with Samuel Johnson LL.D.*. 1785; London: J. M. Dent and Sons, 1931. Print.

Brantlinger, Patrick. *Rule of Darkness: British Literature and Imperialism, 1830-1914.* Ithaca: Cornell U P, 1988. Print.

Burton, Marda. "William Faulkner: Sound and Fury in Mississippi." *Literary Trips: Following in the Footsteps of Fame Vol I*. Ed., Victoria Brooks. Vancouver: Greatescapes.com Publishing, 2000. 147-155. Print.

Buzard, James. *The Beaten Track: European Tourism, Literature, and the Ways to 'Culture' 1800-1918*. Oxford: Clarendon P, 1993. Print.

Byron, Robert. *The Road to Oxiana*. 1937; New York: Oxford U P, 1966. Print.

Calder, Jenni. *Robert Louis Stevenson: A Life Study*. London: Hamish Hamilton, 1980. Print.

Calinescu, Matei. "Rewriting." *International Postmodernism: Theory and Literary Practice*. Eds., Hans Bertens and Douwe Foukkema. Amsterdam: John Benjamin Publishing Company, 1996. 243-248. Print.

Campbell, Joseph. *The Hero with a Thousand Faces*. Princeton: Princeton U P, 1949. Print.

Chatwin, Bruce. *The Songlines*. New York: Viking, 1987. Print.

——. "A Lament for Afghanistan." *What Am I Doing Here*. London: Jonathan Cape, 1989. 286-293. Print.

Cherry-Garrard, Apsley. *The Worst Journey in the World*. London: Chatto and Windus, 1922. Print.

Clark, Steve. "Introduction." *Travel Writing and Empire: Postcolonial Theory in Transit*. Ed., Steve Clark. New York: Zed Books, 1999. 1-28. Print.

Classic Travel Stories. London: Bracken Books, 1994. Print.

Clayton, Jay, and Rothstein, Eric. "Figures in the Corpus: Theories of Influence and Intertextuality." *Influence and Intertextuality in Literary History*. Eds., Jay Clayton and Eric Rothstein. Madison, Wisconsin: The U of Wisconsin P, 1991. 3-36. Print.

Clayton, Jay. "The Alphabet of Suffering: Effie Deans, Tess Durbeyfield, Martha Ray, and Hetty Sorrel." Clayton and Rothstein. 37-60. Print.

Clifford, James. *Routes: Travel and Translation in the Late Twentieth Century*. Cambridge, Mass.: Harvard U P, 1997. Print.

Cohen, Eric. "Contemporary tourism — trends and challenges. Sustainable authenticity or contrived post-modernity?" *Change in Tourism: People, Places, Processes*. Eds., Richard W. Butler and Douglas G. Pearce. London: Routledge, 1995. 12-29. Print.

Coleridge, Samuel Taylor. *Cristabel, &c*. London: John Murray, 1816. Print.

Couser, Thomas. "Authority." *Auto/Biography Studies*, 10:1. (1995): 34-47. Print.

Cowart, David. *Literary Symbiosis: The Reconfigured Text in Twentieth Century Writing*. Athens: U of Georgia P, 1993. Print.

Culler, Jonathan. *Framing the Sign: Criticism and its Institutions*. Oxford: Basil Blackwell Ltd, 1988. Print.

Davies, Hunter. *The Teller of Tales: In Search of Robert Louis Stevenson*. London: Sinclair-Stevenson, 1994. Print.

Delaney, Frank. *A Walk to the Western Isles: After Johnson and Boswell*. London: HarperCollins Publishers, 1993. Print.

Downer, Lesley. *On the Narrow Road: Journey into a Lost Japan*. London: Jonathan Cape, 1989. Print.

Duncan, James, and Ley, David, eds. *Place/Culture/Representation*. London: Routledge, 1993. Print.

Duncan, James. "Sites of Representation: Place, Time and the Discourse of the Other". Duncan and Ley. 39-56. Print.

Duncan, James, and Gregory, Derek. *Writes of Passage: Reading Travel Writing*. London: Routledge, 1999. Print.

Eisenlau, Jennifer. "Rome's Ultimate Guidebook: *I Claudius*." *Literary Traveler*. 30 Nov. 2007. Web. 11 Dec. 2009. <http://www.literarytraveler.com >

Eliot, Thomas, Stearns. *The Sacred Wood: Essays on Poetry and Criticism*. London: Methune, 1920. Print.

Filsnoel, Monique. "Karen Blixen's Kenyan Paradise." *Literary Traveler*. 29 Nov. 2007. Web. 11 Dec. 2009. <http://www.literarytraveler.com >

Fremd, Charles. *Scott of the Antarctic*. Ealing Studios, 1948. Film.

Furnas, Joseph Chamberlain. *Voyage to Windward*. London: Faber, 1952. Print.

Fussell, Paul. *Abroad: British Literary Traveling Between the Wars*. New York: Oxford U P, 1980. Print.

Galván, Fernando. "Travel Writing in British Metafiction." *British Postmodern Fiction*. Eds., Theo D'haen and Hans Bertens. Amsterdam: Rodopi, 1993. 77-87. Print.

Gilmore, Leigh. *Autobiographics: A Feminist Theory of Women's Self-Representation*. Ithaca: Cornell U P, 1994. Print.

Glazebrook, Philip. *Journey to Kars: A Modern Traveller in the Ottoman Lands*. New York: Atheneum, 1984. Print.

Grewal, Inderpal. *Home and Harem: Nation, Gender, Empire, and the Cultures of Travel*. Durham: Duke U P, 1996. Print.

Hamalian, Leo. *Ladies on the Loose*. New York: Dodd, Mead and Co., 1981. Print.

Henderson, Heather. "The Travel Writer and the Text: My Giant Goes with Me Wherever I Go." Kowalewski. 230-248. Print.

Holland, Patrick, and Huggan, Graham. *Tourists with Typewriters: Critical Reflections on Contemporary Travel Writing*. Ann Arbor: Michigan U P, 1998. Print.

Holmes, Richard. *Footsteps: Adventures of a Romantic Biographer*. 1985; New York: Vintage Departures, 1996. Print.

Holmes, Richard. "Biography: Inventing the Truth." *The Art of Literary Biography*. Ed., John Batchelor. Oxford: Clarendon P, 1995. 15-25. Print.

Holt, Kåre. *Kappløpet*. Olso: Gyldendal, 1974. Print.

Huntford, Roland. *Scott and Amundsen*. London: Hodder and Stoughton, 1979. Print.

Huget, Jennifer. "Mark Twain: Connecticut Southerner in Yankee Land." *Literary Trips: Following in the Footsteps of Fame Vol I*. Ed., Victoria Brooks. Vancouver: Greatescapes.com Publishing, 2000. 175-180. Print.

Hutcheon, Linda. *A Theory of Parody: The Teachings of Twentieth Century Art Forms*. New York: Methuen, 1985. Print.

--. *A Poetics of Postmodernism: History, Theory, Fiction*. New York: Routledge, 1988. Print.

Huxley, Elspeth. *Scott of the Antarctic*. 1977; London: Pan Books, 1979. Print.

Höjer, Signe. *Mary Kingsley — forskningsresande i Västafrika*. Stockholm: LTs förlag, 1973. Print.

"In the Footsteps of Amundsen 2010." *Bancroft Arnesen Explore*. N. d. Web 11 Dec. 2009 <http://www.yourexpedition.com/expeditions>

Jameson, Frederick. "Postmodernism, or the Cultural Logic of Late Capitalism." *New Left Review* 146 July-August. (1984): 53-92. Print.

Johnson, Samuel. *A Journey to the Western Islands of Scotland*. 1775; New Haven: Yale U P, 1971. Print.

Kaplan, Caren. *Questions of Travel: Postmodern Discourses of Displacement*. Durham: Duke U P, 1996. Print.

Kinglake, Alexander. *Eothen, or Traces of Travel Brought Home from the East*. 1844; London: Sampson Low, Marston & Co. Ltd, 1913. Print.

Kingsley, Mary. *Travels in West Africa: Congo Français, Corisco and Cameroons*. 1897; Boston: Beacon Press, 1988. Print.

––. *West African Studies*. 1899; London: Frank Cass & Co. Ltd., 1967. Print.

––. "West Africa from an Ethnographical Point of View." *Imperial Institute Journal*, April. (1900). Print.

––. "A Lecture on West Africa." *Cheltenham Ladies College Magazine* 38. Autumn. (1898). Print.

Knight, Alanna. "Introduction." *RLS in the South Seas: An Intimate Photographic Record*. 1900; Edinburgh: Mainstream Publishing, 1986. Print.

Kirshenblatt-Gimblett, Barbara. *Destination Culture: Tourism, Museums, and Heritage*. Berkeley: U of California P, 1998. Print.

Kowalewski, Michael, ed. *Temperamental Journeys: Essays on the Modern Literature of Travel*. Athens: U of Georgia P, 1992. Print.

Kubrick, Stanley. *2001: A Space Odyssey*. MGM, 1968. Film.

Lawrence, Karen R. *Penelope Voyages: Women and Travel in the British Literary Tradition*. Ithaca: Cornell U P, 1994. Print.

Leed, Eric. *The Mind of the Traveler: From Gilgamesh to Global Tourism*. New York: Basic Books, 1991. Print.

––. *Shores of Discovery: How Expeditionaries Have Constructed the World*. New York: Basic Books, 1995. Print.

Lévi-Strauss, Claude. *Tristes Tropiques*. Trans. John and Doreen Weightman. 1955; New York: Atheneum Press, 1975. Print.

Lomax, Judi. *The Viking Voyage: With Gaia to Vinland*. London: Hutchinson, 1992. Print.

MacCannell, Dean. *The Tourist: A New Theory of the Leisure Class*. 1976; Berkeley: U of California P, 1999. Print.

MacKenzie, John, ed. *Popular Imperialism and the Military 1850-1950*. Manchester: Manchester U P, 1992. Print.

Matos, Jacinta. "Old Journeys Revisited: Aspects of Postwar English Travel Writing." Kowalewski. 215-229. Print.

Mear, Roger, and Swan, Robert. *In the Footsteps of Scott*. London: Jonathan Cape, 1987. Print.

Mills, Sara. *Discourses of Difference: An Analysis of Women's Travel Writing and Colonialism*. London: Routledge, 1991. Print.

– –. "Knowledge, Gender, and Empire." Blunt and Rose 29-50. Print.

Minh-ha, Trinh T. "Other than myself/my other self." *Traveller's Tales — Narratives of Home and Displacement*. Eds., George Robertson, et. al. London: Routledge, 1994. 9-26. Print.

Morris, Marry Morris and Larry O'Connor. *The Illustrated Virago Book of Women Travellers* . London: Virago 2003. Print.

Murray, Carl. "The Use and Abuse of Dogs on Scott's and Amundesen's South Pole Expeditions." *Polar Record* 44. (2008): 303-10. Print.

Noble, Andrew. "Introduction." *From the Clyde to California*. By Robert Louis Stevenson. Aberdeen: Aberdeen U P, 1985. Print.

Norwich, John Julius. *A Taste for Travel*. New York: Alfred A. Knopf, 1987. Print.

Ousby, Ian. *The Englishman's England*. Cambridge: Cambridge U P, 1990. Print.

Palin, Michael. *Around the World in 80 Days*. BBC Warner. 11 Oct. 1989. Television.

Pierce, Andrew. "Ben Fogle and James Cracknell beaten to South Pole by Norwegian team." *The Daily Telegraph*. 22 Jan. 2009. Web. 11 Dec 2009. <http://www.telegraph.co.uk >

Pope Hennessy, James. *Robert Louis Stevenson*. London: Jonathan Cape, 1974. Print.

Porter, Dennis. *Haunted Journeys: Desire and Transgression in European Travel Writing*. Princeton, N J: Princeton U P, 1991. Print.

Pratt, Mary-Louise. *Imperial Eyes: Travel Writing and Transculturation*. New York: Routledge, 1992. Print.

Rankin, Nicholas. *Dead Man's Chest: Travels After Robert Louis Stevenson*. London: Faber and Faber, 1987. Print.

Riffenbaugh, Beau. *The Myth of the Explorer.* 1993; Oxford: Oxford U P, 1994. Print.

Rojek, Chris. *Ways of Escape: Modern Transformations in Leisure and Travel.* London: MacMillan, 1993. Print.

Ruskin, John. *The Crown of the Wild Olive; Three Lectures on Work, Traffic and War.* London: Smith, Elder & Company, 1866. Print.

Russell, Alison. *Crossing Boundaries: Postmodern Travel Literature.* New York: Palgrave, 2000. Print.

Russell, Mary. *The Blessings of a Good Thick Skirt: Women Travellers and Their World.* 1986; London: William Collins, 1988. Print.

Said, Edward. *Orientalism.* New York: Vintage Books, 1979. Print.

Schlaeger, Jürgen. "Cult as Culture." Batchelor, ed., 55-71. Print.

Schwartz, Hillel. *The Culture of the Copy: Striking Liknesses, Unreasonable Facsimiles.* New York: Zone Books, 1996. Print.

Scott, Robert Falcon. *Scott's Last Expedition: the Journals.* 1913; New York: Carroll & Graf Publishers, 1996. Print.

--. *The Voyage of the Discovery.* London: Charles Scribner's Sons, 1907. Print.

Severin, Tim. *Tracking Marco Polo.* London: Routledge, 1964. Print.

--. *The Brendan Voyage.* London: Hutchinson, 1978. Print.

--. *The Jason Voyage: The Quest for the Golden Fleece.* London: Hutchinson, 1987. Print.

--. *The Sinbad Voyage.* London: Arrow Books, 1982. Print.

--. *In Search of Genghis Khan.* London: Hutchinson, 1991. Print.

--. *In Search of Moby Dick: the Quest for the White Whale.* London: Little, Brown, 1999. Print.

--. *Seeking Robinson Crusoe.* London: MacMillan 2002. Print.

Spufford, Francis. *I May Be Some Time: Ice and the English Imagination.* London: Faber and Faber, 1996. Print.

Stagl, Justin. *A History of Curiosity: The Theory of Travel 1550-1800.* Chur, Switzerland: Harwood Academic Publishers, 1995. Print.

Steven, Stuart. *Night Train to Turkistan: Modern Adventures along China's Ancient Silk Road.* New York: Atlantic Monthly Press, 1988. Print

Stevenson, Robert Louis. *An Inland Voyage.* 1878; London: Chatto and Windus, 1919. Print.

—. *Travels with a Donkey in the Cevennes*. 1879; London: Chatto and Windus, 1921. Print.

—. *A Child's Garden of Verses*. London: Longmans, 1885. Print.

—. *The Silverado Squatters*. 1890; London: Chatto and Windus, 1920. Print.

—. *From the Clyde to California*. Ed. Andrew Noble. Aberdeen: Aberdeen U P, 1985. Print.

—. *RLS in the South Seas: An Intimate Photographic Record*. Ed. Alanna Knight. 1900; Edinburgh: Mainstream Publishing, 1986. Print.

Thomson, David. *Scott's Men*. London: Allen Lane, 1977. Print.

von Martels, Zweder. *Travel Fact and Travel Fiction: Studies on Fiction, Literary Tradition, Scholarly Discovery and Observation in Travel Writing*. Leiden: E. J. Brill, 1994. Print.

Ware, Vron. *Beyond the Pale: White Women, Racism and History*. 1992; London: Verso, 1996. Print.

Waugh, Evelyn. *When the Going was Good*. 1946; London: Penguin Books Ltd., 1968. Print.

Wheeler, Sara. *Terra Incognita*. New York: Random House, 1996. Print.

Young, Gavin. *In Search of Conrad*. London: Hutchinson, 1991. Print.

INDEX

adventure, 11, 27-28, 35, 70, 81, 92, 94, 96, 103, 106-07, 116, 127, 131, 133, 139-43, 156, 161-62, 167, 171, 174, 181-82, 185, 188, 190

Alexander, Caroline, **111-151**, 12, 16-17, 26, 34, 43-44, 55, 63, 66-67, 69, 80, 107, 153, 175, 185, 191

Amundsen, Roald, 26, 70, 77, 81, 86-89, 91, 103, 110

Antarctica, 26, 44, 68, 79-81, 89, 91-92, 94, 97, 105-06, discursive construction of, 15, 83-84, 189-90, isolation of, 80-81, 83, 91, 100, 110, Cape Evans, 61, 77, 85, 94-98, 107, 149, McMurdo, 99, 106, South Pole, the 15, 17, 26, 68, 70, 77, 79, 81, 85, 87-89, 93-94, 97, 99, 102-04, 106-09, 189

authenticity, 13-15, 18-19, 25, 30, 33, 37-41, 48, 52, 56, 65, 73, 80, 93-94, 108, 113, 179-181, 185, 190-92, search for, 11, 13, 29, 37-38, 79, 128, 133-34, of the past, 14, 18, 24, 27, 29, 41-42, 52, 57, 60, 63, 124, 188, markers of, 32, 38-39, 63, 178-79, discourse, 39-40, 100, in writing, 46, 87, 122, 156-58, 180, authentic experiences, 11, 14, 18, 26, 29, 33, 38, 41, 53, 62-63, 96, 128, 141, 149, 165, 170-71, 179, 183, inauthentic, 39-40, 162, 166, 174-77, 182, 189

autobiography, 120-21, 156-58

belatedness, sense of, 11, 25-26, 31, 35, 48, 53, 55, 58, 71, 73, 170, 189, 192

biography, 15-17, 33, 41-43, 45, 61, 70, 126, 144, 153-60, 166-67, 169-70, 175, 180, 183-4, 191

Boswell, James, 61-63

Bowers, Henry 77, 99, 102-03

Britain, 68, 80, 82-83, 86, 116, 144, 189, 191, British society, identity, 68, 83, 88, 90, 109, 144, 189

Burton, Marda, 73-74

Byron, Lord 32, 57, 75

Byron, Robert, 64

Chatwin, Bruce, 14, 34, 55, 64

citationary structure, 12, 25, 33, 36, 56

Coleridge, Samuel Taylor, 66-67

colonialism, 11, 23, 115-16, 119, 132, 145, 149, 189, colonial discourses, 22, 26, 51, 67, 116, 119-21, 131, 145, 161, 190-91, colonial areas, 16, 26, 128, 130, 133-34, 140

Curzon, Lord, 88-89

de Brazza, Count, 26, 59, 137

Delaney, Frank, 55, 61-63

discourse, 12, 15, 18-19, 22, 27, 35, 49-50, 68, 107, 111, 177, 189-91, converging, conflicting discourses, 18, 22, 27, 30, 40, 146, 188, 191, gendered discourses, 16, 22, 43, 69, 84, 113-23, 130-31, 133, 144-45, heroic discourse, 84, 89, 94, colonial and explorational discourses, 24, 26, 31, 51, 115-20, 130, 145, 189-91, of belatedness, 25, 55, of destinations, 25, of exoticism, 26, of tourism, 27-31, 56, 75, of travel writing, 31-35, 37-38, postcolonial and postmodern discourses, 23, 31, 83, 189, 191

discursive elements, structures, representations, constraints, 12, 16-17, 21, 24, 30, 38-39, 50, 52, 71, 116, 127, 135, 145, 190-91

Eisenlau, Jennifer, 73

Europe, European, 17, 22, 26, 31, 118, 127, 130-32, 135, 137, 140-41, 143, 146-47, 154, 160-61, 164, 180, 191

Evans, Edgar, 77, 101, 105

exhaustion, of travel genre, 11, 35, 51, 59, 187, 192 of destinations, 17, 187, 190, 192

exotic, the, exoticism 25-26, 28, 71, 130, 161, 182

exploration, 11, 15-16, 51-52, 70, 78, 80-81, 84, 86-87, 89-90, 104, 117-19, 130-31, 136, 145, 190-91, explorers, 31, 48, 61, 80-81, 83-84, 88, 130, 144-45, 181 190

Filsnoel, Monique 73-74

France, 15, 154-55, 160-61, 164-65, 177, 190

gender, 15, 22, 69, 87, 112, 114, 116, 120, 128, 130-33, 192, *see also* gendered discourses

Glazebrook, Philip, 55, 58, 60-62, 71

Grand Tour, the, 14, 75

guidebooks, 8, 14, 18, 32, 37, 56- 60, 71-72, 188

heritage, 41-46, 156, 177
  heritage trails, 17, 30, 42-43, 162-63, 176, 178

hero, heroic traveller, heroic journey 15, 18, 22, 44, 51, 56, 67, 69-72, 80-85, 89-94, 99, 101-02, 104, 108, 119, 125, 131, 133, 144-45, 167, 181, 185, 188, 190-91, *see also* heroic discourse

Holmes, Richard, 17, 44-45, 156-57, 159-60, 166-71, 175, 180

home, images of, 11, 12, 15, 22, 56, 67-68, 81, 90, 144-45, 147, 184, 189

Huget, Jennifer, 73-74

identity, identity constructions, 16, 21, 23, 28-29, 49, 56, 67-69, 92, 114-15, 127, 130, 132-34, 145, 148-49, 172-73

intertextuality, 12, 18-19, 37, 48-53, 59-60, 79, 113, 136, 188, intertextual references, intertexts, 36-37, 48-53, 56, 58, 79, 108-09, 159, 188

Johnson, Samuel, 61-63

Kinglake, Alexander, 58-59

Kingsley, Mary, **111-151**, 16-17, 26, 43, 51, 59, 63, 68-70, 80, 87, 153, 175, 185, 189, 191

Lawrenson, Deborah, 74

literary trails, literary tourism, 29, 32, 41

Mear, Roger, and Robert Swan, **77-110**, 15, 17, 43-44, 66, 70, 111, 149, 153, 185, 190

modernism, modernist order, 30-31, 42, 50, 71

museums, 17, 42-43, 96, 149, 156-57, 162, 166, 175-85,

Nassau, Robert, 26, 59, 123, 137-38

nationality, 68, 131, 189

North America, 15, 26, 65-66, 171-73, 180, 190, California, 70, 155-56, 165, 169, 182, San Francisco, 72, 174

nostalgia, 44-45, 55, 64

Oates, Lawrence, 77, 82, 102, 105

originality, 12-14, 17, 31, 35, 44, 47-48, 50-52, 91-92, 118, 130, 161, 188-89, original experiences, 31, 33, 37, 39, 50-51, 130

Other, the, 19, 22-24, 26, 28-29, 31, 33, 69, 133, 161

pilgrimages, 14, 25, 29-30, 46

postcolonialism, 11-12, 132, postcolonial discourses, 23-24, 116-17, 147, 149, 188, 191

postmodernism, 18-19, 31, 36, 42, postmodern forms, 7-8, 13, 30, 33, 50, 56, postmodern discourses, 33-35, 40-42, 46-48, 51-52, 68, 71, 96, 120, 188-89

power, 11, 13, 23, 28, 30, 41-42, 46, 116, 192

Rankin, Nicholas, **153-185**, 16-17, 43-44, 63-64, 70, 80, 96, 107, 149, 191

recycling, 14, 18, 44, 192

repetition, 33, 99, 139, 175, of itinerary, 16, 49, 189, with a difference, 50, 188,

representations, 11-12, 19, 23, 35, 40, 43, 56, 69, 116, 121, 132, 156, 160, 162, 177, 185, textual, 13, 32-33, 44, 57, 71, 118, 151, 190-91

retracing of routes, 12.13, 18, 34-35, 53, 72, 74, 85-86, 94, 123-24, 138, 146-47, 149, 166, 187

Scotland, Scottish, 61, 68, 155, 160, 171-72, Edinburgh, 17, 155, 161-62, 164, 178

Scott, Robert Falcon, **77-110**, 15-17, 26, 43-44, 51, 59, 61, 65, 67-70, 122, 149, 153, 185, 189-90

Severin, Tim 64-65, 79

Shackleton, Ernest 70, 83, 87-88, 100-01

South Seas, 15, 17, Pacific Islands, 26, 155-56, 161, 176, 181, 183, 190

Stevenson, Robert Louis **153-185**, 16-17, 26, 43-45, 59, 63, 68, 70, 80, 96, 149, 189-91, *An Inland Voyage*, 17, 155, 160, 164-65, *From the Clyde to California*, 17, 155-56, 171-75, 185, *In the South Seas*, 17, 26, 155, 161, 181, *Travels with a Donkey in the Cevennes*, 17, 44-45, 153, 155-56, 160, 165-171

Stroud, Michael, 79, 97, 99

temporal distance, 23-24, 39, 45, of first journeys, 29, 49, 61, 137, 146, 188, temporal boundaries, 34, 42

Tolson, John, 79, 97, 99

Trader Horn, 43, 136

Warburton, Eliot, 62, 71

West Africa, 15-16, 26, 59, 111, 116, 119, 122-23, 125-28, 131, 133, 137, 139, 144-45, 148-49, 151, 190, Gabon, 111, 123-25, 129, 137, 143-44, 146-47, 149, Booué, 141,

Franceville, 142, Lambaréné, 127, 134-35, 141, Libreville, 124-25, 129, 134, 137, 143-44, Mount Cameroon, 131, 143, Ndjolé, 137, 140, Ogooué River, 134, 136-37, 140-42, Okota rapids, 133, 139, Remboué, 63, 131, 142, Samba Falls, 136, 150-51

Wheeler, Sara, 12, 34, 56, 61, 84-85

Wilson, Edward, 77, 82, 99, 102

Wood, Gareth, 79, 97, 99

Young, Gavin, 55, 73

Studier i språk och litteratur från Umeå universitet
Umeå Studies in Language and Literature

Publicerade av Institutionen för språkstudier, Umeå universitet
Published by the Department of Language Studies, Umeå University

Redaktion/Editors: Heidi Hansson, Per Ambrosiani

Distribuerade av/Distributed by: eddy.se ab
P.O. Box 1310, SE-621 24 Visby,
Sweden
E-mail: order@bokorder.se
Phone: +46 498 253900
Fax: +46 498 249789

1. Elena Lindholm Narváez, *'Ese terrible espejo'. Autorrepresentación en la narrativa sobre el exilio del Cono Sur en Suecia*. Diss. 2008.
2. Julian Vasquez (ed.), *Actas del Simposio Internacional "Suecia y León de Greiff (1895–1976)"*. 2008.
3. Dorothea Liebel, *Tageslichtfreude und Buchstabenangst. Zu Harry Martinsons dichterischen Wortbildungen als Übersetzungsproblematik*. Diss. 2009.
4. Dan Olsson, *„Davon sagen die Herren kein Wort". Zum pädagogischen, grammatischen, und dialektologischen Schaffen Max Wilhelm Götzingers (1799–1856)*. Diss. 2009.
5. Ingela Valfridsson, *Nebensätze in Büchern und Köpfen. Zur Bedeutung der Begriffsvorstellungen beim Fremdsprachenerwerb*. Diss. 2009.
6. Per Ambrosiani (ed.), *Swedish Contributions to the Fourteenth International Congress of Slavists (Ohrid, 10–16 September 2008)*. 2009.
7. Therese Örnberg Berglund, *Making Sense Digitally: Conversational Coherence in Online and Mixed-Mode Contexts*. Diss. 2009.
8. Gregor von der Heiden, *Gespräche in einer Krise. Analyse von Telefonaten mit einem RAF-Mitglied während der Okkupation der westdeutschen Botschaft in Stockholm 1975*. Diss. 2009.

9. Maria Lindgren Leavenworth, *The Second Journey: Travelling in Literary Footsteps*. 2010.

Skrifter från moderna språk (2001–2006)
Publicerade av Institutionen för moderna språk, Umeå universitet
Published by the Department of Modern Languages, Umeå University

1. Mareike Jendis, *Mumins wundersame Deutschlandabenteuer. Zur Rezeption von Tove Janssons Muminbüchern*. Diss. 2001.
2. Lena Karlsson, *Multiple Affiliations: Autobiographical Narratives of Displacement by US Women*. Diss. 2001.
3. Anders Steinvall, *English Colour Terms in Context*. Diss. 2002.
4. Raoul J. Granqvist (ed.), *Sensuality and Power in Visual Culture*. 2002. NY UPPLAGA 2006.
5. Berit Åström, *The Politics of Tradition: Examining the History of the Old English Poems* The Wife's Lament *and* Wulf and Eadwacer. Diss. 2002.
6. José J. Gamboa, *La lengua después del exilio. Influencias suecas en retornados chilenos*. Diss. 2003.
7. Katarina Gregersdotter, *Watching Women, Falling Women: Power and Dialogue in Three Novels by Margaret Atwood*. Diss. 2003.
8. Thomas Peter, *Hans Falladas Romane in den USA*. Diss. 2003.
9. Elias Schwieler, *Mutual Implications: Otherness in Theory and John Berryman's Poetry of Loss*. Diss. 2003.
10. Mats Deutschmann, *Apologising in British English*. Diss. 2003.
11. Raija Kangassalo & Ingmarie Mellenius (red.), *Låt mig ha kvar mitt språk. Den tredje SUKKA-rapporten. / Antakaa minun pitää kieleni. Kolmas SUKKA-raportti*. 2003.
12. Mareike Jendis, Anita Malmqvist & Ingela Valfridsson (Hg.), *Norden und Süden. Festschrift für Kjell-Åke Forsgren zum 65. Geburtstag*. 2004.
13. Philip Grey, *Defining Moments: A Cultural Biography of Jane Eyre*. Diss. 2004.
14. Kirsten Krull, *Lieber Gott, mach mich fromm ... Zum Wort und Konzept „fromm" im Wandel der Zeit*. Diss. 2004.

15. Maria Helena Svensson, *Critères de figement. L'identification des expressions figées en français contemporain*. Diss. 2004.
16. Malin Isaksson, *Adolescentes abandonnées. Je narrateur adolescent dans le roman français contemporain*. Diss. 2004.
17. Carla Jonsson, *Code-Switching in Chicano Theater: Power, Identity and Style in Three Plays by Cherríe Moraga*. Diss. 2005.
18. Eva Lindgren, *Writing and Revising: Didactic and Methodological Implications of Keystroke Logging*. Diss. 2005.
19. Monika Stridfeldt, *La perception du français oral par des apprenants suédois*. Diss. 2005.
20. María Denis Esquivel Sánchez, *"Yo puedo bien español". Influencia sueca y variedades hispanas en la actitud lingüística e identificación de los hispanoamericanos en Suecia*. Diss. 2005.
21. Raoul J. Granqvist (ed.), *Michael's Eyes: The War against the Ugandan Child*. 2005.
22. Martin Shaw, *Narrating Gypsies Telling Travellers: A Study of the Relational Self in Four Life Stories*. Diss. 2006.

Umeå Studies in Linguistics (2001–2006)
Publicerade av Institutionen för filosofi och lingvistik, Umeå universitet
Published by the Department of Philosophy and Linguistics,
Umeå University

1. Leila Kalliokoski, *Understanding Sentence Structure: Experimental Studies on Processing of Syntactic Elements in Sentences*. Diss. 2001.
2. Anna-Lena Wiklund, *The Syntax of Tenselessness: On Copying Constructions in Swedish*. Diss. 2005.
3. Fredrik Karlsson, *The Acquisition of Contrast: A Longitudinal Investigation of Initial s+Plosive Cluster Development in Swedish Children*. Diss. 2006.

PHONUM (1990–2005)
Publicerade av Institutionen för lingvistik, Umeå universitet (1990–1998) och av Institutionen för filosofi och lingvistik, Umeå universitet (1999–2005)
Published by the Department of Linguistics, Umeå University (1990–1998) and by the Department of Philosophy and Linguistics, Umeå University (1999–2005)

1. Eva Strangert & Peter Czigler (eds.), *Papers from Fonetik –90 / The Fourth Swedish Phonetics Conference, Held in Umeå/Lövånger, May 30–31 and June 1, 1990*. 1990.
2. Eva Strangert, Mattias Heldner & Peter Czigler (eds.), *Studies Presented to Claes-Christian Elert on the Occasion of his Seventieth Birthday*. 1993.
3. Robert Bannert & Kirk Sullivan (eds.), *PHONUM 3*. 1995.
4. Robert Bannert, Mattias Heldner, Kirk Sullivan & Pär Wretling (eds.), *Proceedings from Fonetik 1997: Umeå 28–30 May 1997*. 1997.
5. Peter E. Czigler, *Timing in Swedish VC(C) Sequences*. Diss. 1998.
6. Kirk Sullivan, Fredrik Karlsson & Robert Bannert (eds.), *PHONUM 6*. 1998.
7. Robert Bannert & Peter E. Czigler (eds.), *Variations within Consonant Clusters in Standard Swedish*. 1999.
8. Mattias Heldner, *Focal Accent – f_0 Movements and Beyond*. Diss. 2001.
9. Mattias Heldner (ed.), *Proceedings from Fonetik 2003: Lövånger 2–4 June 2003*. 2003.
10. Felix Schaeffler, *Phonological Quantity in Swedish Dialects: Typological Aspects, Phonetic Variation and Diachronic Change*. Diss. 2005.